# Commercialization and Agricultural Development

# Commercialization and Agricultural Development

## Central and Eastern China 1870–1937

### LOREN BRANDT

*University of Toronto*

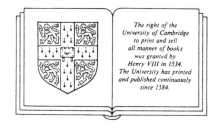

The right of the
University of Cambridge
to print and sell
all manner of books
was granted by
Henry VIII in 1534.
The University has printed
and published continuously
since 1584.

CAMBRIDGE UNIVERSITY PRESS
Cambridge
New York   Port Chester
Melbourne   Sydney

CAMBRIDGE UNIVERSITY PRESS
Cambridge, New York, Melbourne, Madrid, Cape Town, Singapore, São Paulo

Cambridge University Press
The Edinburgh Building, Cambridge CB2 2RU, UK

Published in the United States of America by Cambridge University Press, New York

www.cambridge.org
Information on this title: www.cambridge.org/9780521371964

First published 1989
This digitally printed first paperback version 2005

*A catalogue record for this publication is available from the British Library*

*Library of Congress Cataloguing in Publication data*

Brandt, Loren.
Commercialization and agricultural development: central and
eastern China, 1870–1937 / Loren Brandt.
p.   cm.
Bibliography: p.
ISBN 0-521-37196-1
1. Agriculture – Economic aspects – China – History.   I. Title.
HD2097.B73    1989
338.1´0951–dc19      89-739      CIP

ISBN-13 978-0-521-37196-4 hardback
ISBN-10 0-521-37196-1 hardback

ISBN-13 978-0-521-02286-6 paperback
ISBN-10 0-521-02286-X paperback

# Contents

# Tables

# Figures and Maps

## Figures

## Maps

# Acknowledgments

This book began as a Ph.D. dissertation that was completed at the University of Illinois in October 1983. During the course of the dissertation and subsequent revisions, I benefited greatly from the help of a number of individuals, a few of whom I would like to single out. Of course, I alone assume responsibility for any errors of fact or interpretation contained in this volume.

At Illinois, Larry Neal and Peter Schran, my Ph.D. supervisor, were very influential in the formative stages of this project. Shortly after the dissertation was completed, I received long letters from Ramon Myers, of the Hoover Institution, Stanford University, and Thomas Rawski, then of the University of Toronto, providing new inspiration and detailed comments for subsequent revisions. In fact, based on their recommendation, I decided, after having been at St. Olaf College for only a month, to apply for an American Council of Learned Societies/Social Science Research Council fellowship in order to begin the arduous task of revision. During the last four years, their assistance has been enormous, and to both I owe a large personal, as well as intellectual, debt. To those who have read Myers's *The Chinese Peasant Economy* (Harvard University Press, 1970), and who will peruse Rawski's *Economic Development in Prewar China* (University of California Press, forthcoming), this debt will be fairly obvious.

My research was supported with fellowships from St. Olaf College; the American Council of Learned Societies/Social Science Research Council; and the Hoover Institution, where most of the revisions were made between 1985 and 1987, and where I was a National Fellow during the 1986-87 academic year. My three years at that institution will always be looked on fondly, and to its staff I extend my thanks. I would also like to express my gratitude to Hersh Sheffrin for providing me the opportunity while there to teach intermittently at the Leavy School of Business, University of Santa Clara, and thus help extend what was to have been a one-year visit to three.

Others whose comments have contributed to this book and the papers that preceded it include Sandra Archibald, Shannon Brown,

Nicholas Lardy, Barry Naughton, Barbara Sands, and Tim Wright. Also, the students in my class on the Chinese Economy at Stanford University in the fall of 1987 helped me see important connections between developments in rural China during the nineteenth and early twentieth centuries and those in the post-1978 era. I have benefited, too, from feedback obtained at seminars sponsored by the universities of California-Berkeley, California-Davis, California-San Diego, Michigan, Minnesota, Toronto, and Stanford; the Chinese Academy of Social Sciences, Beijing; and the Shanghai Academy of Social Sciences. I would also like to thank Margaret Mirabelli for her editorial assistance, and Lorraine Nelson for her aid in preparing the graphics. Special thanks also go to the publishers of *Explorations in Economic History* and the *Journal of Economic History* to use previously published materials.

Finally, I owe an enormous debt to my wife, Carol, and our three children, Matt, Katie, and Kyle. They gave up much so that this book could be completed and, when progress seemed unbearably slow, helped to keep everything in perspective. To them, this book is dedicated.

LOREN BRANDT

# Weights and Measures

Except as noted, 1 *picul* equals 110 pounds; 20 *piculs* equal 1 metric ton; and 1 *picul* contains 100 *chin* or *catties*. A *shih* is a volume measure and in the case of grain equals approximately 160 *catties*. 1 *shih* equals 10 *tou*; 1 *tou* equals 10 *sheng*. 1 *mou* equals 0.1647 acre, which equals 0.0666 hectare. Six *mou*, therefore, equal 1 acre; 15 *mou* equal 1 hectare.

# Commercialization and Agricultural Development

# 1

# Introduction

Since 1978 the Chinese agricultural sector has achieved remarkably high growth rates of output and factor productivity. Although there is room for debate, technological change and substantially increased usage of modern inputs do not appear to have figured prominently in this growth. Rather, it has come from an accelerated commercialization and specialization in the rural sector, both fostered by a comprehensive set of rural reforms.[1] Within just six or seven years, agricultural output (in constant prices) increased by nearly two-thirds and real incomes perhaps by even more.[2] This far surpasses the growth achieved over the previous two decades, during which new high-yielding varieties (especially rice) were widely disseminated, along with modern inputs, such as chemical fertilizers and certain types of farm machinery.

This episode of accelerated commercialization is not unique in Chinese history. Historians and economic historians almost unanimously agree that slightly less than a century earlier China's rural sector had embarked on a similar course, which lasted almost fifty years before being interrupted by the Sino-Japanese War (1937–45) and then by civil war (1945–9). Although opinions differ as to how rapidly commercialization advanced and the exact nature of the forces underlying the process, very few scholars doubt its enormous impact on the agricultural sector. Most analysts, however, believe commercialization expanded rural poverty rather than possibly helping to relieve it. In an extensive literature on the subject, dating back to the 1920s and 1930s,[3] the importation of inexpensive manufactured goods and a decline in rural handicrafts, the loss of self-sufficiency, exposure to market volatility, and shifting terms of trade against agriculture are the most frequently cited factors in support of this view.[4]

Over time, views on the disruptiveness of commercialization on China's rural sector have moderated, the reassessment of the impact of manufactured yarn imports beginning in the late nineteenth century on the handicraft textile sector being a case in point.[5] Nonetheless, a common perception remains that Chinese agriculture experienced enormous difficulty over this period in accommodating

a relatively modest growth in population. Dwight Perkins's estimates of the rate of growth of agricultural output seem to justify
such a view; between the late nineteenth and early twentieth centuries, Chinese agriculture merely kept pace with population
growth, estimated to be only 0.6 percent per year.[6] Because much
of this growth in output actually occurred in Manchuria (Northeast
China), agriculture presumably did not even fare this well in other
parts of China, where there was much less room to extend cultivated
area.[7] It is, of course, from such a perspective, when the Chinese
population exceeded half a billion, that R. H. Tawney observed in
1932: "The fundamental fact, it is urged, is of terrible simplicity. It
is that the population of China is too large to be supported by existing
resources."[8]

In many respects, agricultural development, or the lack of it, in
Central and East China seems to typify China outside of the Northeast. Composed of the provinces of Kiangsu, Chekiang, Anhwei,
Kiangsi, Hupei, and Hunan, the Central-East region had by the
early 1930s a population exceeding 160 million (see Map 1.1). Historically, it supplied the rest of China with critically needed surplus
grain, a happy circumstance that it owed to highly fertile soil, a
long growing season, and a well-developed water transport system
centered on the Yangtse River. The river system feature figured
prominently in G. B. Cressey's geographical description of the
Yangtse Plain, which encompassed much of the six provinces:

The Yangtse Plain is a land of rivers and canals. Probably nowhere else in
the world is there an area with so many navigable waterways. The Yangtse
Kiang (Yangtse River), the Hwai Ho, and their tributaries provide a splen-
did highway through the length of the region. In addition to the many rivers
there are a series of great lakes, chief among which are Tungting, Poyang,
Tai, and the Hungtse Hu. It is the canals, however, which give the most
characteristic note to the landscape. These canals are the very arteries of
life.[9]

This elaborate network of interior waterways and canals not only
linked much of the six provinces together, allowing us to conceive
of Central and East China as a single region, but, even before the
opening of China to the West, this transportation system made the
Yangtse more commercialized than other parts of the country.[10]
Despite these "natural" advantages, the early twentieth century saw
a dissipation of the Yangtse region surplus – it sent much smaller
shipments of rice to South China and Peking – and it even occasionally imported grain. Between 1893 and 1933, the cultivated area
reportedly did not expand, and grain production estimates for the

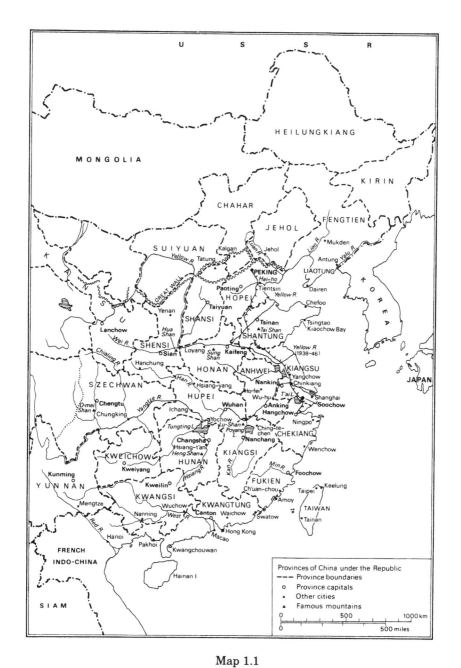

Map 1.1

China: 1930s Provincial Boundaries

region reveal a marked decline in per capita grain availability between 1914–18 and 1931–7.[11] Cotton imports from the United States and India also increased in the 1920s and 1930s to supply the textile mills in Shanghai and the rest of the Lower Yangtse. Either the rate at which commercialization proceeded has been exaggerated or commercialization was not the catalyst it has been more recently.[12]

This book rejects both these views and offers new perspectives on the commercialization of agriculture in Central and East China – on both the forces underlying it and its impact on agricultural growth and distribution during the late nineteenth and early twentieth centuries. Between the 1890s and 1930s, the agricultural sector did become more highly commercialized. And in the process not only did agricultural output grow much more rapidly than previously believed – my estimates suggest that between the 1890s and the 1930s output probably grew at least twice as rapidly as population and that marketed output, a measure of the rate at which commercialization proceeded in the farm sector, grew even faster – but also the benefits of the commercialization process were much more evenly distributed among rural households than previously believed. In other words, I do not think that rural commercialization was economically polarizing, as others have long held that it was.

Underlying this critical reassessment are alternative perspectives on several key issues about the region's rural economy that are at the center of existing intepretations.[13]

## New Ties with the International Economy

In trying to explain the accelerated commercialization of agriculture and the new higher levels of farm household participation in the market, much of the existing literature has concentrated on expanded international demand for Chinese agricultural goods.[14] In both North and Northeast China, for example, railroad development in the early twentieth century opened up substantial areas of the interior to the international market. But, although there were areas highly specialized in production for export, and despite rapid growth in them, Chinese agricultural exports never amounted to more than about 4 percent of total agricultural output. In other words, increasing international demand played a very modest role in the accelerated commercialization of agriculture. This was especially true for Central and East China.

Nonetheless, concurrent with the late nineteenth-century expansion in China's treaty port system,[15] development of the steamship offered importers and exporters quicker and cheaper access to world markets, and the telegraph swiftly conveyed market information. Not only did this involve tea and silk, historically China's major exports, but also rice, cotton, and oilseeds, farm products that the country traded internationally in much smaller quantities. At the same time, similar innovations were acting as powerful forces integrating China at both the regional and national level. Shanghai, ideally situated at the mouth of the Yangtse River, was a revolving door through which much of the information passed back and forth between the region and the world. Tientsin played a similar role in the north and Canton in the south.

Because China had only modest tariff protection, competition between internal and external sources of supply rapidly emerged within the nation and exposed internal markets to outside market forces. Although this competition frequently was centered in treaty ports like Shanghai, international market forces penetrated the interior as well. Competition in overseas export markets only reinforced this new relationship, with consequences much more profound for China than an occasional rise in domestic market prices because of a supply shock in the world economy, or a fall in domestic prices because of a sharp contraction in international demand.[16] Through the operation of commodity price arbitrage, domestic agricultural prices, both in the treaty ports and in the interior markets, became systematically tied to international market prices. This was as true for rice and cotton as it was for China's major exports. Equally important, because the currencies of its major trading partners were tied to gold while China's was linked to silver, changes in the gold price of silver came to systematically influence internal market prices. Although on occasions the comparatively smooth workings of this system were stayed by political developments,[17] integration with the international economy substantially diminished the role of internal demand and supply factors in domestic price determination in many markets and simultaneously increased the importance of the behavior of agricultural commodity prices as well as the gold price of silver in the world market.

## Growth in the Domestic Nonagricultural Sector

Although new international market forces by the turn of the century heavily influenced the behavior of agricultural prices, the domestic economy still remained the primary outlet for agricultural products, as the relatively small percentage of agricultural output that was exported overseas demonstrates. But what was happening to domestic demand? After the 1890s, Central-East China experienced a

rapidly growing demand for agricultural goods, only a small percentage of which was required by expansion of the local farm population. Much more important was the rapid growth of the domestic
nonagricultural sector – a key component of which was the treaty
port sector – which continued unabated through the mid–1930s.[18]
Shanghai and the Kiangnan area of the Lower Yangtse was one of
China's two major growth centers; the other was southern Liaoning.
Thomas Rawski's revised estimates show that between 1914 and
1936 output in China's nonagricultural sector grew in excess of 2.5
percent per annum.[19] No doubt growth in the Lower Yangtse was
even greater. Over a slightly longer period, the number of people in
the nonagricultural sector in Central and East China increased several times more rapidly than the regional population did.

This sector not only demanded grain to feed its growing population, but also required cash crops to supply its rapidly expanding
consumer-goods industry. Overseas demand increased for some products like silk. Dwight Perkins suggests that imports fed the growing
population, but in Central and East China this was unequivocally
not the case; despite occasional overseas grain imports (much of
which was actually reexported to other parts of China), the region
remained a net exporter of grain throughout the entire period. Regional agriculture not only accommodated a more than doubling in
the nonagricultural population, but expanded its cash-crop production as well. Because nothing indicates that poorer rural households
consumed less over this period – in fact, the secular behavior of real
wages paid long-term agricultural workers suggests the exact opposite – these observations go far toward discrediting those regional
output estimates that show declining per capita food grain availability and output for the period and imply the exhaustion of almost
all possibilities for expanding agricultural output.

How exactly did these new internal and external forces interact
to accelerate commercialization? No sooner did Chinese agricultural
markets integrate with the world economy than the structure of
prices facing the rural sector began to change. Domestic agricultural
prices began rising and continued to do so through the late 1920s.
They rose not only absolutely, but also relative to the price of nonagricultural goods, except during World War I. Between the mid–
1880s and the late 1920s, the terms of trade rose in agriculture's
favor by more than two-thirds. Over the same period, international
market forces also influenced the relationship among the prices of
raw cotton, cotton yarn, and cotton cloth.

The combination of changed price structure and new market opportunities – many of them associated with the region's ongoing urbanization and industrialization – had a profound impact on the organization of economic activity in the countryside. Most importantly, they provided rural households powerful incentives for redirecting economic activity toward the market. Specialization increased as rural households expanded production, increased their marketed output, and used the market to procure goods that the nonagricultural sector (or even other farm households) could supply more efficiently. This was as true for rural households still actually farming as it was for those involved with handicraft textiles, who found it profitable to substitute manufactured for homespun yarn.

Reflecting these trends, urban-rural and intrarural exchange expanded several times over, generating a host of new income-earning opportunities that further commercialized the rural sector. Although parts of the Yangtse region are noted for having achieved relatively high degrees of specialization and commercialization much earlier in time, I will show that the level rose considerably between the 1890s and 1930s. The percentage of agricultural output that was marketed increased from less than 30 percent shortly before the turn of the century to between 45 and 50 percent by the mid–1930s.

The signs of increasing specialization in the rural sector were not lost on some observers. Sixty years ago, Friedrich Otto pointed out:

The Chinese farmer is fairly quick to notice his own advantage provided he is left alone and is sure that the fruits of his labor become his. One need only point to the tremendous increase in the cultivation of groundnuts in the neighborhood of the Tsinan-Tsingtao railway, or of soya bean and wheat along the Manchurian railway, or to the transformation of agriculture around Shanghai: wheat and cotton instead of rice, in order to realize that the passiveness even of the northern Chinese farmer is by no means due to the dullness of perception.[20]

Yet, the ability of Yangtse agriculture to feed its own increasing population, as well as a more than doubled nonagricultural population, while at the same time marketing more nongrain crops, reveals a rural responsiveness to new market opportunities that even Otto did not imagine. My estimates suggest that agricultural output grew between 1.2 and 1.5 percent per annum, and that the market surplus grew even faster. Associated with these increases, of course, were rising incomes. Although data limitations prevent us from quantifying the contributions of various factors, the returns to this increasing specialization and exchange based on comparative local or regional advantage no doubt figured prominently, much as they have more recently.[21]

## Rural Market Structure and Distributive Consequences

In any economy, buyers or sellers occasionally enjoy greater market power as a consequence of the limited opportunities or information of other economic agents. In rural China, observers frequently attribute such power to the landlord, who is often the sole provider of off-farm wage opportunities, rentable land, or maybe even credit. Analysts have argued that such power enables a very small group to monopolize the benefits of rural commercialization and thus in the process polarize the community economically. Yet, market expansion and integration – two factors often associated with commercialization either as causal factors or as corollaries – would actually weaken the market power of any one individual. By providing new opportunities both on and off the farm and access to new sources of information, commercialization would undermine existing sources of market power and help markets work more smoothly and competitively.

Examples of highly imperfect product and factor markets in rural China abound in the literature. Yet, as Albert Feuerwerker noted several years ago, few studies document these common assumptions about local markets.[22] I agree. Certainly the data on rural product and factor markets for the early twentieth century examined in this book reveal those features usually associated with competitive market conditions: many buyers and sellers, freedom of entry and exit, mobility of resources, and so forth. Although exceptions no doubt existed, in the commercialized areas of the Yangtse and China more generally, markets were well established and competitive, a trait that I believe the accelerated commercialization of the late nineteenth and early twentieth centuries only reinforced.

The implications of this feature for the rural economy cannot be underestimated. Obvious efficiency gains arise because markets helped allocate resources to their highest value uses. Yet, there are equally important distributive consequences. Market expansion and the commercialization of agriculture was in many respects a "labor-using" process. The shift to labor-intensive crops of higher value, the intensification of production, and higher levels of marketing all increased the demand for labor in the rural sector, as did the growing variety of nonagricultural rural activities. Rising real wages in many localities reflect the fact that rising demand for labor outpaced the supply increases provided by an expanding population.

How much any one farm household benefited from the opportunities offered by commercialization and market expansion depended for the most part on the decisions it and other households made with respect to the crops grown, the amount marketed, and the allocation of resources (especially labor) more generally. If most households made similar decisions under similar circumstances, it would not only suggest that competitive markets existed but also that the gains from commercialization were much more evenly distributed among rural households than previously believed.

Farm-level survey data for the 1920s and 1930s in fact reveal only modest differences among households in agricultural decision making. Farms of all sizes seem to have taken equal advantage of the opportunities offered by cash cropping and market expansion. Even land-poor households benefited from the increasing labor demand and higher wages, if not by working their own land more intensively, then by hiring out on someone else's farm or pursuing a nonagricultural sideline. Both factors had income-equalizing tendencies and weakened the influence of land distribution on income distribution. Data that I will present strongly suggest that land distribution did not worsen between the 1890s and 1930s and lead me to believe that income differentials actually narrowed at the local level. This, of course, is not to say that other kinds of differentials may not have widened. Because access to low-cost transportation varied, all localities did not enjoy equally the gains offered by market expansion and commercialization. Such, however, have not been the differentials that have concerned the literature linking commercialization with increasaing inequality.

Through a very detailed study of the rice market, Chapter 2 addresses questions relating to the timing and extent of integration of Chinese agricultural markets with the international economy. Although Shanghai did not import any rice from overseas until the 1920s and never exported rice overseas at all, by the late nineteenth century it had become tightly integrated with markets in Monsoon Asia, the center of the international rice market. During this period, new links were also forged between the international market and Chinese markets in cotton and other key agricultural goods.

Once one acknowledges the relatively high degree of integration achieved by the turn of the century, price movements and commodity flows can no longer be explained solely in terms of domestic market forces. Drawing on the theory of international commodity arbitrage, Chapter 3 analyzes how the interaction of international and domestic market forces influenced the rice and cotton markets. Although changes in international agricultural prices and in the gold price of silver explain much of the price variability of these two commodities in China, output of both was primarily earmarked for domestic consumption. Moreover, whereas imports of rice and cotton occasionally increased, output and marketing of both increased substantially over the period to accommodate growing domestic demand.

Chapter 4 takes a more general view of the commercialization process. I not only estimate the percentage of agricultural output that was marketed in the 1890s and 1930s, in order to measure how rapidly commercialization advanced, but I also examine in more detail how the interaction of internal and external market forces gave rise to this acceleration. Critical here is the household-level reorganization of economic activity with regard to the market.

Chapter 5 investigates the implications that commercialization had for productivity and output in the rural sector. Drawing on a wide variety of data, I provide estimates of productivity change and of increased output in agriculture between the 1890s and 1930s. Despite the dissimilar methods that I used, and allowing for some error, a set of estimates emerges that solidly establishes in the aggregate substantial long-run growth in labor productivity and per capita agricultural output.

Chapter 6 analyzes how the increases in incomes associated with rising output and productivity were distributed among rural households; it pays particular attention to the role of rural market structure. By all indications, commercialization and market forces helped reduce inequality in the rural sector by diminishing the influence that own landholdings had on income.

The alternative interpretation this book provides should help to redress a serious historical imbalance in previous assessments of the pre–1949 economy and the severity of problems posed by distribution. Without question, many households benefited significantly from the growth in the rural sector and found themselves much better off shortly before the Sino-Japanese War than they had been forty to fifty years earlier.

At the same time, this book provides a richer historical perspective to the enormous costs that self-sufficiency and highly restrictive commercial policies had for the rural sector between the mid–1950s and 1970s.[23] Through an examination of product and factor markets, we obtain a better idea of how markets worked in the rural economy before 1949 to facilitate a remarkably high degree of specialization and division of labor in an economy with such low incomes. Rather than being a source of inefficiency, these highly articulated markets had just the opposite impact.

Despite the more favorable assessment I present, however, it certainly goes without saying that rural incomes remained very low, that households still suffered from the vagaries of nature and other uncertainties, and that some parts of China remained largely isolated from the forces this book describes. Moreover, the rural sector would doubtless have benefited substantially from public investment in agriculture and a calmer political environment. The fact that it did not makes the achievements of the rural sector even more impressive.

# 2

# Chinese Agriculture and the International Economy

Within a decade in the latter part of the nineteenth century, developments in transportation and communications fundamentally altered how business was carried out in Chinese import and export markets. The Maritime Customs *Decennial Reports* for 1882–91 observed how "in old times business was done in Shanghai by men having command of large amounts of capital, who bought heavy consignments and stored them till there was a chance for a sale," but that more recently "a very large and increasing amount of foreign produce is bought on commission, orders being conveyed abroad by telegrams and the total price and rate of exchange settled before the order is despatched."[1] Similar remarks were made regarding operations in export markets. The report noted how this situation "facilitates the carrying on of trade with small or no capital" and "promotes a sharpness in business and keenness in competition which tend to make getting business a more important consideration than how it is got."[2]

Yet, the influence of these new technologies went much further than simply changing how business was conducted. By tying more closely Chinese markets in these export commodities into the international market, they also influenced how Chinese prices were set. For the late 1850s, S. Wells Williams observed of the domestic silk market:

The quantity [of silk] produced to supply the native consumption is so enormous, that not withstanding the vast increase in exports during the past 10 years, the average of prices is lower than when the export was but one-fourth of its present amount. The silk grower looks to the home market for fixing the value of his produce, and prices range according as the demand is active or dull; little or no effect being produced by the foreign exportation, except among the speculative holders at the ports.[3]

But, by the late nineteenth century, as Chinese economist D. K. Liu has noted, prices in Shanghai were much more influenced by prices prevailing in Lyon, New York, or Yokohama than they were by internal market conditions.[4] T. R. Banister, in his "A History of the External Trade of China, 1834–1881," makes exactly the same point about the tea market:

The opening of the Suez Canal and the completion of the through telegraph line from Shanghai to London radically changed conditions in the tea market. In earlier years the price of tea was ruled by conditions in China, quantity and quality of the crop, demand and supply at Shanghai, Foochow, Hankow, etc. In subsequent years the price of tea, speaking broadly, was governed by the state of the London market – quantity of stocks in hand, demand in England and Europe, estimated requirements for the future, etc.[5]

Despite these changes, most scholars have tended to discount any influence that the international economy was exerting on China's agricultural sector during the late nineteenth and early twentieth centuries. After all, the nation's foreign trade in agricultural products was small and production for the foreign market was geographically confined to a few key areas. Dwight Perkins estimates that even at its peak, after growing in real terms at almost 4 percent per annum for almost forty years, raw and processed agricultural exports never amounted to more than 3 to 4 percent of the gross value of agricultural output in the early twentieth century.[6] High transportation costs within China are frequently cited as the principal limitation on this trade.

Such reasoning would imply, in turn, that other agricultural markets in China, such as those for rice, cotton or even wheat – commodities that China either imported or exported in relatively small amounts (both absolutely and as a percentage of total output) – were also fairly far removed from developments in the international economy. Studies have, in fact, assumed this and concentrated almost exclusively on the domestic economy when trying to explain changes in prices, output, and trade. Thomas Rawski expressed a widely held view when he wrote: "[T]he fundamental point . . . is that the specific influence of foreign activity on the size and composition of farm output, on prices . . . and on other important economic magnitudes was generally small."[7]

I wish to offer an alternative view of the relationship between the home and overseas markets. By the late nineteenth and early twentieth centuries, despite the fact that only relatively small amounts were ever imported or exported, markets for such commodities as rice, wheat, cotton, and oilseeds had in many parts of China become inseparably tied to the international economy.[8] This development was part of the same process described for tea and silk. In Central and East China, approximately 85 percent of the cultivated area, or more than one-half of the sown area, was devoted to the first three of these crops alone. Integration with international markets in these commodities was predicated on a centuries-old, low-cost water transport system that was complemented in the early twentieth century by railroad development, the introduction of the steamer and developments in communications, and on a marketing structure that allowed for the relatively efficient transmission of price information.[9]

To demonstrate in any detail that domestic markets in each of these commodities was integrated with the international economy would take a book in itself. Rather, I will concentrate on establishing this phenomenon for one major crop, rice, and then explain why I believe that similar forces were operating in the other commodity markets as well. Historically, rice had been the most important crop grown in Central and East China. During the late nineteenth and early twentieth centuries, approximately 50 percent of acreage in the region was planted in rice, often as a summer crop following a winter crop of wheat, barley, or even rapeseed.

To establish that the rice market was affected by the international economy, I will investigate whether major rice markets in China, such as those in Canton and Shanghai, were integrated with the international markets. If they were, then I will examine whether integration was unique to a few treaty ports, or whether it extended to interior markets as well. Finally, I will look at the local markets in the hinterland where farm households sold their output. Through a detailed analysis of price data and an examination of rural market structure, I will show that markets throughout the Yangtse were integrated with each other, with markets elsewhere in China, and with the international grain market. In later chapters, I will take up the consequences this integration had for agriculture and the rural sector in Central and East China. I begin by looking at the link between the markets of South China and the international rice market.

## South China and the International Market in Rice

John Latham and Larry Neal have examined the formation of an international market in rice and wheat between 1868 and 1914.[10] On the basis of a detailed analysis of price data and rice flows, they have suggested that rice moved within an integrated international market during this period. Moreover, fluctuations in the rice market were tied to those in the wheat market, not because the two grains were substitutes in the international market (they were not), but "through the intervention of the vast Indian market where they were."[11]

Throughout the period Latham and Neal examined, China ap-

Table 2.1 *Chinese rice imports and Monsoon Asia exports, 1901–10*

| Year | Exports of Indo-China Cochin-China, India, and Siam (in millions of cwts.) | Chinese Imports (in millions of cwts.) | Chinese Imports As % of Exports |
|------|------|------|------|
| 1901 | 75.77  | 5.25  | 6.93% |
| 1902 | 98.07  | 1.15  | 1.17  |
| 1903 | 77.25  | 3.33  | 4.31  |
| 1904 | 96.25  | 3.99  | 4.15  |
| 1905 | 78.45  | 2.65  | 3.38  |
| 1906 | 79.05  | 5.37  | 7.08  |
| 1907 | 99.49  | 15.19 | 15.27 |
| 1908 | 85.19  | 8.02  | 9.41  |
| 1909 | 90.60  | 4.52  | 4.99  |
| 1910 | 107.53 | 10.97 | 10.20 |

*Sources:* Chinese rice imports: Hsiao, *China's Foreign Trade Statistics,* pp. 32–3; exports of Indo-China, Cochin-China, India, and Siam: Latham and Neal, "The International Market in Rice and Wheat," p. 278.

pears to have been only a minor participant in the international rice market, usually importing between 5 and 10 percent of the total exports of Siam, Cochin-China, Indo-China, and India. Table 2.1 displays total exports from the four major rice-exporting countries, Chinese imports, and the percentage Chinese imports represented for the ten years between 1901 and 1910.[12] Over the period, Chinese rice imports averaged approximately 6 million hundredweights, less than 7 percent of the total exported by the four countries.

According to China's Imperial Maritime Customs, most of the rice imported was destined for the southern part of the country and the markets of Amoy, Canton, Kowloon, Lappa, and Swatow. Amoy is situated on the southeastern coast of Fukien, and the four remaining ports are located in Kwangtung province. Overseas rice shipments helped supplement domestic sources, which for the Canton delta included other parts of Kwangtung, the neighboring province of Kwangsi, and the distant Yangtse provinces. Amoy also drew on rice from the Yangtse. It should be noted, nonetheless, that total rice imports represented a very small percentage of provincial rice production.[13]

Kowloon received more than 80 percent of the rice imported into China during the 1890s, a high percentage of which was then transshipped for Canton.[14] By the first decade of the twentieth cen-

Table 2.2. *Port of entry of Chinese rice imports, 1901–10*

| Port | % of Total Rice Imports |
| --- | --- |
| Amoy | 7% |
| Canton | 6 |
| Kowloon | 57 |
| Lappa | 10 |
| Swatow | 7 |
| Total | 87 |

*Source:* Chinese Imperial Maritime Customs, *Returns of Trade and Trade Reports,* 1901–10.

tury, the percentage of rice entering through Kowloon had dropped off, but a high percentage of imports continued to be shipped into the five markets,[15] as Table 2.2 clearly reflects.

The question nevertheless remains as to how integrated or well connected these markets were with their international counterparts. Table 2.3 provides simple correlation coefficients between the unit values of Chinese rice imports and the price of rice exports of four leading rice-exporting economies of Monsoon Asia in four subperiods between 1870 and 1936 and in the overall period. Correlation coefficients are one of several measures of market integration that are frequently used and were relied on by Latham and Neal. Prices for the same good in two markets that are integrated should be separated by a constant reflecting transportation/transactions costs, but otherwise move together. Thus, the better integrated the markets, the higher the correlation coefficient between their respective price series. Price correlations for the international wheat market, frequently cited as an efficient commodity market in the late nineteenth century, offer a measure as to how high the rice price correlations must be to infer a "good" market integration.[16] Until the 1920s, almost all of China's rice imports were destined for the southern part of the country, so the import price of rice can be used as a proxy for the price of rice prevailing in southern markets, and the correlation coefficients can be taken as a measure of how integrated markets in the Monsoon Asia rice-exporting economies were with the major grain markets in South China.

The results presented in Table 2.3 are informative in a number of respects. First of all, the changes that occur in the correlation coefficients between the subperiods 1870–92 and 1892–1914 suggest

Table 2.3. *Rice price correlations between South China and Monsoon Asia, 1870–1936*

| Country | 1870–92 | 1892–1914 | 1914–36 | 1870–1914 | 1870–1936 |
|---|---|---|---|---|---|
| South China/Siam | .69 | .84 | .81 | .79 | .87 |
| South China/Burma | − .07 | .82 | n.a. | .49 | n.a. |
| South China/India | .23 | .75 | .89 | .56 | .89 |
| South China/Saigon[a] | .90 | .74 | .96 | .80 | .94 |

[a]Saigon price data are not available until 1876.
*Sources:* For the years prior to 1914: Latham and Neal, "The International Market in Rice and Wheat," Appendix I, pp. 276–7; for later years, Siam: Ingram, "Thailand's Rice Trade and the Allocation of Resources," pp. 120–1, and *Economic Change in Thailand Since 1850*, p. 337; for later years, China: Hsiao, *China's Foreign Trade Statistics*, pp. 32–33 and 190–1; for later years, India, *Statistical Abstract for British India*; and for later years, Saigon, *Annuaire Statistique de L'Indochine*.

increasing integration in the prewar period. Only in the case of Saigon is $r_{xi}$ $r_{xj}$ lower for the latter half of the prewar period than it is for the first. Between 1870 and 1892, rice markets in South China were most closely tied to Siam and French-Indochina, the source of probably 80 percent or more of its rice imports.[17] Between 1892 and 1914, on the other hand, though most rice imports continued to originate in Siam and French-Indochina, the markets in South China were as integrated with Burma and India as they were with either Siam or French-Indochina. The average correlation coefficient is .79, or just slightly below that for the North Atlantic wheat market. Indeed, this attests not only to South China's increasing integration with Monsoon Asia, but to the growing integration throughout Monsoon Asia and in the international economy that Latham and Neal documented. After 1914, the correlation with Siam is marginally lower than that for the period immediately preceding the war, but higher for both Saigon, the rice exporter nearest to South China, and India. Given the high correlations for the years between 1892 and 1914 and the fact that the correlations for the post–1914 period were not substantially higher, I believe that South China had integrated into the rapidly evolving international rice market centered in Monsoon Asia by the turn of the twentieth century.

Table 2.4. *Rice price correlations between Shanghai and Monsoon Asia, 1870–1936*

| Country | 1870– 92 | 1892– 1914 | 1914– 36 | 1870– 1914 | 1870– 1936 |
|---|---|---|---|---|---|
| Shanghai/Siam | .53 | .80 | .69 | .67 | .80 |
| Shanghai/Burma | .29 | .85 | n.a. | .42 | n.a. |
| Shanghai/India | .06 | .69 | .94 | .46 | .93 |
| Shanghai/Saigon[a] | .89 | .85 | .86 | .80 | .89 |
| Shanghai/South China | .84 | .61 | .87 | .68 | .90 |

[a]Saigon price data are not available until 1876.
*Source:* For Shanghai, see Note 18, Chapter 2; for other data, see Table 2.3.

## Shanghai's Early Link to Monsoon Asia and the International Rice Market: South China As an Intermediary

Not only were markets in South China integrated with Monsoon Asia by the twentieth century, but also, as Table 2.4 shows, simple correlation coefficients between rice prices in Shanghai and the price of rice exports of Siam, Saigon, India, and Burma demonstrate similar integration. The price for Shanghai, an internal price for non-glutinous rice, was calculated on the basis of price reports that appeared several times each month in *Shen-pao*, a Shanghai newspaper.[18] The correlation coefficient between the price in Shanghai and the unit value of Chinese imports is also given.

Tables 2.3 and 2.4 show a great deal of similarity. With the exception of Saigon, Shanghai was only loosely tied to the Monsoon Asia rice markets during the years between 1870 and 1892. At the same time, Shanghai and South China markets were closely linked, though for reasons I cannot explain the relationship between their prices is weaker for the latter half of the prewar period than it is for the first half. By the beginning of World War I, Shanghai was just as integrated with Monsoon Asia as were the markets in South China.

Additional information about market integration between Shanghai and Monsoon Asia can be obtained by regressing the price of rice in Shanghai on the price prevailing in each of the other four markets. The regression coefficient can be taken to measure the degree of integration and the intercept to estimate transactions costs. A value of one for the slope signifies that the two markets are

Table 2.5. *Regression results of test of integration between Shanghai and Monsoon Asia rice exporters*

| Exporter—Years | Constant | Slope | R2 |
|---|---|---|---|
| *Siam* | | | |
| 1870–1892 | .13 | 0.68(.24) | .28 |
| 1892–1914 | .08 | 0.77(.13) | .64 |
| 1870–1914 | .10 | 0.73(.12) | .44 |
| 1870–1936 | .06 | 0.96(.09) | .64 |
| *Burma* | | | |
| 1870–1892 | .28 | 0.13(.46) | .01 |
| 1892–1914 | − .04 | 1.23(.16) | .73 |
| 1870–1914 | .15 | 0.63(.21) | .17 |
| *Saigon* | | | |
| 1876–1892 | .10 | 0.65(.20) | .79 |
| 1892–1914 | − .08 | 1.35(.18) | .73 |
| 1876–1914 | .03 | 0.91(.11) | .63 |
| 1876–1936 | .07 | 0.89(.06) | .79 |
| *India* | | | |
| 1870–1892 | .17 | 0.55(.39) | .09 |
| 1892–1914 | .01 | 0.97(.22) | .52 |
| 1870–1914 | .12 | 0.64(.19) | .21 |
| 1870–1936 | − .05 | 1.29(.06) | .86 |

*Note:* Standard errors are in parentheses.
*Source:* Same as Table 2.4.

highly integrated and that monopoly elements did not interfere with arbitrage.

Several predictions can be made about the values these coefficients should assume. Cross-sectionally, the intercept terms should reflect the differences in the average transactions costs incurred in shipping rice from each of these Monsoon Asia rice-exporting countries to Shanghai. Naturally, the farther the market from Shanghai, the greater these costs should be. Over time, these costs should fall with the reduction in transport costs, developments in communications, and other technological improvements during the early twentieth century.

Table 2.5 presents the regression results of the tests for the prewar period, its two subperiods, and the entire period between 1870 and 1936. In evaluating these results, it must be remembered that not only are measurement errors present in the price variable, but also that the relationship was continually changing because of the reasons cited. Nonetheless, the results conform nicely to expectations, especially for the pre-1914 period. The estimated transactions costs of shipping rice to China, for example, were lowest for Saigon (0.03 for the period between 1870 and 1914), and increased for sources of rice farther west (Siam, 0.10; Burma, 0.12; and India, 0.15). In addition, it was usually the case that costs were falling and the degree of integration increasing over time, as signified by the fall in the value of the intercept between the prewar subperiods and the behavior of the slope coefficient and its standard error. For the longer period between 1870 and 1936, the statistical results are not nearly so neat; the intercept term for India, for example, is negative. On the key question of market integration, however, 95-percent confidence intervals for the slope coefficient binds the critical value of 1 for both Saigon and Siam and just fails to include it in the case of India.

Both the price correlations and the regression tests point to a high degree of integration between Shanghai and Monsoon Asia by the turn of the century. This result no doubt seems paradoxical when one considers that Shanghai was a thousand miles farther from these markets than Canton; Shanghai began importing rice from Monsoon Asia in the 1920s, and then only occasionally; and it never exported rice overseas over this period. (Historically, the overseas export of rice had been prohibited.) In other words, Shanghai had no direct ties with these markets.

How, then, did Shanghai become so integrated with Monsoon Asia? Historically, the Lower Yangtse area had a deficit in grain. Rice from the Middle and Upper Yangtse provinces passed through a hierarchy of markets on its way down the Yangtse to the lower delta. Until the mid-1800s, a fairly high percentage of the rice appears to have been destined for Soochow, the administrative center for southern Kiangsu and the cultural and commercial capital of Southeast China. Situated on the Grand Canal, Soochow had become the preeminent inland port of the entire Grand Canal system by the late imperial period. Beginning in the 1850s and 1860s, however, many of the city's functions shifted to Shanghai.[19] During the remainder of the nineteenth century and through the early twentieth century, Shanghai became one of the most rapidly growing urban areas in the region and in China generally. According to Hsi-an Kúng, Shanghai's population grew at an annual rate of 4 percent in the early twentieth century and exceeded 3.5 million by the

1930s.[20] As a major consumer of grain and because of its access by steamer, the city soon became the major grain market in the region.

Shanghai and the Lower Yangtse were not the only outlets for the grain surplus of the Middle and Upper Yangtse provinces. The annual trade reports of the Yangtse and South China treaty ports reveal that substantial amounts of rice arrived in Canton and other southern markets from Changsha, Kiukiang, and Wuhu. This rice was either shipped directly by steamer from the Yangtse treaty ports or was transported to Shanghai by junks outside the authority of Maritime Customs, and then conveyed by steamer to South China through Maritime Customs. In the 1890s and 1900s, between 6 and 9 million hundredweights were shipped annually through Maritime Customs,[21] and the total may have been even higher because a significant portion of the Yangtse trade went unenumerated.

Throughout the late nineteenth and early twentieth centuries, the four rice-exporting economies of Monsoon Asia both increased rice production and greatly expanded their exports. Between 1870–4 and 1901–5 average annual rice exports from Siam, Cochin-China, and India increased from 27 million hundredweights to 71 million.[22] This growth continued in the early 1900s, the product of both government policy and technological change. In French-Indochina, public work projects expanded the canal network in Central and Western Cochin China by over 1,300 kilometers, facilitating the transport of paddy to the processing centers of Cholon and Saigon. They also permitted the reclamation of previously uncultivated lands because of the effects of the canals on drainage and irrigation. Between 1900 and 1937, the area under cultivation increased from 1.18 million acres to 2.20 million acres, and rice exports more than doubled.[23] In Siam, several measures encouraged the cultivation of new lands. Tax revisions lowered the land tax; the government expanded the railway and undertook irrigation works; government regulations concerning the disposition of unclaimed lands were liberalized; and the corvée was eliminated. Between 1905–6 and 1935–6, land under rice cultivation increased from 3.6 acres to 8.4 million, and rice exports increased commensurately.[24] In both countries, it can be argued that government policies effectively lowered the costs of production and transport and thereby increased the returns to rice cultivation. In addition, the introduction of the steamship helped continuously reduce long-distance shipping costs.[25]

The increasing competition that this fostered in South China grain markets initially tied Shanghai and the other markets in Central and East China to developments in Monsoon Asia, more than a thousand miles away. The sensitivity of the Yangtse markets is perceptively captured in two separate reports by the commissioner of the treaty port of Wuhu. The first, reviewing the rice trade in 1893, notes:

In my report for 1892 I observed that the price of rice in the southern markets declined toward the close of the year, and thus caused a check to the export of this article from Wuhu; consequently a considerable quantity of grain remained on the market at the end of December, waiting for a rise of price during 1893. The first six months of the year, however, passed by without bringing about any great briskness of trade. Although the first quarter showed an increase in the export, the second and third quarters' Returns exhibited a falling off in comparison with the corresponding periods of the previous year, and large quantities remained stored, waiting for better times. This long lull in the rice trade was doubtless caused by exceptionally good harvests of Rice in Siam and Annam, coupled with the fact of these countries having suspended laws interdicting the export of Rice, which enabled Canton to draw largely from abroad at cheap rates, thereby causing such a fall in the market prices that the Wuhu merchant was unable to ship grain at a remunerative figure.[26]

In 1897 the commissioner of Wuhu similarly reported:

The rice trade during the year under review was subjected to a great deal of fluctuation and uncertainties, which proved rather baffling to our merchants and acted adversely to our export trade ... Large quantities of Rice from Saigon and further supplies from Kwangsi, where the opening of Wuchow and Samshui is said to have facilitated the down-river traffic in Rice, flooded the Canton market to such an extent that the prevailing rates there fell at times to a point actually lower than the prices ruling here. The uncertainties of the Canton market and the narrow margin of profit left on the exported article after the payment of all charges induced traders in the interior to seek other outlets.[27]

Although Shanghai and the Lower Yangtse had a grain deficit, the prices they paid depended heavily on the price the surplus of the Middle and Upper Yangtse markets commanded in South China and, therefore, the price prevailing in Monsoon Asia and the international rice market.

By the early Republican period (1912–49), if not sooner, the influence of Monsoon Asia and the international market in rice on Shanghai and the Yangtse markets became more direct. The volume of rice shipments out of Hunan, Kiangsi, and Anhwei destined for South China fell precipitously, and in some years the Yangste provinces actually imported rice from Monsoon Asia. Shanghai, not Canton, became the new focal point of the competition between internal and external sources. The complex reasons for this change and their implications will be taken up more fully in the next chapter. Here it is sufficient to notice that the way in which the international economy was influencing the markets of Central and East China had changed slightly.

### Interior Markets and the International Market in Rice

So far, I have shown that Shanghai and the major markets in South China were highly integrated with the international market. But was integration limited to a few treaty ports or did it extend into the interior? Moreover, what was the relationship between the prices that prevailed in these markets and the prices received by farm households? If the prices these households received can be systematically linked to those prevailing in higher order markets, it is possible to assert that the influence of the international economy was more pervasive than previously believed.

The *Wuhu Trade Report*, quoted earlier, clearly suggest that at least one interior market – approximately 225 miles upstream from Shanghai on the Yangtse River – was very sensitive to developments in the international market. Unfortunately, I have yet to uncover data that would permit tests for market integration similar to those for Shanghai. Nonetheless, other evidence suggests that interior markets, which themselves appear to have been integrated, were closely linked to the international market.

Chuan and Kraus have argued on the basis of price and grain trade data that as early as the eighteenth century a highly integrated market operated in rice in the Yangtse region. According to their estimates, shipments of rice from Middle and Upper Yangtse provinces destined for the Lower Yangtse averaged roughly 15 to 20 million *picul*. Most came from Hunan, Hupei, Kiangsi, and Anhwei, with the remainder from distant Szechwan. Critical to this trade was the efficient and inexpensive water-transport system that facilitated the distribution of the surplus.[28]

By the turn of the twentieth century, Shanghai had become the Lower Yangtse's major grain market. Rice ceased to be shipped from Szechwan, but substantial amounts still came from Hunan, Kiangsi, and Anhwei. That the region's markets continued to demonstrate a high degree of integration is shown in a lengthy passage taken from the Maritime Customs *Report of Trade* for 1931. It details how effectively the market coped with the shortfall in production that occurred following the severe flooding of the Yangtse that year:

As some ten provinces or more suffered from the most disastrous inundations that have been experienced in 60 years, the period under review will probably be known for a long time to come as the year of the great flood; and yet we find the quantity of foreign rice imported just about half that brought in during 1930. The explanation for the apparent anomaly may be found in a study of the Customs reports from the regions concerned. To take the Yangtse Valley and Tungting Lake terrain alone: Chungking reports a recovery in Szechwan from the drought of 1930, when the rice crops were only 40% of normal; Shasi reports that, as rice crops are mostly grown on higher grounds, the low-lying fields being surrendered to cotton, the harvests of grain were excellent; Changsha reports that, although 54 out of the 75 districts of Hunan were affected by the floods, the real calamitous inundations occurred only in the northeast of the province and that the grain garnered in the districts outside the latter areas was sufficiently plentiful to make Hunan independent of outside supplies; Hankow reports that stocks were obtained without difficulty from districts bordering on the Han River in North Hopeh and South Honan, where harvests were abundant, instead of from Hunan and Anhwei as formerly, while less foreign rice was imported and that only by speculators; Kiukiang reports that the first harvests in Kiangsi were excellent and that, despite the ruination of the second crop, only 840 piculs of foreign rice were imported; Wuhu, which depends for its existence on the agricultural products of the surrounding districts of Anhwei, was able to export 2.4 million picul as against only 1.7 million piculs in 1930, due to the surplus carried over from the super-excellent crops of the previous year; and Chinkiang was able to report that, despite the inundations in the Yangtse and Grand Canals regions, only 672 piculs of foreign rice were imported owing to good harvests of rice in the hilly districts.[29]

This "natural" working of demand and supply in the regional rice trade neatly reflects the extent of integration achieved among markets throughout the region.

Monthly price data for the relatively short period between 1928 and 1932 reveal a similarly high degree of integration between Yangtse markets. Table 2.6 provides simple correlation coefficients between prices in Shanghai and four other secondary markets in the region: Hangchow, Wuhu, Nanchang, and Changsha. The price data they are based on appear in Figure 2.1.

As can be seen from the correlation matrix, all the price series show a relatively high degree of integration. Had there been prices for the same variety of rice for all five markets, the degree of correlation might have been even higher. In addition, occasional market disruption during this period also affected price relationships.[30]

Aside from showing a high degree of integration, the results in Table 2.6 corroborate the view that Shanghai was indeed the re-

Table 2.6. *Rice price correlations between major Yangtse markets, 1928–33*

| City | Wuhu | Changsha | Shanghai | Nanchang | Hangchow |
|------|------|----------|----------|----------|----------|
| Wuhu | 1.00 | | | | |
| Changsha | .62 | 1.00 | | | |
| Shanghai | .92 | .80 | 1.00 | | |
| Nanchang | .84 | .60 | .89 | 1.00 | |
| Hangchow | .89 | .76 | .94 | .87 | 1.00 |

*Sources:* For Shanghai and Nanchang, Institute of Social and Economic Research, *Shang-hai mi-shih tiao-ch'a* for Wuhu, Cheng Wu, *Wan-chung tao-mi ch'an-hsiao chih tiao-ch'a;* for Changsha, Jen-chia Cheng, *Konan no kokumai* (Tokyo, 1940); and for Hangchow, Hsi-chou Chu, ed., *Mi.*

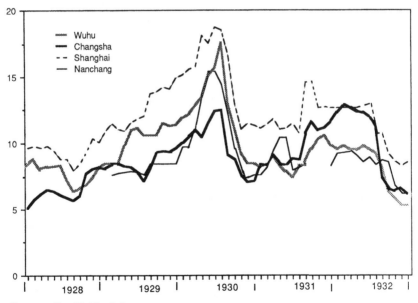

*Source:* See Table 2.6.

Figure 2.1

Monthly Rice Prices for Selected Yangtse Markets, 1928–32
(*yuan* per *shih*)

Table 2.7. *Distance from and correlation with Shanghai*

| City | Correlation with Shanghai | Distance from Shanghai (in miles) |
|------|---------------------------|-----------------------------------|
| Hangchow | .94 | 100 |
| Wuhu | .92 | 225 |
| Nanchang | .89 | 525 |
| Changsha | .80 | 850 |

*Sources:* Same as Table 2.6.

gion's major market. In fact, the price series for Hangchow, Wuhu, Nanchang, and Changsha are each most highly correlated with the Shanghai series: the correlation coefficient between prices in Changsha and Nanchang, for example, is 0.60, between Changsha and Wuhu 0.62, and Changsha and Hangchow 0.76, but between Changsha and Shanghai 0.80. Although both Wuhu and Nanchang are closer to Changsha, prices in Changsha were still more highly correlated with Shanghai, several hundred miles downriver from Wuhu. This same kind of relationship holds true for the other three markets as well. Not only does such behavior indicate Shanghai's role in the regional market, but it also reflects informational flows in the region. At the same time, the correlation with Shanghai is a decreasing function of distance, as Table 2.7 reveals.[31]

Given that an integrated market existed in the Yangtse as early as the eighteenth century and that by all indications it was operating effectively in the late 1920s and early 1930s, there is every reason to believe that during the late nineteenth and early twentieth centuries there was also one. In fact, the degree of integration probably increased after the 1890s because of developments in transportation, communication, marketing, and even banking, all of which helped to further reduce transactions costs.[32] The introduction of the steamer reduced the time it took to ship grain to Shanghai; the introduction of the telegraph and telephone better linked buyer and seller and reduced business uncertainty;[33] the expansion in warehousing facilities helped to eliminate some seasonal variability; and the development of a modern banking system in China and the spread of branch banks in many of these markets made for more efficient financing of the rice trade.[34]

If I am correct in assuming that a highly integrated regional market in rice existed in the late nineteenth and early twentieth centuries and that the interior markets were closely linked to Shanghai, it follows logically that these markets would have also been tied to the international market either directly or indirectly. Regional price formation may thus be viewed as a simultaneous process in which prices were determined in Shanghai and prices in the interior markets (such as Wuhu, Nanchang, and Changsha) set to reflect the transport and transactions costs of shipping rice to Shanghai.[35] The price in Changsha would have been less than that in Wuhu because of its greater distance from and hence higher costs in shipping rice to Shanghai.[36] Prices graphed in Figure 2.1 generally bear this out; prices are a decreasing function of distance from Shanghai. As noted earlier, between 1928 and 1932 the markets were occasionally disrupted, so the differentials between Shanghai and the secondary markets were not always maintained.[37]

### The Rural Hinterland and the International Market: A Question of Market Structure

One final question remains: Were the prices in the rural hinterland linked to those in the major markets in such a way that one might assume economic decision making and the well-being of rural households was seriously influenced by the international economy? Long-run time series on the prices farmers received are available for a single locality, Wuchin *hsien*, located approximately 125 miles from Shanghai.[38] Most of the data are retail prices. Nonetheless, inferences about the relationship between the prices farmers received and those in larger markets can still be made, on the basis of additional information concerning the relationship between retail prices in major markets and those in smaller market towns and the nature of market structure and rural marketing in China. If retail prices in market towns were tied to those in higher-order markets, then the link between the prices farmers received and those prevailing in major commercial centers comes down to a question of local market structure and rural marketing. In other words, were local rice markets and, more generally, agricultural markets in China competitive, or were there monopolistic or monopsonistic elements that might have severed the link between the price in Chaohsien (a major collection center for rice located northwest of Wuhu on the east bank of the Lake Chao), for example, and the price received by the farmer whose rice was first shipped to Chaohsien on its way to Wuhu?

Before pursuing these two points, I will first examine the price

Table 2.8. *Correlations between prices paid and received:*
*Wuchin* hsien

|  |  | Prices paid for: | | |
|---|---|---|---|---|
|  |  | Pai-mi | N'o-mi | Shan-mi |
| Prices | Pai-mi | .997 | .976 | .978 |
| received | N'o-mi | .980 | .988 | .963 |
| for: | K'eng-tao | .924 | .928 | .924 |

*Source:* Based on price data contained in Lu-luan Chang, "Chiang-su Wuchin wu-chia chih yen-chiu."

data for Wuchin, which include prices received by farmers for three
varieties of rice over the period 1894–1932 and prices paid in the
market by rural households for three varieties of rice for the shorter
period 1910–32. What was the relationship between producer prices
(what the farmers received) and retail prices, and what was the link
between Shanghai and Wuchin prices?

Carrying out the same kind of tests as before, I find that the
correlation between the prices farmers received and retail prices
was exceptionally high (see Table 2.8). But what does the behavior of producer and retail prices actually say about local market
structure? Under competitive market conditions, the marketing
margin between producer and retail prices should be independent
of price and the difference between the two more or less constant
(assuming no change in transactions costs). This would imply, in
turn, that in a linear regression of retail prices on producer
prices the slope coefficient should not be significantly different
from one.[39] Such a test was run on two varieties of rice, and the
results were generally consistent with the hypothesis of competitive market conditions.[40] In Figure 2.2, producer and retail prices
for one of these varieties has also been graphed and offers additional confirmation that marketing margins remained fairly constant over the period.[41]

Retail prices in Wuchin were also highly correlated with Shanghai
retail prices (0.994, 0.960, and 0.979, respectively, for the period
between 1910 and 1932), as were the prices farmers received for the
years between 1894 and 1932 (0.995, 0.983, and 0.966, respectively).
The results of these limited tests, therefore, point to the relatively
efficient transmission of information between Shanghai and farm
households in the Wuchin area. Naturally, there are dangers in

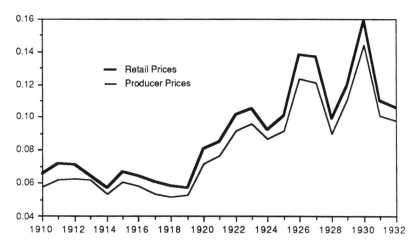

Source: Lu-luan Chang, "Chiang-su Wu-chin wu-chia chih yen-chiu," pp. 189–216.

Figure 2.2

Producer and Retail Prices: Wuchin *hsien*, Kiangsu, 1910–32
(*yuan* per *sheng*)

generalizing on the basis of one locality. Nonetheless, the price data for Wuchin suggest that a link between retail prices in major markets and outlying market towns would, with the support of additional information on local market structure, verify that prices received were inevitably tied to those in Shanghai and the international rice market.

## The Central Anhwei Rice Market

A wonderfully detailed 1936 survey of the Central Anhwei rice market makes this possible.[42] Investigators conducting the survey were not only concerned with detailing (and quantifying) the movement of rice from outlying *hsien* north and south of the Yangtse into Wuhu, but were also equally interested in the institutional aspects of the market. Monthly rice price data were also compiled for a number of *hsien* city and market towns that were major collection points in the distribution system.

Rice moved into Wuhu from outlying areas in the following fashion (see Map 2.1). Approximately 70 percent of the rice shipped out of the city originated from *hsien* north of the

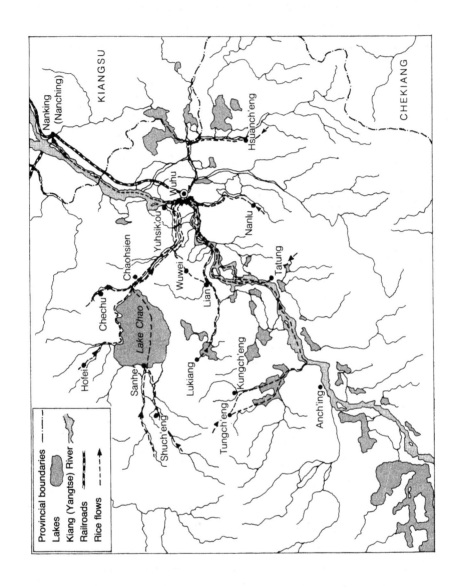

Map 2.1
Central Anhwei
Rice Market

Table 2.9. *Correlations between Central Anhwei market towns, 1928–32*

| Town | Wuhu | Sanhechen | Shuanghe | Chaohsien | Hsuancheng |
|------|------|-----------|----------|-----------|------------|
| Wuhu | | | | | |
| Sanhechen | .77 | | | | |
| Shuanghe | .79 | .90 | | | |
| Chaohsien | .91 | .88 | .91 | | |
| Hsuancheng | .89 | .73 | .71 | .85 | |
| Nanlu | .68 | .64 | .62 | .66 | .80 |

*Source:* Based on price data contained in Cheng Wu, *Wan-chung tao-mi ch'an-hsiao chih tiao-ch'a.*

Yangtse; the remainder, from those south of it. Sanhechen, on the west bank of Lake Chao, was the major collection point for rice north of the Yangtse. Rice passed into Sanhe from smaller market towns such as Shuanghe (Liuan *hsien*), Paishihshan (Lukiang *hsien*), Sucheng, and the southwestern corner of Hofei, and was then shipped on to Wuhu by small junk. The two other major collections points were Lukiang *hsien* and Wuwei, with rice shipments reportedly totaling 1 million *picul*. South of the Yangtse, the two major markets were located in Hsuancheng and Nanlu *hsien*. Hsuancheng produced approximately 2.5 million *shih*, some of which was shipped south to southeastern Anhwei and Chekiang, but presumably more was shipped north to Wuhu. Most of the rice from Nanlu destined for Wuhu was shipped out of either the county seat (Nanluchen) or Chingtaichiang.

How closely were prices in these market towns tied to those in Wuhu and with each other? The monthly price data permit the computation of correlation coefficients between prices in some of these markets.[43] Table 2.9 provides the correlation matrix. Three points of qualification are in order. First, in some cases the lunar calendar was used to report rice prices, but in others the solar calendar was used. Because there is no easy way to adjust the series for the slight differences involved, I have used the series as reported. Second, the prices for Wuhu are for *t'zu mi*, and those for all remaining markets are for *t'sao mi*, or unpolished rice. Third, the survey conveys the impression that over the period (1928–32) the market was not always operating at optimal efficiency. It cites as disruptive factors the severe flooding of the Yangtse in 1931, banditry, and tightness of the local money market. All the same, the prices still demonstrate a fairly high degree of correlation. Moreover, during the period studied, prices rose as high as 17–18 *yuan* per *shih* in 1930, but fell to between 4–5 *yuan* per *shih* by the end of 1932. No obvious explanation clarifies the weaker correlations for Nanlu, especially because the correlation with Hsuancheng, the other market town south of the Yangtse, is 0.80 – nearer the other correlation levels.

In regard to the institutional aspects of the market, until recently conventional wisdom held that neither factor or product markets in rural China were very competitive. Tawney pointed to the weak bargaining position of the local farmer and his lack of market information as factors that made him "easy prey" for the local monopolist.[44] Thirty years later, Feuerwerker echoed this sentiment in his frequently cited survey of the Republican economy:

The local market tended to be monopsonistic for what the peasant sold and monopolistic for what he bought. He was subject to considerable price manipulation, which was intensified by the fact that the supply would naturally be larger at harvest time when he wanted to sell and smaller in spring when he wanted to buy ... In general, the marketing process aggravated an already skewed distribution of the agricultural product between producer and others.[45]

Lately, however, a number of scholars, including Ramon Myers, Thomas Rawski, and William Rowe, have called attention either explicitly or implicitly to the competitive nature of rural markets throughout much of China. Rawski's work is noteworthy because he has tried to reconcile the competing views on this subject by loosely drawing on the distinction between core and peripheral areas as applied to China by Skinner.[46] Acknowledging that monopolistic and monopsonistic elements were present in some markets, Rawski points out that core areas with well-developed networks of traditional transport, communication, and marketing and with a high level of commercial activity and expanded economic opportunities were less likely to deviate from competitive market conditions. Feuerwerker's recent contribution to the *Cambridge Economic History of China* agrees that few studies have been able to document monopolistic and monopsonistic elements in local markets.[47] Was this true for the rice market?

The Central Anhwei rice-marketing system was characterized by a hierarchy of middleman, rice mills, and rice-trading firms similar in a number of respects to the system William Rowe found marketing tea in Hankow.[48] Most of the time, the farmer himself shipped his rice to a market town for sale to a *mi-hao*, or middleman. Sometimes, however, *mi-fan*, or rice peddlers, would buy up small amounts of rice in the countryside to sell in the market town. When the market was exceptionally good, the *mi-hao* would actually send representatives into the countryside to procure rice rather than wait for farm households to deliver it themselves. Although in some cases *mi-hao* behaved like small independent entrepreneurs, using working capital of several thousand *yuan* to buy rice and organize its shipment to Wuhu, most acted on behalf of larger middlemen from Sanhe or Wuhu in return for a modest commission.[49] The rice was milled in a *nien-mi chang*, or rice mill, several of which would be found in the market town. Often these mills simply milled rice for others, but sometimes mill owners acted as agents for outside buyers or small entrepreneurs themselves, buying and milling rice for resale. At the market town level, then, there was some overlap in the roles each economic actor played, a feature that contributed to the overall competitiveness of the local market.

After passing up through these smaller market towns into San-hechen, Wuwei, and so forth, the rice was shipped to Wuhu, where two kinds of middlemen handled it: *hsiao-shih hang* and *chiang-kuang hang*. The former, who numbered over a hundred, acted primarily as middlemen between farmers within Wuhu *hsien* and the larger *chiang-kuang hang*. They also fulfilled a similar role for a comparatively small number of farm households from southern markets who transported their rice to Wuhu themselves. All the rice shipped into Wuhu for eventual export passed through the hands of the *chiang-kuang*. Numbering almost fifty in 1934, the *chiang-kuang* procured rice for outside buyers. Their primary customers were twenty-seven *mi-hao*, or rice-trading firms, which bought rice for shipment to markets in South China, the Lower Yangtse, and North China. With warehouses, or godowns, situated along the south bank of the Yangtse, the *mi-hao* typically had working capital of about 10,000 *yuan* and were themselves organized into *pangs*, or guilds, which were constituted along geographical lines. The four major *pangs* were Canton, with six members, three of which had recently suspended operation; Wuhu, with eight members; Yentai, with five; and Ningpo, with three. In addition, the Shanghai *pang* had four members and the Tientsin *pang* had one. Unfortunately, the surveyors did not examine the formal or informal ties between *pang* and their respective markets. Were they representatives of firms that also had agents throughout Monsoon Asia? If so, they were then part of an important network through which information about the price of rice in the international market was transmitted to the interior.

Finally, Wuhu also had two kinds of mills: *nien-mi chang* and *lung-fang*. The former not only milled rice for others, but owned warehouses and extended credit to customers, using their rice as collateral. As of 1933, there were nine in operation. Substantially smaller in size and less mechanized, but more numerous (over forty of them) were the *lung-fang*. They were usually owned by landlords and fulfilled many of the same functions as their larger counterparts.

One cannot help noticing how this situation fits the textbook description of competitive markets: a large number of participants operating on both sides of the market, freedom of entry and exit, mobility of capital and other resources, and so forth. These features not only characterized the rice market in Wuhu, but also the smaller market towns that fed rice into the city. Despite the fact that the rice would change hands several times before finally leaving Central Anhwei, a lively competition appears obvious at every stage of the marketing process.

The number of firms operating in each market does not inform us of any one firm's market power or the likelihood of collusion between firms. This cannot be entirely ruled out, but, given the relatively modest working capital of the parties involved, collusion seems rather unlikely. A Japanese description of the Hankow rice market in 1913–14, quoted by Ramon Myers, tends to substantiate this view:

Rice exchange in Hankow is no different than in Shanghai, where it is handled through rice brokerage firms... There are at least 20 rice brokerage firms... However, there is no case whereby these firms buy large quantities of rice at a fixed time, or send agents to the rice producing areas to corner the rice supply. Nor are there any examples whereby they resort to cunning means to collude with various shops which buy rice. We can say that these practices simply do not exist on a yearly basis, and for Chinese merchants this is one of their noteworthy characteristics.[50]

By all indications, the same can be said for the market centered in Wuhu.

To return to my original concern, I believe this assessment of the market operation and structure, combined with the price data, lets me reasonably link the prices farmers received to those prevailing in larger market towns and Wuhu. The farm household either delivered its rice to one of these markets or sold it to a middleman operating in a highly competitive environment. It seems unlikely that the price changes occurring in Wuhu were not mirrored in those that households received for their rice.

Throughout the Yangtse drainage basin and even beyond it, the prices farmers received were closely tied to those prevailing in larger markets and Shanghai. Given that Shanghai was highly integrated with the international market, it seems reasonable to believe that the prices farmers received were also tied to the international market. But how many farm households would this mean?

This kind of price-setting behavior was primarily confined to areas linked together by cheap water transport (and to a lesser extent rail); in other words, they were core areas. Slightly less than half of the Middle and Lower Yangtse counties belonged in the core. Given a slightly higher population density in these areas, a conservative estimate would extend the analysis to one-half the population. But because some key areas that I discussed fall totally outside Skinner's core – Central Anhwei being a case in point – the analysis may be applicable to two-thirds of all rural households in the region.

## Summary

Over the course of the late nineteenth and early twentieth centuries, agricultural markets throughout the Central and Lower Yangtse provinces became vitally linked to the international economy. This integration can best be viewed as part of the same process that fundamentally altered how Chinese markets for tea and silk related to the international economy and was facilitated by developments in transportation and communications, both those inside China and those linking it with the rest of the world.

Although the focus of attention of this chapter has been on rice markets, certainly other markets such as those in cotton and wheat were similarly integrated.[51] In the early twentieth century, for example, China's domestic textile industry grew rapidly and generated in the process a great increase in cotton demand. As the center of the nation's expanding textile industry, Shanghai was the focal point of the competition that developed between internal and external sources of supply. Cotton shipped from Honan, Hopei, Hupei, and from within Kiangsu competed in Shanghai with supplies from the United States and British India.[52] In a similar manner, domestic wheat competed in Shanghai with supplies from Canada, Argentina, and the United States.[53]

This interpretation raises many new questions about price formation in domestic agricultural markets as well as the influence of the international economy on domestic trade and output more generally.

# 3

# Price Formation, Marketing, and Output in Agriculture

Historically, the provinces of the Middle and Upper Yangtse produced a grain surplus. Rice and to a lesser extent wheat passed through an elaborate network of interior waterways into Changsha, Hankow, and Wuhu for shipment down the Yangtse River. During the late nineteenth and early twentieth centuries, shipments of rice down the Yangtse River through Maritime Customs increased.[1] In 1880–1 they averaged 6 million Maritime Customs *picul*, but by 1903 they had almost doubled. Although some of the increase reflects the expanded coverage of Maritime Customs, most of it probably represents an actual increase in the amount of rice marketed due to the reduction in long-distance transport costs that accompanied the introduction of the steamship as well as the increased demand for rice in South China.

During the last few years of the Ch'ing (1644–1911), however, rice exports from the region began to decline. In 1908–9 they averaged 8 million Maritime Custom *picul*, but in 1910–12 they sank to 5 million, and by 1913–14 they had fallen to only 3–4 million Maritime Customs *picul*. With few exceptions, most notably 1919, they remained at this level for the next twenty years. Simultaneously, overseas rice imports began to increase, first into South China and then in the twenties and thirties into Central and East China.

Much has been made of this decline. It has often been taken as symptomatic of the inability of agriculture to increase output at the same rate as population growth and to increase quantity marketed at the rate the urban population was growing – an annual average of 2 to 2 1/2 percent throughout the early twentieth century.[2] Perkins's estimates of rice production for the six provinces of East-Central China are consistent with this interpretation: he shows that average rice output declined by 75 million *picul* between 1914–18 and 1931–6, or slightly less than 10 percent of average output. Combined with an estimated 15 percent population increase,[3] this implies a fall in per capita rice consumption of a quarter. Some contemporary observers attributed the more than doubling of rice prices in Shanghai between the late 1890s and early 1930s to these same developments.

39

In addition to utilizing some questionable data, such interpretations fail to recognize the nature of the rapidly emerging relationship between the domestic and international markets documented in Chapter 2. At the same time, they have often ignored, or underestimated, the substantial growth in demand for agricultural goods by the nonagricultural sector. In this chapter, I examine price formation, marketing, and agricultural output in light of Chapter 2 and the changes occurring simultaneously within the domestic economy. I focus on the markets in rice and cotton.

## The Question of Price Determination

In a closed economy, agricultural prices are determined solely through the interaction of internal demand and supply, so price movements and agricultural output are typically inversely related. A less-than-average harvest produces a rise in agricultural prices, and prices fall with a bumper crop. In any locality with a poor harvest, the price rise would depend on whether the locality was isolated or was integrated with a larger marketing area and how easily grain could be brought in from areas with a surplus. The higher prices that appear in the deficit area either in anticipation of or after the actual shortfall provide outside suppliers with an incentive to supply the needed grain, which in the process eliminates any price differential (less transport costs) that has arisen between areas. An analogous set of events would occur if the locality harvested a surplus. The more closely an individual locality is tied to other areas and markets, the smaller the role demand and supply in that particular locality would play in agricultural price formation and the larger the role demand and supply in the wider geographic area would assume.

This analysis can be extended to an entire economy. Upon integration with the international market, domestic prices would cease to depend principally on internal demand and supply; instead, they would come to be heavily influenced by prices prevailing in the international market. If the country's imports or exports amounted to a relatively small percentage of the trade in a particular commodity, the country would be a price taker in the international market – that is, its trade would not influence international prices.

### Commodity Arbitrage

The theory of commodity arbitrage and the law of one price offers a slightly idealized view of how prices and commodity flows would be linked in a perfectly integrated international market and, in turn, how prices in China would have been influenced by international market forces. Any price differential that arises between two markets (or countries) outside of what are commonly referred to as import and export points would be arbitraged away.[4] Trading agents quickly spot the opportunities associated with these "excessive" price differentials and profit from them by shipping goods between the markets.[5] In the process, price differentials that had existed outside the import and export points are eliminated, thereby ensuring similar prices (in a common currency) for similar goods between countries.[6]

Prices in an integrated market are no longer determined by demand and supply in the domestic market, but by a similar set of forces (demand for imports, supply of exports) operating in the international market. And, if a particular country has few imports or exports relative to the total volume of trade, its transactions in the international market will not alter prices and it will become a price taker.

What exactly did this mean for China? Take the case of the rice market in Shanghai. If it was as integrated with the international market as I have suggested, prices would ultimately have been determined by demand and supply conditions in major rice-exporting economies. The price of Shanghai rice could never exceed the price at which grain could be imported from Monsoon Asia. If $P_M$ represents the price of rice prevailing in Monsoon Asia, in equilibrium the Shanghai price, $P_S$, would equal $P_M + T$, where T represents the transport and transactions costs for shipping rice to Shanghai. If $P_S$ rose above $P_M + T$ in expectation of a less-than-average rice crop and a decline in the quantity marketed in the region, imports would presumably increase in order to clear the market. A bumper crop in Monsoon Asia would lower prices in Shanghai.

On the other hand, if the price of rice in Shanghai was actually less than that in Monsoon Asia, an increase in demand in southern markets (which historically imported rice from Monsoon Asia) would eliminate the differential. Commodity arbitrage between Shanghai and other domestic markets and between Shanghai and Monsoon Asia would have closely tied prices in Shanghai and the interior Yangtse markets to those in the international market. Changes in the international market as reflected by prices in Monsoon Asia, therefore, should have heavily influenced Shanghai prices.

In Figure 3.1 the average export price of rice for Saigon, India, and Siam shows the changes that occurred in the international market between 1876 and 1936. Throughout most of the late nineteenth

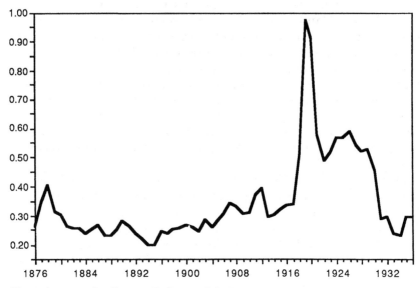

*Note:* Average for Saigon, India, and Siam.
*Source:* See Table 2.3.

Figure 3.1

Average Export Price of Rice from Monsoon Asia, 1876–1936
(in £/cwt.)

century, rice prices expressed in pounds sterling were actually falling. In the mid–1890s they began to recover and for the next thirty
years, rice prices in the international market rose. This increase
can be associated with the long-term decline in transport costs and
the increase in the world demand for agricultural products. The year
1926, however, marked the beginning of a sharp eight-year decline
in rice prices, which ultimately fell below their 1900 level.

Throughout most of the period, the price of rice in the international market was determined independently of the rice market in
Shanghai or China more generally. China faced an infinitely elastic
supply curve for imports, with its own demand for rice imports generally too small to influence international prices. Table 3.1 presents
the nation's rice imports for the years between 1870 and 1936. Data
cited in Chapter 2 show that between 1901 and 1910 these imports
averaged less than 7 percent of the total exported by the four major
rice exporters. In the teens, China's rice imports were only 8 percent
of the total,[7] but between 1921 and 1935 the country's average an-

Table 3.1 *Chinese overseas rice imports, 1870–1936 (in thousands of Maritime Customs* picul)

| Year | Quantity | Year | Quantity | Year | Quantity |
|------|---------|------|---------|------|---------|
| 1870 | 141   | 1893 | 9,475  | 1915 | 8,476  |
| 1871 | 248   | 1894 | 6,441  | 1916 | 11,284 |
| 1872 | 659   | 1895 | 10,096 | 1917 | 9,387  |
| 1873 | 1,156 | 1896 | 9,415  | 1918 | 6,984  |
| 1874 | 6     | 1897 | 2,104  | 1919 | 1,810  |
| 1875 | 85    | 1898 | 4,645  | 1920 | 1,152  |
| 1876 | 576   | 1899 | 7,365  | 1921 | 10,629 |
| 1877 | 1,051 | 1900 | 6,207  | 1922 | 19,156 |
| 1878 | 298   | 1901 | 4,412  | 1923 | 22,435 |
| 1879 | 249   | 1902 | 9,732  | 1924 | 13,198 |
| 1880 | 30    | 1903 | 2,802  | 1925 | 12,635 |
| 1881 | 198   | 1904 | 3,357  | 1926 | 18,701 |
| 1882 | 233   | 1905 | 2,228  | 1927 | 21,092 |
| 1883 | 253   | 1906 | 4,686  | 1928 | 12,656 |
| 1884 | 152   | 1907 | 12,765 | 1929 | 10,823 |
| 1885 | 317   | 1908 | 6,737  | 1930 | 19,891 |
| 1886 | 1,944 | 1909 | 3,798  | 1931 | 10,741 |
| 1887 | 7,132 | 1910 | 9,221  | 1932 | 22,487 |
| 1888 | 4,271 | 1911 | 5,303  | 1933 | 21,419 |
| 1889 | 7,574 | 1912 | 2,700  | 1934 | 12,749 |
| 1890 | 4,685 | 1913 | 5,415  | 1935 | 21,436 |
| 1891 | 3,948 | 1914 | 6,814  | 1936 | 5,132  |
| 1892 | 3,948 |      |        |      |        |

*Source:* Hsiao, *China's Foreign Trade Statistics,* pp. 32–3.

nual rice imports almost tripled, to a million metric tons, or approximately 13.5 percent of total rice exports of Monsoon Asia. This figure is slightly misleading, however, for a number of reasons.

First, international prices were formed in an integrated market for both rice and wheat. As a result, information on China's rice imports alone would naturally exaggerate its influence on the market. Between 1921 and 1935, the nation's combined imports of rice and wheat averaged less than 1 1/2 million metric ton, or just over 5 percent of the international trade in these two goods.[8] Second, between 1911–15 and 1931–5, rice exports increased from 4.3 million to 7.5 million metric tons. Although I do not want to rule out entirely the role demand played in this growth, much was due to government policies in these rice-exporting countries that effectively lowered the costs of production and encouraged exports.[9] This ultimately made the importation of rice into China less expensive.[10] Finally, something very similar was occurring in both India and Japan. Between 1931 and 1935, India's rice imports averaged 1.4 million metric tons, or almost five times their level between 1911 and 1915. Over the same period, Japanese rice imports almost tripled. These increases reflected the changing market conditions in Monsoon Asia and the international rice market.

## Gold and Silver

Rice prices in Monsoon Asia were not the only external factor influencing Shanghai prices; changes in the international gold price of silver also affected internal rice prices.[11] Although both copper and silver served as monetary units in China, silver was the medium used for foreign trade. Silver circulated as silver dollars, *sycee* (silver ingots cast in the form of shoes), and subsidiary coins; prices were quoted in *taels* of silver. Every one of hundreds of commercial centers had its own *tael*, each defined as so many grains of silver of a particular fineness. The fictitious Haikwan *Tael* (HKT), the unit of account used by Chinese Maritime Customs, was designated equal to 584 grains of silver of 992.3 fineness.[12] Even with the increase in the use of *yuan* bank notes in the early twentieth century, silver remained the numeraire. China was on a silver standard, and up through 1935 bank notes could be redeemed for silver at the bank of issue for an amount equal to their face value. The national *yuan*, for example, was equal to 0.8166 standard ounces or 0.7553 fine ounces.[13]

Whereas China was tied to silver, Monsoon Asia economies and most of China's trading partners were tied to gold. In the United States, gold was fixed at $20.67 per ounce between 1879 and 1934, making each dollar equal to 0.0484 ounces of gold. In Great Britain, gold remained at 3 pounds, 17 shillings, and 10.5 pence per ounce for most of the 200-year period ending in 1931. Consequently, over this period the price of foreign exchange as expressed in terms of either silver or *yuan* was effectively determined by the international gold price of silver. When the gold price of silver fell, the price of foreign exchange (in terms of either silver or *yuan*) rose.[14] Shanghai was an integral part of this market, and arbitrage assured that the Shanghai price of silver (in terms of either gold or foreign exchange) never deviated far in this period from the international market price given in London, New York, or Yokohama.[15]

How, then, did a change in the gold (or foreign exchange) price of silver affect the price of a domestic good such as rice traded in the international economy? When the gold price of silver fell in the international market, the price of the domestic commodity would fall below its foreign counterpart also expressed in silver. When the gold price of silver rose, the commodity price would rise. If the two markets were highly integrated, the price of the domestic item would soon be bid up or down because of the higher or lower price of the imported item. In general, one would expect a fall in the exchange rate to be followed by a rise in the price of the domestic good by a similar percentage (or a rise in the exchange rate to be followed by a fall in price) in order to maintain the equilibrium between the internal and external price. Assuming no restrictions to trade, arbitrage would assure this continuous equilibrium, which in turn suggests that an inverse relationship should exist between changes in the price of tradables and the gold price of silver.

Over the late nineteenth and early twentieth centuries, the world economy gradually reduced the role of silver in the international financial system as both a medium of exchange and store of value; economies increasingly tied their currencies to gold.[16] As the demand for silver declined, so did its price relative to gold. This downward trend – and a fair amount of volatility – are reflected in the sterling/ HKT exchange rate (see Figure 3.2). Because the HKT represented 581.83 grains of silver and Britain was on a gold standard, the exchange rate between sterling and the HKT makes an excellent proxy for the changing gold price of silver. By the 1930s, the exchange rate had fallen to approximately one-quarter of its level during the 1870s.

What effect did China have on the international gold price of silver? Elsewhere it has been argued that the country had none whatsoever.[17] It must be remembered, however, that China was the largest silver-standard economy in the world. Its primary demand would be for coinage and for industrial use. No industrial estimates appear to have been made, but estimates on China's net coinage requirements have been found for the relatively short period between 1922 and 1931. They represent approximately 20 percent of total silver production and governmental sales of silver for these years.[18] Net silver imports may give a better measure of Chinese demand because this would reflect not only monetary and industrial demand, but also the role of silver in the nation's balance of payments. Between 1920 and 1932, it was consistently a net importer of silver: imports averaged 78.3 million fine ounces, or 23.7 percent of total silver production and sales by governments. Although the country was a major silver consumer in the 1920s, it is hard to

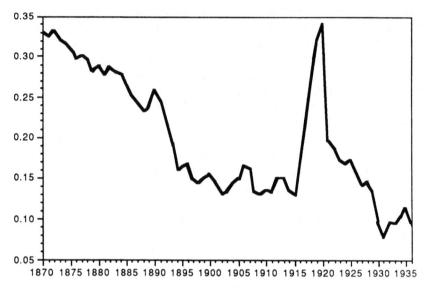

*Source:* Hsiao, *China's Foreign Trade Statistics*, pp. 190–2.

Figure 3.2

Sterling–Haikuan *Tael* Exchange Rate, 1870–1936

ascertain the effect that it had on silver's international price because silver prices were falling so rapidly. Prior to 1920, however, China was just as likely to be a net exporter as a net importer. Maritime Customs data show net silver imports between 1889 and 1919 at one-third their level between 1919 and 1933. I believe Chinese demand had only a weak influence on the gold price of silver in the international market during this period.

## The Model

My previous analysis clearly suggests that, because of China's integration with the international economy, exogenous changes in the international price of rice and the gold price of silver should have been exerting a major influence on rice prices in Shanghai. Theoretically, arbitrage in both the silver and the rice markets would have tied the internal and external price together. It is possible to

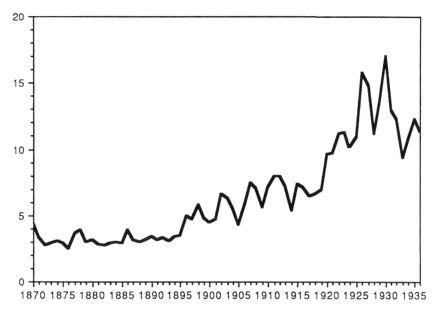

*Source:* See Note 18, Chapter 2.

Figure 3.3

Rice Prices in Shanghai, 1870–1936

test this proposition and determine how much the behavior of the rice price reflected these external changes rather than internal changes in demand and supply. Figure 3.3 graphs the price of rice in Shanghai between 1870 and 1936.

Assuming that China was integrated into the international market and faced an infinitely elastic supply curve for imports, that is, China was a price taker, the price of rice in Shanghai and the international market should have been linked by the following relation:

$$P_S = T(P_I/R) \tag{1}$$

where $P_S$ is the Shanghai price of rice expressed in silver, $P_I$ is the international price expressed in gold, $R$ is the exchange rate between gold and silver, and $T$ is the transactions cost of shipping rice from the international market to Shanghai, measured as a percentage of the international price. The extent to which this relationship was actually the case and the overall influence of T, $P_I$, and R on $P_S$ can be ascertained by taking logs of equation (1) and estimating the equation:

$$\ln P_S = a_0 + a_1 * \ln T + a_2 * \ln P_I + a_3 * \ln R + u_i \qquad (2)$$

In equation (2), $a_1$, $a_2$ and $a_3$ are just elasticities and measure the percentage change in the price in Shanghai for a percentage change in T, $P_I$ and R. If Shanghai was isolated from the international market and commodity arbitrage did not go on, all three coefficients would have been equal to zero. On the other hand, if internal and external markets were integrated, $a_0$ should be equal to zero, and $a_1$ and $a_2$ equal to 1, but $a_3$ should be equal to $-1$ because of the inverse relationship between prices in Shanghai in silver and the gold price of silver.

Unfortunately, because I lack a time series on T, it is not possible to estimate equation (2) as it is. Nonetheless, it can be argued that T and $P_I$ and R should be unsystematically correlated, and, therefore, ordinary least squares (OLS) can be used to obtain unbiased estimates of $a_2$ and $a_3$ through the estimation of equation (3) with T now omitted.

$$\ln P_{S,HKT} = a_0 + a_1 * \ln P_M + a_2 * \ln R_{\pounds/HKT} + u_i \qquad (3)$$

In equation (3), $P_{S,HKT}$ is the Shanghai price of rice expressed in HKT, and $P_I$ is the international price proxied by the price in Monsoon Asia expressed in sterling. The appropriate exchange rate, R, is that between the British pound sterling and the HKT. The coefficients $a_1$ and $a_2$ measure the rate at which Shanghai prices were adjusting to changes in the international price of rice and the gold price of silver, respectively. Finally, the $R^2$ for the model would provide us with an estimate of the percentage of the variability in Shanghai prices that can be explained by external factors. A high $R^2$ would confirm the belief that with integration external factors came to play the predominant role in domestic price formation.

Table 3.2 reports the estimation results. Two proxies have been used for the international price: first, the average of the export price of rice of Saigon, India, and Siam; and, second, the price of exports from India separately on the rationale that it was the nexus of the international market in rice and wheat. The model was estimated using OLS. The findings strongly support the view that Shanghai was highly integrated with the international market and sensitive to changes in international rice prices and changes in the gold price of silver through commodity arbitrage. When the average price of rice exports was used, not only did I accept the null hypothesis that

Table 3.2. *Regression results for arbitrage model*

| | | Rice, 1870–1936 | | |
|---|---|---|---|---|
| | | OLS | | OLS |
| Intercept | | 0.231 | Intercept | 0.432 |
| | | (0.095) | | (0.121) |
| WPR1 | | 1.105 | WPR | 1.141 |
| | | (0.054) | | (0.068) |
| SHKT | | −0.983 | SHKT | −0.887 |
| | | (0.045) | | (0.054) |
| $\bar{R}^2$ | | 0.928 | $\bar{R}^2$ | 0.895 |

| | | | Cotton | | |
|---|---|---|---|---|---|
| | | 1900–36 | | | 1913–36 |
| Intercept | 0.262 | | −0.633 | | 0.284 |
| | (0.294) | | (0.449) | | (0.487) |
| WPC | 0.854 | 0.936 | 1.125 | 0.935 | 0.880 |
| | (0.093) | (0.015) | (0.135) | (0.013) | (0.140) |
| DHKTR | −1.179 | −1.1274 | −1.356 | −1.140 | −.965 |
| | (0.137) | (0.085) | (0.167) | (0.073) | (0.192) |
| Dummy, WW I | | | | | −0.239 |
| | | | | | (0.079) |
| $\bar{R}^2$ | 0.718 | 0.726 | 0.753 | 0.763 | 0.821 |

*Note:* In the regressions for rice, WPR1 is the average price of rice exports for Siam, French-Indochina, and India; WPR2 is the price for India only; and SHKT is the sterling-HKT exchange rate. In the regressions for cotton, WPC is the price of cotton in the United States, and DHKT is the dollar-HKT exchange rate.
*Source:* See text.

the elasticities $a_1$ and $a_2$ were equal to 1 and −1, respectively, but both point estimates (1.100 and −0.978, respectively) were also actually very close to these values. In addition, I failed to reject the hypothesis that the absolute values of the two coefficients were equal, implying an underlying symmetry in the way prices in Shanghai were adjusting to changes in $P_I$ and R. In general, I believe that information on external changes was rapidly assimilated and reflected in Shanghai rice prices: a fall in the international price of rice would lead to a decline in Shanghai, but a fall in the gold price of silver would have exactly the opposite effect.

Over sixty years, the influence of these external and otherwise exogenous changes on rice prices in China appears to have been substantial. The adjusted $R^2$ ($\overline{R}^2$) suggests changes in the international price of rice and the gold price of silver explain between 80 and 90 percent of the variability in Shanghai, leaving only a small residuum to be explained by other factors. In its analysis of Shanghai rice prices between 1912 and 1931, the Institute of Social and Economic Research attributed almost all the change to internal factors.[19] Only for the last few years does it acknowledge that the international market had any influence and then only because the volume of rice imports had markedly increased. The systematic influence of changes in silver prices appears to have gone unnoticed.

In Chapter 2, I showed that Shanghai not only integrated with the international market, but was also at the core of a highly integrated market operating within central and eastern China. Because the excellent functioning of the internal marketing system helped to tie prices in the interior markets to Shanghai, the influence of external factors was not confined to that city, but was similarly reflected in the interior markets, and ultimately in the price the farmer received. Prices in the Middle and Lower Yangtse markets reflected Shanghai prices less the transasctions costs incurred in shipping rice to Shanghai. The farther the market from there, the longer it may have taken for local prices to fully capture external changes; in distant locales, external factors may have even played a marginally smaller role. Even compensating for these considerations, however, external factors still explain about 75 percent of the annual variability in Changsha, a market more than 800 miles upriver from Shanghai. In Wuhu and markets nearer to Shanghai, the percentage was even higher.

With the regression results in mind, Figures 3.1–3.3 can be used to help explain the secular behavior of Shanghai rice prices. From the 1870s until the mid–1890s, the "inflationary" consequences of the fall in the gold price of silver helped offset the decline in the Monsoon Asia rice price and contributed to a slight rise in China's internal rice price. Over the next twenty-five to thirty years, this increase accelerated; prices rose at an annual rate of 3 to 4 percent, the product of both the continuing fall in silver prices in terms of gold and the rise in Monsoon Asia's rice prices, each factor contributing about half to the increase. In the late 1920s, rice prices in Monsoon Asia began to fall precipitously, but, because the price of silver was falling even more rapidly, rice prices in Shanghai in silver actually rose and thereby insulated China temporarily. In the early

1930s, however, a sharp rise in silver prices and continued depression in the international commodity market put severe downward pressure on prices. Rice prices in Shanghai fell between 35 and 40 percent.

This is not to say that changes within China ceased to influence domestic prices – they did. In 1926 and 1927, for example, the Civil War severely disrupted market activity in the Yangtse. In both years, rice could not be moved from the interior to Shanghai, which relied heavily on overseas rice to meet consumption needs. The residuals from the regression analysis point to the fact that prices in 1926 and 1927 were substantially higher than what one would have predicted given the rice price prevailing in Monsoon Asia and the gold price of silver. In other years, such as 1907, a very poor harvest in China put extraordinary pressure on domestic prices that could not be totally relieved through imports. At any given time in any one of hundreds of markets at various levels, domestic factors could and did exert themselves.[20] Over the longer run, however, the market mechanism in areas linked by water and rail worked reasonably well and arbitraged away price differentials in excess of transactions costs. Consequently, throughout most of the region external factors came to play the predominant role in rice price formation, and changes in internal demand and supply became secondary.

## Changes in Marketing

Integration with the international market had implications not only for price formation, but for rice flows in China as well. The reason rice shipments out of the Yangtse declined was not related to any drop in production; in fact, production and marketing appear to have increased substantially over this period. Instead, the region's competition from the rice-exporting countries of Monsoon Asia intensified as the export surplus of these countries grew. With Indochina only a few hundred miles away and Siam less than a thousand, it became less expensive for markets in South China to import rice from these countries than from the Yangtse.

Maritime Customs data for six South China markets (Amoy, Canton, Lappa, Kongmoon, Kowloon, and Swatow) in Table 3.3 capture the increasing substitution of foreign for domestic rice. Over a thirty-year period, overseas rice imports increased about two and one-half times, while domestic rice shipments through Maritime Customs declined by a factor of four. The composition of imports in 1919 and 1920, however, represents an interesting departure. In 1919 a major crop failure in Monsoon Asia, followed by a ban on rice exports out

Table 3.3. *Rice shipments into South China through Maritime Customs, 1901 – 1935 (in Maritime Customs* picul)

| Period | Total Imports | Domestic | Overseas |
|---|---|---|---|
| 1901–1905 | 10,058,424 | 6,151,754 | 3,906,670 |
| 1906–1910 | 8,875,563 | 3,356,077 | 5,522,486 |
| 1911–1915 | 6,971,999 | 2,082,165 | 4,889,834 |
| 1916–1920 | 9,787,711 | 4,141,957 | 5,372,754 |
| 1916–1918 | 10,565,559 | 2,433,048 | 8,132,511 |
| 1919–1920 | 8,620,941 | 7,387,821 | 1,233,120 |
| 1921–1925 | 13,736,115 | 1,869,390 | 11,866,725 |
| 1926–1930 | 8,984,613 | 932,657 | 8,051,956 |
| 1931–1935 | 12,856,610 | 1,752,678 | 11,103,932 |

*Source:* Chinese Imperial Maritime Customs, *Returns of Trade and Trade Reports,* 1901–19; *Annual Trade Report and Returns,* 1920–31; *Domestic Trade: Analysis of Interport Movement of Chinese Produce,* 1932–5.

of Siam that remained in effect until 1922, forced the South China markets to look once again in 1919 and 1920 to the Yangtse for rice.

These data alone, however, do not capture the entire picture. Grain from the neighboring province of Kwangsi began to supply Canton in the late nineteenth century, in the process coming to compete with rice from the Yangtse and overseas. The changes in this trade cannot be easily quantified, but one source notes that by the 1920s rice shipments out of Kwangsi had declined to approximately 2 million *shih* (approximately 3 million *picul*), or one-half their earlier level because of overseas competition and an increased demand in Kwangsi itself.[21] In addition, junks carried on trade entirely outside the authority of Maritime Customs that cannot be measured either. If rice shipments from Kwangsi averaged approximately 4–6 million *picul* in the early 1900s, but then fell to half that by the 1920s, then over most of the period rice shipments into the six southern markets would have totaled between 14 and 16 million *picul*: two-thirds from domestic and one-third from foreign sources early in the century, but one-fourth from domestic and three-fourths from foreign sources twenty-five to thirty years later.

One must also analyze the decline in rice exports through the Yangtse treaty ports in terms of any increase within the Yangtse region itself. With the growth and industrialization of the Lower Yangtse, the demand for rice undoubtedly increased. Perkins estimates that the population of the largest urban areas (those in excess of 100,000) in Chekiang and Kiangsu alone increased by approximately 4 million in the early twentieth century.[22] A number of Middle Yangtse cities, including Wuhan (the combined name for Hankow, Wuchang, and Hanyang) and Changsha, grew perhaps by as much as a million. Wuhan served both as a treaty port and as the terminus of the first inland railroad. To feed these 5 million new mouths would have required an additional 20 to 25 million *picul* of husked grain (roughly 16 to 20 million Maritime Customs *picul*), presumably much of it rice.[23] Yet, as I show in the next chapter, this figure substantially underestimates the region's increased demand during this period for rice, and for grain more generally. The increased number of people living in cities over 100,000 may represent no more than a fourth or fifth of the increase that occurred in the nonagricultural population over a slightly longer period running from the 1890s to the 1930s.

What part did foreign imports supply of the possibly more than 20 million *picul* required? Table 3.4, which displays overseas rice imports into the region, shows that until the 1920s they were negligible, and increased only in the 1920s and 1930s. Yet, even this rise needs to be qualified. The 1922–3 increase reflects Siam's recovery from earlier crop failure and a return to previous export levels. Indeed, over these two years, Siamese exports increased from 4 million to 20 million Maritime Customs *picul*. Interestingly, Maritime Customs *Trade Reports* show 1922 to have provided an excellent harvest in China and 1923 to have been average. In 1926 and 1927, civil war disrupted normal marketing activity within China and required an unusually high level of imports into Shanghai. In 1931 severe flooding throughout the Yangtse and in 1934 a major crop failure also necessitated increased rice imports the following year. Between 1920 and 1936, imports averaged 3.20 million Maritime Customs *picul* or 3.9 standard *picul*; excluding 1926 and 1927 from the calculations because of the "exceptional" events of those two years (though the same could be said of a few other years), imports averaged slightly more than 3 million standard *picul*. This represents only a small fraction of the increased rice that the population living in cities over 100,000 would have required. Even subtracting the rice freed up by the decline in shipments from the Middle and Upper Yangtse provinces to South China, marketing of rice in Central and East China increased substantially in order to accom-

Table 3.4. *Overseas rice imports into East-Central China, 1903–36* (*in Maritime Customs* picul)

| Year | Imports | Year | Imports |
|------|---------|------|---------|
| 1903 | 983 | 1920 | 17,404 |
| 1904 | 685 | 1921 | 105,996 |
| 1905 | n.a. | 1922 | 2,567,159 |
| 1906 | 126,002 | 1923 | 2,324,111 |
| 1907 | 1,291,299 | 1924 | 20,685 |
| 1908 | 149,48 | 1925 | 650,114 |
| 1909 | 925 | 1926 | 8,811,822 |
| 1910 | 475,934 | 1927 | 6,245,609 |
| 1911 | 5,640 | 1928 | 528,869 |
| 1912 | n.a. | 1929 | 1,198,319 |
| 1913 | 17,012 | 1930 | 10,327,750 |
| 1914 | 4,499 | 1931 | 1,266,377 |
| 1915 | 145,499 | 1932 | 5,773,233 |
| 1916 | 1,758 | 1933 | 941,723 |
| 1917 | 2,026 | 1934 | 1,899,260 |
| 1918 | 433 | 1935 | 11,735,123 |
| 1919 | 478 | 1936 | 294,725 |

*Note:* n.a.—not available.
*Source:* Chinese Imperial Maritime Customs data; see Table 3.3.

modate growing demand. Estimates that I have made elsewhere of the rice surplus of Anhwei, Hunan, and Kiangsi in the 1930s are consistent with an increase in domestic rice marketing.[24]

## A Reexamination of Changes in Output

Increased domestic rice marketing of this magnitude could be reconciled with a simultaneous reduction of output. Farm household income might have been falling either as part of a secular decline in the economy or as part of worsening income distribution and a rise in tenancy. A fall in incomes would have forced farm households to shift consumption to inferior, less-expensive grains (or other foods like potatoes that had a high caloric value), and the rise in tenancy and rental payments in kind would have put more rice into the hands of landlords for resale to the nonagricultural population. If rents were in cash, farm households would have been forced to sell more output to meet these obligations. I do not believe this was the case,

Table 3.5. *Rice production in East-Central China, 1914–18 and 1931–7 (in thousand* mou *and* picul)

| Province | 1914–18 | | 1931–7 | |
|---|---|---|---|---|
| | Acreage (*mou*) | Output (*picul*) | Acreage (*mou*) | Output (*picul*) |
| Kiangsu | 33,590 | 139,730 | 32,690 | 136,000 |
| Chekiang | 32,470 | 158,800 | 25,860 | 126,500 |
| Anhwei | 26,540 | 96,100 | 26,540 | 96,100 |
| Kiangsi | 43,820 | 124,000 | 31,640 | 89,500 |
| Hupei | 26,730 | 124,300 | 26,730 | 124,300 |
| Hunan | 50,390 | 171,190 | 46,520 | 158,600 |
| Total | 213,540 | 814,120 | 189,980 | 731,000 |

*Source:* Perkins, *Agricultural Development in China,* pp. 249 and 276. I have revised the original data in two ways. First, output in Anhwei in 1914–18 should have been 96.1 million *picul* rather than 108.6. Perkins has assumed that yields in both periods were the same as they were in the 1950s. Because acreage in 1914–18 and 1931–7 were the same, the level of output should also have been the same. Second, output in Kiangsu for both 1914–18 and 1931–7 has been recomputed using the yield estimate provided for the 1950s. For some unknown reason, a substantially lower figure was originally used by Perkins.

however. I will examine changes in income and distribution more fully in Chapters 5 and 6, but, regarding tenancy, the consensus is that no rise occurred over the late nineteenth and early twentieth centuries.[25]

The problem resides in the output data. In constructing the totals shown in Table 3.5, Perkins has drawn heavily on contemporary Chinese estimates on acreage. Rice yields in the two periods were assumed to be the same as in the 1950s, thereby making changes in acreage the sole source of output changes. The acreage data for the years between 1914 and 1918, however, were based on estimates contained in *Nung-shang t'ung-chi piao* and are very weak, as the following examples attest.

In the case of Chekiang, Perkins's data show that acreage in rice cultivation declined by more than 25 percent between 1914–18 and 1931–7, from 32.47 million *mou* to 25.86 million *mou*. Another way of saying this is that rice acreage declined as a percentage of cultivated area from almost 100 percent to roughly 75 percent. If this were the case, it would single out Chekiang as the only one of twelve southern provinces in which rice output in 1957 was below that in 1914–18, despite an increase in double-cropping over this period. Given the huge investments landowners made in paddy fields, it seems highly unlikely that a quarter of all cultivated acreage was taken out of the production of rice and shifted into some other crop within a relatively short time period. Further suspicion is cast by the fact that I have yet to find any qualitative data pointing to a reduction in cultivated acreage between 1914–18 and 1931–6.

The data for Kiangsi pose similar problems. According to Perkins, rice acreage declined from 43.82 million *mou* between 1914–18 to 31.64 in the 1930s, a reduction of 28 percent. Population reportedly declined by a million and a half, from roughly 18 million to 16.5 million, so a modest reduction would not be out of the question. But the acreage figure for 1914–18 implies the unreasonably high level of total rice output of 124 million and, assuming a population of 18 million, a per capita consumption of 7 *picul*. Such consumption would be exceptionally high for China at this time and is inconsistent with the relatively modest level of rice exports during this period. By comparison, in the mid-1950s output was the same, but rice exports reportedly equaled roughly 20 million *picul*.[26] Alternatively, if the rice-acreage figure for the 1930s is accurate, a multiple-cropping index of less than 150 is implied for Kiangsi. For the six localities in Kiangsi that Buck surveyed, the average was almost 180.[27] From both perspectives, there appears a major inconsistency between the rice estimates for 1914–18 and 1931–6.

More examples could be cited to highlight the weaknesses of Perkins's estimates for 1914–18. A recent compilation by Tao-fu Hsu of many earlier estimates actually points to substantial increases in rice output in some of the same provinces for which Perkins shows reductions.[28] Moreover, data presented by Buck fail to show a decline in the percentage of acreage sown to rice over the slightly longer period between 1904–9 and 1930–3.[29] The returns to working with these early estimates to arrive at new totals for 1914–18 are probably marginal. Nonetheless, even on the basis of the evidence so far adduced, a decline in rice output seems unlikely.

## The Case of Cotton

Although some of the particulars differ, many of the findings regarding rice markets carry over to domestic cotton markets as well. These include both the role of external factors in cotton price formation and evidence of substantial increases in cotton output as well as marketing.

## Marketing and Output

The changes that occurred in the production and marketing of cotton over this period were inseparably tied to changes in China's domestic textile industry. Within fifteen to twenty years of the opening up of the country's interior to overseas yarn imports in the late nineteenth century, more than a third of handicraft yarn production was displaced by manufactured yarn imports for use in handicraft cloth production. At first, much of this foreign yarn came from Bombay spinning mills; later, it was supplemented by imports from Japan. The success of yarn imports was relatively short-lived, however. Import substitution soon followed and factory production of yarn in China increased from less than 100,000 *piculs* in 1890 to almost 10 million by the mid-1930s.[30] In the late 1920s, the nation actually became a net exporter of yarn.[31]

Although cotton imports increased in the twenties and thirties, a high percentage of the increased demand for cotton was accommodated by increased Chinese output. Figure 3.4 graphs estimates of cotton consumption by the country's modern yarn factories less net exports. This implicitly represents the amount of cotton domestic agriculture supplied. The total increased from less than a million *picul* in the 1890s to an average of almost 10 million *picul* in the mid-1930s.

Modern manufacturers of yarn were not the only source of demand. Cotton continued to be in demand by handicraft manufacturers for spinning, for padding in clothing, for the manufacture of munitions, and for medicinal purposes. Drawing on a 1910 Japanese estimate, Richard Kraus has estimated the cotton consumed for padding alone at 3 million Maritime Customs *picul*, or 3.63 standard *picul*.[32] Because handicraft manufacturers did not grow all their own cotton, we can conservatively add an additional 3 to 4 million *picul* for these other uses to the estimates suggested by Figure 3.4 to arrive at an estimated total amount of cotton marketed by the mid-1930s of between 13 and 14 million *picul*. A recent estimate by Cheng-ming Wu for these same years suggests the slightly higher figure of 15 million *picul*.[33]

Over the long run, this increase in marketed cotton appears to have been accompanied by an almost equal increase in output. I have no annual data on cotton output, but Feuerwerker has put average output between 1901–10 at 7 million Maritime Custom

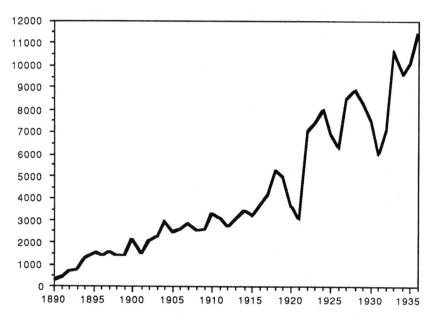

*Note:* Following the calculations in Table 3.7, I have assumed it took 4.287 picul of *raw* cotton to produce 1 bale of yarn.
*Source:* Based on yarn production estimates for China contained in Takamura, *Kindai Nihon mengyō to Chugoku,* p. 98, and data on cotton imports and exports in Hsiao, *China's Foreign Trade Statistics,* pp. 38–9 and 85–6.

Figure 3.4

Cotton Consumption by China's Modern Textile Industry,
Less Net Exports, 1890–1936
(in 1,000 *piculs*)

*picul,* or 8.5 standard *picul.*[34] By contrast, a host of estimates for the 1930s suggest an average output level in the vicinity of 18 million.[35] These estimates would imply that output more than doubled during the early twentieth century. An increase of this magnitude is not out of line with Buck's finding that in the twenty-seven cotton-cultivating localities he surveyed, the percentage of total crop area (sown area) in cotton increased from 11 percent in 1905–9 to 18 percent between 1924 and 1929 to 20 percent between 1929 and 1933. With sown area rising slightly over this period due to an

Table 3.6. *Distribution of manufactured yarn production, 1930 (output in bales of yarn)*

| Nationality | Location | | | | |
|---|---|---|---|---|---|
| | Shanghai | Kiangsu[a] | Hupei | Region | China |
| Chinese | 529,353 | 812,507 | 262,235 | 1,179,742 | 1,500,248 |
| Japanese | 581,410 | 0 | 23,000 | 581,433 | 825,407 |
| British | 119,522 | 0 | 0 | 129,522 | 129,522 |
| Total | 1,230,285 | 812,507 | 285,235 | 1,890,697 | 2,455,177 |

[a]Not including Shanghai.
*Source:* Fong, *Chung-kuo chih mien-fang chih-yeh,* Appendix Table 1.

increase in double-cropping, total acreage and output in cotton could have more than doubled, assuming of course that yields did not decline or fell only marginally.[36]

With output averaging approximately 18 million *picul* between 1933 and 1936, marketed cotton would have amounted to at least three-quarters of output and may have been as high as 85 percent.[37] At the turn of the century, on the other hand, total marketing by Chinese farm households would have been nearer to 4 million *picul*, or slightly less than half of total output.[38] Unmistakably, cotton marketed increased in absolute terms – perhaps by as much as a factor of three and a half – and in percentage terms.

### Influences on Regional Output and Marketing

By all indications, the growth of the modern textile industry encouraged cotton production and marketing in the Yangtse region, not a very surprising fact because Shanghai and the Lower Yangtse were at the center of this rapid growth. In 1930, a year for which we have very detailed information, 62.1 percent of all manufactured yarn was produced in Kiangsu (50.1 percent of it in Shanghai). An additional 10.6 percent was produced in Hupei. If one includes production in the four remaining provinces, more than three-quarters of all domestically manufactured yarn was produced in the region. These data are presented in Table 3.6.

Data provided in *Chung-kuo mien-fang t'ung-chi shih-liao* (His-

torical Data on Spinning and Weaving in China) for the period 1919–
36 suggest that the region produced roughly this same percentage
of China's manufactured yarn output for much of the early twentieth
century.[39] These data permit us to estimate the maximum amount
of cotton that the region was supplying to accommodate the industry
and overseas demand. Column 3 of Table 3.7 contains the region's
estimated raw cotton requirements for the industry for the years
between 1912 and 1936. Column 4 provides data on overseas imports
into the region, almost all of which were earmarked for Shanghai.
Cotton imports increased almost continuously until 1931. They hit
4.795 million *picul* in that year, but fell sharply subsequently. Column 5 is the difference between columns 3 and 4 and represents the
use of domestic cotton by factories in the region. Demand increased
from less than 2 million *picul* before World War I to an average of
7 million by the mid-1930s. Growth was fairly regular, though some
years, such as 1920–1 and 1930–2, experienced substantial drop-
offs. Some of the region's cotton supplied mills in other parts of China
or was exported overseas. Column 6 captures the portion of this
trade that went through the treaty ports; the figure equals exports
(overseas and domestic) out of the region less imports from other
treaty ports (most notably Tientsin) into the region. The sum of
columns 5 and 6 (column 7), then, represents an upper limit on the
amount of cotton the region could have been supplying both for
export and for use in manufactured yarn production. Like column
5, column 7 implies substantial growth, from a low of 2 million *picul*
to over 7 million. In the early 1890s, the figure was approximately
1 million.

How much of the increasing demand from then until the 1930s
was actually supplied by the region, however? Obviously, the
Yangtse supplied no more than it produced. Did the region have the
capacity to accommodate such expanded demand? There are numerous indications that cotton acreage increased. In eastern and
southeastern Kiangsu, for example, salt farms abandoned toward
the end of the nineteenth century were reclaimed in the teens and
twenties by land-reclamation companies for cotton production.[40]
Hsu's data on cotton acreage for the years 1914–16 and 1934–6 and
reported in Table 3.8 suggest the increase that occurred. They imply
a growth in acreage of almost 60 percent, from 15.45 million *mou*
to 24.61 million. If only the estimates for 1914 and 1915 are used,
a growth rate of 70 percent is inferred.[41] Throughout the period,
yields (expressed in terms of ginned cotton) averaged approximately
30 *chin* per *mou*, thus implying an increase in output from 4.5 million *picul* to almost 7.5 million.

Table 3.7. *Estimated regional demand for domestic cotton, 1912–36 (unit: thousands)*

| 1 Year | 2 Yarn Production (bales) | 3 Cotton Requirements (picul) | 4 Overseas Imports (picul) | 5 (364) (picul) | 6 New Domestic Exports Plus Overseas Exports (picul) | 7 (3 − 4 + 6) (picul) |
|---|---|---|---|---|---|---|
| 1912 | 488 | 1,569 | 309 | 1,260 | 540 | 1800 |
| 1913 | 541 | 1,740 | 132 | 1,608 | 492 | 2100 |
| 1914 | 645 | 2,074 | 121 | 1,953 | 573 | 2526 |
| 1915 | 645 | 2,074 | 395 | 1,679 | 309 | 1988 |
| 1916 | 726 | 2,335 | 465 | 2,092 | 772 | 2864 |
| 1917 | 795 | 2,557 | 332 | 2,225 | 717 | 2942 |
| 1918 | 928 | 2,984 | 192 | 2,792 | 1,199 | 3991 |
| 1919 | 918 | 2,952 | 250 | 2,702 | 756 | 3458 |
| 1920 | 927 | 2,981 | 694 | 2,258 | 327 | 2585 |
| 1921 | 1,011 | 3,251 | 1,786 | 1,465 | 398 | 1863 |
| 1922 | 1,905 | 6,126 | 1,796 | 4,330 | 479 | 4809 |
| 1923 | 1,898 | 6,104 | 1,657 | 4,447 | 620 | 5067 |
| 1924 | 1,891 | 6,081 | 1,204 | 4,876 | 1,060 | 5936 |
| 1925 | 1,909 | 6,139 | 1,816 | 4,323 | 469 | 4792 |
| 1926 | 1,979 | 6,364 | 2,722 | 3,641 | 233 | 3874 |
| 1927 | 2,248 | 7,229 | 2,229 | 5,000 | 967 | 5967 |
| 1928 | 2,306 | 7,416 | 1,861 | 5,555 | 712 | 6267 |
| 1929 | 2,381 | 7,657 | 2,375 | 5,283 | 657 | 5940 |
| 1930 | 2,456 | 7,898 | 3,349 | 4,549 | 82 | 4631 |

Table 3.7. (*continued*)

| 1 Year | 2 Yarn Production (bales) | 3 Cotton Requirements (picul) | 4 Overseas Imports (picul) | 5 (364) (picul) | 6 New Domestic Exports Plus Overseas Exports (picul) | 7 (3 − 4 + 6) (picul) |
|---|---|---|---|---|---|---|
| 1931 | 2,487 | 7,998 | 4,795 | 3,203 | −128 | 3075 |
| 1932 | 2,525 | 8,120 | 4,042 | 4,078 | −232 | 3846 |
| 1933 | 2,625 | 8,442 | 2,248 | 6,194 | −6 | 6188 |
| 1934 | 2,676 | 8,606 | 1,826 | 6,780 | −134 | 6638 |
| 1935 | 2,458 | 7,905 | 823 | 7,082 | 137 | 7219 |
| 1936 | 2,680 | 8,618 | 643 | 7,975 | n.a. | n.a. |

*Note.* n.a.—not available.

*Source:* Yarn production data for China are from Takamura, *Kindai Nihon mengyō to Chūgoku*, p. 98. I have assumed that the region consistently produced three-quarters of this and that it took 1.123 *picul* of cotton to produce one *picul* of yarn to arrive at the estimates in column 3. A bale of yarn of 420 pounds, therefore, required 4.287 *picul* of yarn. The input requirements are based on survey data contained in Tzu-chien Wang and Chen-cheng Wang, *Ch'i-sheng hua-sheng sha-ch'ang tiao-ch'a pao-kao* (Shanghai: Commercial Press, 1935). Data on overseas imports and exports and inter-treaty-port shipments (the basis for columns 4 and 6) are from the annual reports of China's Imperial Maritime Customs.

Table 3.8. *Cotton acreage, 1914-16 and 1934-6 (in thousands of mou)*

| Years | Kiangsu | Chekiang | Anhwei | Hunan | Hupei | Kiangsi | Total |
|---|---|---|---|---|---|---|---|
| 1914–1916 | 9,204 | 1,010 | 467 | 765[a] | 3,599 | 404 | 15,499 |
| 1934–1936 | 11,796 | 2,015 | 2,115 | 1,289 | 6,391 | 915 | 24,609 |

[a]For 1914–15 only.
*Source:* Tao-fu Hsu, *Chung-kuo chin-tai nung-yeh sheng-chan chi mao-yi t'ung-chi tzu-liao* (Shanghai, 1983), pp. 203–14.

The output figures are informative in two respects. First, with regional industrial demand plus net exports alone averaging almost 7 million *picul* in the mid-1930s, it is most unlikely that regional production alone satisfied demand. County-level marketing data for the 1930s show, however, that five to six million *picul* of cotton were shipped from within Hupei, Kiangsu, and Chekiang to major centers of demand, including Shasi, Hankow, Shanghai, Wuhsi, and Ningpo.[42] This would leave a minimum of several million *picul* for producers outside the region to supply.[43] Second, an increase in regional cotton output of 3 million *picul* represents 50 to 60 percent of the increase implied by column 7 of Table 3.7.

But column 6 of Table 3.7 reveals one other interesting development: in the early 1930s, net domestic exports through Maritime Customs plus overseas exports became negative, implying a net import of domestic cotton into the region through Maritime Customs. The most likely explanation is that the continued growth in the region's textile industry now absorbed the cotton formerly destined for export. The figures for the 1920s and 1930s imply that up to a million *picul* may have been redirected towards regional consumption. Adding this to the estimated increase in output suggests that the region accommodated around two-thirds of the five million *picul* increase in demand given in column 7.


## Prices

The same kinds of factors that determined rice prices in the region determined cotton prices. The mechanism underlying the sensitivity of domestic cotton prices to external forces was also the same: international commodity arbitrage. The role of international market forces is very explicit in a 1935 description of price formation in the Shanghai cotton market:

The price of cotton fluctuates with the American staple, cent for cent. The price of the Hankow standard ... is always from 10 to 15 dollars per *picul* lower than the American staple, ex-wharf, Shanghai, regardless of any unforeseen factors. Without artificial manipulation in the Cotton Goods Exchange, the China cotton always follows the New York market cent for cent except when during a time of local political disturbance, tightness of the local money market and violent fluctuations of foreign exchange, affect the price. Before deciding to purchase China cotton, every millowner must scrutinize the New York quotations and their causes of drop or advance. Abnormal conditions may prevail for a time, but sooner or later an adjustment in prices between China and American staples must be reached.[44]

One can almost see this arbitrage at work in several passages taken from Maritime Customs. In 1929 the agency reported: "The rise in the price of Chinese cotton caused by a failure in local crops and the comparatively cheap price ruling for infinitely better Indian staple were responsible for heavy imports of Indian cotton."[45] Indian imports that year totaled almost 1.5 million Maritime Custom *picul*. In 1932, on the other hand, the agency remarked: "As in the previous year, price was the great inducement in the case of purchases from America: five gold dollar cents per pound, the lowest recorded price since 1894, was reached at one time during the year in review."[46] Between July 1931 and June the following year, the price of cotton in Tientsin declined from 55.94 *yuan* per *picul* to 34.03 *yuan*.[47] At the end of the year, prices were only slightly higher. American imports exceeded 3 million Maritime Customs *picul* that year and represented more than 80 percent of China's cotton imports. By contrast, American cotton exports in 1932 were over 2 million tons, or approximately 36 million Maritime Custom *picul*.[48] Figure 3.5 provides a slightly stylized representation of how these various forces interacted to determine prices and the level of cotton imports over this period.

China also exported cotton. In the 1920s and 1930s, these exports averaged between 5 and 10 percent of domestic output. Typically inferior to Indian or American varieties, Chinese cotton found a market overseas in the production of lower-quality yarns, for padding, as a woolen mixture, and for use in making gunpowder. Domestic cotton prices were exposed to developments in the international market both through competition in export markets and through competition that domestic sources faced from Indian and American imports in markets like Shanghai and Tientsin.

Tests of commodity arbitrage in cotton markets identical to those performed for rice are reported in Table 3.2. The domestic price data for cotton, however, are not nearly so good as the rice-price data. Aside from data on the unit values of cotton exports (much of it through Yangtse ports), the only other time series of any length on cotton prices is for Tientsin (beginning in 1913). Nonetheless, using the dollar price of cotton exports from the United States as a proxy for the world price, the role of commodity arbitrage in domestic price determination is borne out. The model was estimated using the unit value of Chinese cotton exports (much of it through Shanghai) for the period between 1900 and 1936 and the price of cotton in Tientsin between 1913 and 1936, all expressed in HKT. The appropriate exchange rate is that between the dollar and the HKT. A number of alternative versions of the model were run: with and without

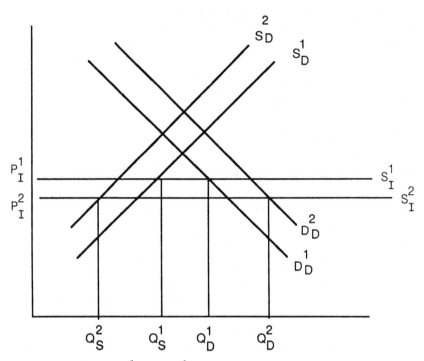

*Note:* In Figure 3.5, $S^1_D$ and $D^1_D$ represent the domestic demand and supply of cotton, and $S^1_I$ the infinitely inelastic international supply of cotton facing China. At the prevailing international price of $P^1_I$, demand in China is $Q^1_D$ and supply is $Q^1_S$. The difference, $Q^1_D - Q^1_S$, represents net imports. The domestic supply shock and continued growth in domestic demand are represented by the shifts in the curves to $S^2_D$ and $D^2_D$, and the increase in supply in the international market by the downward shift in the inelastic supply curve to $S^2_I$. Price in the domestic market falls to $P^2_I$, and net imports rise to $Q^2_D - A^2_S$. Recovery of domestic supply would be reflected by rightward shifts in the domestic supply curve.

Figure 3.5

Chinese Cotton Market, circa Early 1930s

intercepts, a dummy for the war years, and so forth, some of which are reported in Table 3.2.

In general, the results support the role attributed to international commodity price arbitrage in domestic price formation. The coefficients on WPC (the world price of cotton as proxied by the unit value of cotton exports from the United States) and DHKTR (the exchange

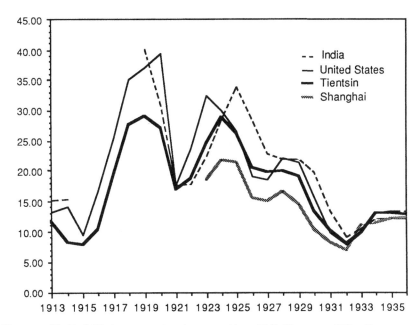

*Sources:* United States, export price on cotton: U.S. Bureau of the Census, *The Statistical History of the United States*, p. 546; India, export price of cotton: *Statistical Abstract of British India*, selected years; Tientsin, wholesale price of cotton: *Nan-kai chih shu tzu-liao hui-pien*, pp. 74–5; Shanghai, wholesale price of cotton: *Shang-hai chieh-fang ch'ien-hou wu-chia tzu-liao hui-pien*, p. 229.

Figure 3.6

Cotton Prices in China and the International Market, 1913–36
(U.S. $ per *picul*)

rate between the dollar and the HKT) are of the correct sign. In general, it is not possible to reject the hypothesis that the coefficients were equal to one and negative one, respectively. Finally, the adjusted $R^2$ ($\overline{R}^2$) for the models suggest that external factors explain approximately three-quarters of the variability in domestic cotton prices. In the model for Tientsin in which a dummy was included for the war years, the adjusted $R^2$ was even higher (0.821).

Further confirmation is provided by Figure 3.6, which graphs the price of cotton in Tientsin and Shanghai and the unit value of American and Indian cotton exports, all denominated in dollars, for the years between 1913 and 1936. Data exist for every year for Tientsin and the United States, but India lacks observations for 1916–18, and Shanghai has only annual observations based on monthly data for the period 1923–36. The 1924 data include only June and August, and for several other years less than twelve months are provided. It is immediately obvious, nonetheless, that price movements in Tientsin and Shanghai mimicked those in the international cotton market. The relatively low Shanghai price in 1924 appears related to the missing observations for the first five months, a period during which cotton prices continued to rise. The tendency for price changes in India to frequently lag behind those in either the United States or China simply reflects differences in the reporting period.[49] There is every reason to believe that a longer time series for cotton prices in Shanghai would reveal the same kind of behavior as Tientsin. Moreover, the competitiveness of the market structure in the region and comparatively low transport costs there all suggest that price movements in interior cotton markets paralleled those in the treaty ports.

## Summary

In much of the work on early twentieth-century Chinese agriculture, analysts have sought to explain price movements and commodity flows in terms of domestic market forces. Once one acknowledges the relatively high degree of market integration achieved by the turn of the century, however, this can no longer be justified and a model must be adopted that allows as well for the systematic influence of the international economy on domestic markets through commodity arbitrage. The analysis presented here of the rice and cotton markets reveals the power such a model has to explain developments in both commodity markets.

Although commodity arbitrage may not have always worked smoothly, price changes in the international rice and cotton markets and changes in the gold price of silver go far in explaining the variability of prices during the late nineteenth and early twentieth centuries.[50] For the millions of farm households that sold their output on the market, the implications of this fact are potentially enormous. The same interaction of internal and external market forces explicit in the theory of commodity arbitrage also helps explain short-run behavior of imports and exports. This is nicely illustrated in the Chinese cotton market between 1930 and 1932: a domestic supply shock combined with growing domestic demand and rapidly falling prices in the international economy to produce a rise in imports but a fall in prices. Domestic output recovered subsequently, and the volume of imports fell. The substitution of overseas for Yangtse rice in South China provides an example of how these forces interacted over an even longer period.

Equally important, this analysis clearly shows that, despite occasional increases in rice and cotton imports, output and marketing of both of these crops increased substantially in the region over the period. The view that regional rice and maybe even cotton production declined and thus required increased imports to meet domestic demand simply cannot be sustained.

# 4

# The Accelerated Commercialization of Agriculture

It is generally acknowledged that during the late nineteenth and early twentieth centuries China's rural economy became more commercialized.[1] Resources devoted to cash-crop production and such subsidiary activities like sericulture increased significantly as did the percentage of farm output that was marketed. In moving away further from self-sufficiency, farm household decision making naturally became more market-oriented and incomes highly dependent on market outcomes. Despite scholarly agreement on these tendencies, questions remain regarding the forces underlying the process, its absolute level and rate of increase, and its implications for productivity as well as for the level and distribution of incomes.

The problem arises in part because much of the work on the commercialization of Chinese agriculture during this period has focused on North China and the role the railroads played in opening the interior of that region to international markets.[2] Between the 1890s and 1930s, almost 10,000 miles of railroad were constructed, mostly in North China and Manchuria.[3] Central, East, and South China saw very modest development, for tens of thousands of miles of interior waterways already provided comparatively cheap transport; the introduction of the steamship to the Yangtse and to the Pearl River only made the system more efficient.[4] Moreover, agricultural exports, largely in the form of soybeans from Manchuria, never amounted to more than 4 percent of the total value of China's agricultural output, and agricultural exports from Central and East China amounted to an even lower percentage of that region's agricultural output.[5] Did the Yangtse region experience a particularly rapid commercialization of agriculture, or were there factors contributing to this process that we have ignored?

It becomes immediately obvious that how rapidly Chinese agriculture was commercialized is important to understanding the forces underlying the process as a whole. One measure would be the amount of agricultural output that farm households were marketing and its growth over time. A number of estimates exist of the percentage of agricultural output that was marketed in the 1930s, but not for the rate at which marketed farm output rose during the late nineteenth and early twentieth centuries. Moreover, the 1930s estimates often confuse the marketed output with market surplus. Marketed output is the total amount of agricultural produce that farm households put on the market. Market surplus, however, deducts from this total any resales (primarily grain) back to the agricultural population. Although these resales play a major role in facilitating the commercialization process, market surplus is arguably a better indicator of the ability of agriculture to accommodate external demand (defined here as the sum of export demand and domestic nonagricultural demand), and of the agricultural sector's potential demand for manufactured or processed agricultural goods. Early in the economic development process, the farming population represents a major market for the products of the nonagricultural sector, and hence the volume of farm sales to the nonagricultural sector and the income farms derived from these sales is important.

I begin by estimating the Yangtse region's agricultural market surplus and marketed output for the 1890s and 1930s. This not only helps measure the rate of commercialization, but also reveals much about the forces underlying the process itself.

## Market Surplus and Marketed Output in Agriculture

Rather than use the conventional method of multiplying the value of each crop times its marketing rate, and then subtracting resales (primarily grain) to the agricultural population to find market surplus, I have employed a simpler method with fewer data requirements. Aside from the grain required by the agricultural population, the demand for farm products came as the nonagricultural population's demand for grain and the demand for cash crops such as fibers and oilseeds. Chapter 3 noted evidence of demand increases from both sources. Because the region remained a net exporter of grain throughout the period,[6] the size of the nonagricultural population and information on cash-crop production and marketing can help estimate roughly the market surplus for the 1890s and the 1930s. Adding on grain resales gives an estimate of marketed output.

## Changes in the Size of the Urban and Nonagricultural Populations

G. William Skinner's work on regional urbanization in late nineteenth-century China provides a baseline for estimating the urban population increase.[7] In 1893 the percentage of China's population living in urban areas (or "central places," to use Skinner's terminology) larger than 2,000 was slightly more than 25 million, or approximately 6 percent of the entire population.[8] In the Lower Yangtse, the rate of urbanization exceeded 10 percent, but the Middle Yangtse, at 5.7 percent, fell slightly below the national average. These rates produce an urban population in Central and East China of roughly 9.5 million, or just over 7 percent of the region's population around 1893.[9]

Comparable estimates do not exist for the 1930s, but it is possible to make them in a number of ways. The first draws on data from the 1950s. At the time of the nationwide census in 1953, the estimated urban population was 78 million or 13.3 percent of the entire population.[10] Although the criterion used in demarcating urban areas is not clear, Chan and Xu have recently pointed out that, of the total 5,402 cities and towns, 920 had a population under 2,000, implying that those remaining had a population of at least 2,000.[11] Estimates based on the population of locations over 2,000 would be comparable to Skinner's data, though I can not rule out the possibility that in 1953 some towns with more than 2,000 may have been excluded by some other criterion. Subtracting the population of these 920 towns and the population of Manchuria (which Skinner's estimates exclude), the urban population of China proper would have been between 60 and 61 million in 1953, or 2.4 times larger than it was in the 1890s; in Central and East China, it was between 23 and 24 million.[12]

How should this growth be apportioned over the sixty-year period? We know that the rate of urbanization rose sharply from 10.6 percent to 13.3 percent between 1949 and 1953, but part of this growth no doubt reflects a movement back into cities and towns after almost twelve years of war.[13] Moreover, because war had also disrupted the economy and industrial activity, very likely the annual growth rate of the urban population was lower between 1937 and 1949 than it had been over the preceding forty years.[14] This reasoning leads me to believe that the urban population in China proper (China excluding Manchuria) residing in towns larger than 2,000 at least doubled between 1890s and the 1930s, increasing from approximately 25 million to 50 million, or at an annual rate of just under 2 percent. This would put the urban population of China proper as a percentage of the total population at 10.5 percent, or the same urbanization rate as that for all the country in 1949. Of course, growth could have been even faster.

In Central and East China, the growth rate probably exceeded 2 percent because the Yangtse region was at the center of the accelerating economic and commercial development that occurred in the early twentieth century. Conservatively, between the 1890s and 1930s the region's urban population increased by at least 10 million, pushing the total urban population slightly over 20 million, or approximately 12 percent of the region's population as a whole.

Fragmentary data compiled by Dwight Perkins for the 1930s suggest urban population estimates at least this high.[15] In Kiangsu, over 6 million people were estimated to have been living in cities over 100,000 in 1938, and in Central and East China roughly 11 million people were. If I knew the percentage of the urban population living in cities over 100,000, I could easily obtain an estimate for the urban population. Although I do not have an estimate for the 1930s, Kirkby estimates that 51.7 percent of China's urban population in 1953 was living in cities larger than 100,000.[16] Applying this percentage to Perkins's estimate also produces an urban population in the region of over 20 million. Suffice it to say that the urban population there at least doubled in absolute terms and maybe even as a percentage of the entire population.

What about changes in the nonagricultural population? The terms nonagricultural and urban are not synonymous, nor, for that matter, are the terms rural and agricultural. The urban population has already been defined as those living in cities and towns over 2,000; the nonagricultural population was made up of those households that were either not engaged in agriculture or for whom farming did not represent the primary source of income. Many such households lived in urban areas, but even in rural areas substantial numbers of households made a living in such nonagricultural occupations as handicraft industry, commerce, and transportation. I believe this number increased substantially with the commercialization process.

In the early 1930s, 24.5 percent of China's population was nonagricultural, though in Central and East China that figure was 28.2 percent.[17] With the overall populations of 503 million for China and 163 million for the region, nonagricultural populations would have been 123 million and 46 million, respectively. The Yangtse's nonagricultural population in the 1930s would thus have been over twice the size of the urban population, a relationship true of the early 1950s also.[18] Lacking information on the size of the nonagricultural population for the early 1890s, I have assumed that the ratio between the nonagricultural and urban populations remained the same between the 1890s and 1930s, which would mean that the nonagricultural population grew at the same rate, or just under 2 percent. This would put China's nonagricultural population in the early 1890s at 13 or 14 percent, or 50–55 million; in Central and East China, it would have been 1 or 2 percent higher, or roughly

20 to 21 million out of an estimated 130 million. The second estimate implies that roughly two-thirds of the region's population increase between the 1890s and 1930s was absorbed by the nonagricultural sector. Data on changes in average farm size for twenty-one localities are consistent with this small but important sectoral shift in the composition of the population.[19]

In order to know how rapidly the sector's grain surplus grew (measured here as a percentage of total agriculture output), we need to know grain's share of total agricultural output. Perkins's data for the region suggest that approximately 70 percent of agricultural output (excluding the output of animal husbandry) was in grain. Assuming that per capita grain consumption in the two sectors of the population were roughly the same, the percentage of output required to meet the grain demands of the nonagricultural population would have increased from 11.2 percent (0.70*16 percent) in the 1890s to 19.6 percent (0.70*28 percent) in the 1930s, or 8.4 percent. If the nonagricultural population consumed somewhat less grain per capita than the agricultural sector, only a marginal adjustment downward is necessary.[20]

This estimate, however, assumes that grain made up the same percentage of agricultural output in the two periods, but there are many indications that acreage devoted to cash crops – cotton, soybeans, rapeseed, sesame, tobacco – increased substantially between the 1890s and 1930s. Calculations performed on the data in Hsu suggest that cash crops' share of agricultural output increased by at least 7 to 8 percent, which would mean that cash crops accounted for 23 percent of the value of agricultural output in the 1890s.[21] In that case, it would be necessary to revise upwards to 12.3 percent (16 percent*0.77) the estimate of the percentage of output marketed in the form of grains in the 1890s.

To arrive at the agricultural sector's total market surplus, estimates for grains must be added to cash-crop output that was marketed. Buck's marketing ratios suggest typically that half or more of the cash crop was marketed. Yet, as I pointed out in Chapter 3, his data probably underrestimate aggregate marketing ratios. In the seventy-six localities that grew cotton, for example, they reported only 35 percent sold, or less than half the percentage suggested by alternative calculations. For this examination, I have assumed that roughly half of cash-crop output was marketed in the 1890s, but that in the 1930s it was nearer to two-thirds.[22]

What does this imply? In the 1890s, agriculture's market surplus would have amounted to 23.5 percent of total agricultural output: 12.3 percent in the form of grains to feed the nonagricultural population, and the remainder in the form of cash crops. By contrast, in the 1930s the market surplus would have been nearer to 40 percent, 19.8 percent in the form of grains and roughly 20 percent in the form of cash crops. Over the intervening years, market surplus measured as a percentage of agricultural output would have increased by roughly 16 percent, from 23.5 to 39.8 percent. Assuming that the region's per capita agricultural output remained at least constant, this would have meant a more than doubling of the sector's market surplus in absolute terms, or annual increases around 2 percent. The assumption that per capita consumption of agricultural output did not decline, but in fact increased, is substantiated more fully in the next chapter.[23]

Finally, how did the percentage of agricultural output marketed overall change? To estimate marketed output from market surplus, we need to know how much agricultural output was resold to the farming population. The major item would be grains sold to households of all sizes specializing in cash-crop production and to households whose landholdings were too small for self-sufficiency.[24] Buck's nutritional surveys showed that the region's farm households obtained 15 to 20 percent of their grain for consumption from the market. He found a similar percengage in the North.[25] With slightly more than a quarter of grain output going to feed the nonagricultural population, farm household grain consumption would have amounted to between 7.5 and 10 percent of agricultural output (that is, $0.70*[1 - .28]*0.20$, where 0.70 is grain's share of total agricultural output). Assuming no overlap in categories – that Buck's consumption estimates apply to the farming population alone, not to any households otherwise classified as nonagricultural – these calculations suggest that in addition to the grain marketed to feed the nonagricultural population and the cash crop sales, as much as 7.5 to 10 percent more of agricultural output was marketed, putting marketed output at roughly 45 to 50 percent of agricultural output.

This estimate is higher than ones for China in the aggregate, but lower than what a number of farm surveys undertaken in the 1920s and 1930s found for areas in the region.[26] In a survey of localities along the Peking-Hankow Railroad, for example, owner-operated farms marketed on average 52.7 percent of farm output (in value terms); and tenant farmers exhibited an even higher rate of commercialization, marketing more than 65 percent.[27] In a 1921–5 survey of eight east-central localities, Buck found that on average 62.8 percent of farm output was marketed. By comparison, the average for nine localities in North China was 43.5 percent.[28] And, finally, a Chinese National Agricultural Research Bureau (NARB) investigation of 161 farm households in four localities in East China found that on average more than 60 percent of farm output was marketed.[29]

Because specialization in the rural economy increased between the 1890s and 1930s, grain sales to households specializing in cash-crop production were probably smaller in the 1890s than in the 1930s. If nearly 50 percent of the region's agricultural output was marketed in the 1930s, in the 1890s it was probably less than 30 percent. Even allowing for error, these calculations point to a sub-stantially more commercialized agriculture in the 1930s than in the 1890s. Equally important, they imply unprecedented growth in agriculture's market surplus, which averaged at least 2 percent per annum and maybe reached as high as 2 1/2 percent, far in excess of annual population growth, which was only 0.6 percent.

## Underlying Forces

The estimation of agriculture's market surplus confirms the view of earlier observers that the region's agriculture experienced rapid commercialization. At the same time, the estimate identifies one major factor contributing to this process: the increased demand for agri-cultural goods from the nonagricultural sector and from overseas demand. Growth in the nonagricultural sector is reflected both in the increased size of its population and expansion of its output. Between 1914–18 and 1931–6, nonagricultural output in China grew at 2.6 percent per annum; that in the more narrowly defined "modern" sec-tor, however, expanded at two times this rate.[30] Over roughly the same period, John Chang has estimated that the output of modern in-dustry in China grew at an annual rate of 9.4 percent.[31] Consumer-goods production that relied heavily on raw materials from agricul-ture expanded most rapidly, increasing its share of net value added in modern industry from 21.9 percent in 1912 to 44.3 percent in 1936.[32]

Shanghai and the Lower Yangtse were at the center of this growth, producing one-half of China's industrial output even as late as the 1930s. In all probability, nonagricultural output in the region grew much faster than 2.6 percent per annum. The cumulative influence of this process is partially reflected in the relative contributions by the 1930s of the agricultural and industrial sectors to total output in the lower Yangtse core.[33] Agriculture's share of total output was 43.3 percent; that of factories, utilities, and mines combined was 12.4 percent; for the rest of China, by comparison, the percentages were 67.6 percent and 2.3 percent, respectively.[34] These estimates suggest a level of development in the Lower Yangtse core very sim-ilar to that achieved by the Japanese economy in the 1890s.[35]

Yet, increased nonagricultural demand is only part of the picture. Equally important for explaining the substantial growth in agriculture's market surplus and the commercialization process more generally were changes in the structure of prices facing farm households, most notably, in the form of the terms of trade. In Hymer and Resnick's stylized model of an agrarian economy, it is a combination of increase in demand outside the farm sector and a secular rise in the terms of trade in agriculture's favor that gives rise to a growing market surplus.[36]

## Agricultural Prices

Chapter 3 analyzed the predominant role that external factors came to play in domestic rice and cotton price formation. Indeed, prices for many other agricultural commodities that either competed with imports or were themselves exported were similarly influenced by changes in the gold price of silver and international commodity prices in an analogous manner. Besides rice, cotton, tea, and silk, the list of regional crops traded internationally included wheat, soybeans, peanuts, rapeseed, sesame, tobacco, and sugarcane. Like rice or cotton, the percentage exported (or imported) was comparatively low, but nonetheless these eleven crops represented more than 80 percent of the value of crop output in Central and East China. Arbitrage in related markets may very well have tied prices for remaining crops to changes in the international economy as well.[37]

Unfortunately, data for these other crops is inadequate for tests analogous to those performed for rice and cotton. Is it possible to say anything more generally about external influences and the long-run behavior of agricultural prices in the region? Chapter 3 discussed the behavior of silver prices in the late nineteenth and early twentieth centuries. Except for two brief interludes in the late teens and early 1930s, silver prices fell almost continuously. And wholesale agricultural prices in the United State give some indication of the behavior of agricultural prices in the international economy. Throughout most of the late nineteenth century, U.S. farm prices were declining at an average annual rate of 2 percent. Beginning in the mid-1890s, however, came a thirty-year period of price increases (interrupted only at the conclusion of World War I) that ended abruptly in the late 1920s and early 1930s when prices dropped by more than 50 percent. Between 1928 and 1933, the index of wholesale prices for farm products fell from 105.9 to 51.4, 1926 being equal to 100.[38] After bottoming out early in 1933, prices finally began to rise again and by 1936 approximately one-half of the earlier loss had been recovered. Were these movements reflected in Chinese agricultural prices?

No long-run time series on agricultural prices dating back to the 1870s appear to exist for China. The best known and most frequently cited index, the Nankai series, does not begin until 1913.[39] In order to remedy this, I have constructed a weighted agricultural price index that allows observation of the direction in agricultural prices over the sixty-year period between 1876 and 1936. The index uses both domestic prices (Shanghai price of rice and wheat) and export unit values (cotton, tea, tobacco, soybeans, sesame, silk, and groundnuts) and weights based on 1930s data. The nine commodities represent 78 percent of total farm output and 80 percent of marketed farm output in the 1930s, respectively.[40] Because the agricultural markets in Central and East China were closely linked (and to other parts of China for that matter), the single index captures the secular behavior of prices reasonably well.[41]

This index is graphed in Figure 4.1 along with the Nankai index for agricultural goods for the years 1913—36. The first half of the 1890s marks a critical turning point for agricultural prices; they began a rise that continued until 1930. This secular rise was due to the depreciation of silver and the general rise in agricultural prices in the international market. During the 1870s and 1880s, these two factors had roughly offset each other. The upward trend in agricultural prices was interrupted only twice – once during World War I and during the early 1930s when agricultural prices fell between 35 and 40 percent. Agricultural prices in the international market had actually begun to fall several years earlier, but the continued decline in silver prices through the late 1920s helped delay the onset of deflation in China. Over the 35–40 year period ending in 1930, agricultural prices rose over threefold at an annually compounded rate in excess of 3 percent. Then in the early 1930s the price of silver suddenly began to rise; combined with the fall in international agricultural prices, this sharply cut Chinese agricultural prices.[42] Both indices graphed in Figure 4.1 show that within four years agricultural prices fell 35 percent, or to the level of the teens. An index for agricultural prices in Shanghai and numerous other local indices for these years suggest a decline of the same magnitude.[43] By 1936, agricultural prices had recovered significantly.

## Nonagricultural Prices

So far, I have only discussed the link between international and domestic agricultural prices. Yet, models such as Hymer–Resnick

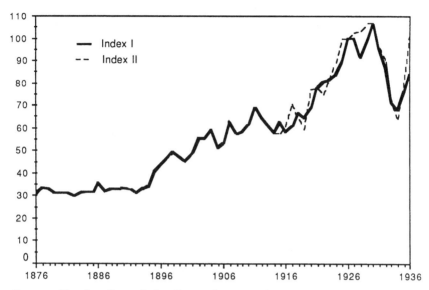

*Sources:* For details on Index I, see the appendix to this chapter. Index II
is the Nankai index for North China and is taken from *Nan-kai chih-shu
tzu-liao hui-pien* (Peking, 1958), pp. 12–13.

Figure 4.1

Agricultural Prices in China, 1876–1936
(1926 = 100)

also direct our attention to changes in the terms of trade – that is,
the price of agricultural goods relative to the price of manufactured
or nonagricultural goods.[44] The same kind of argument I made for
agricultural goods can be extended to numerous manufactured, nonagricultural goods, and even some processed agricultural goods. This
would include such items as yarn, cloth, heating fuels, salt, sugar,
and so forth. Recent scholarship by People's Republic of China historians points to the fact that by the mid-to-late eighteenth century
a national market was already operating in a number of these commodities.[45] Although a major proportion of this interregional trade
was in products of high unit value, such as cloth, sugar, or salt, the
trade also included some lower-unit value commodities like cotton
or timber.[46] In general, the high unit values of most of these commodities effectively reduced the implicit tax that high transportation costs levied.

By the late nineteenth century, many of these nonagricultural items were being imported. This was most evident in the case of textiles, where domestically produced yarn and cloth (both handicraft and manufactured) competed with imports from India, Japan, and Britain. At the turn of the century, approximately 40 percent of the yarn and 25 percent of the cloth consumed in China was imported.[47] Cheng-ming Wu has argued on the basis of just this sort of relationship that the prices of key nonagricultural and processed agricultural goods domestically produced and consumed became closely tied to import prices and therefore tended to follow the price in the international market.[48]

Drawing on the notion of an established and expanding national market and of links between the domestic and international market for nonagricultural goods, I have constructed a price index for manufactured and processed agricultural goods primarily utilizing unit values for imports and exports.[49] Although it is unrealistic to expect this index to accurately reflect all the year-to-year changes, it offers a fairly realistic impression of the secular change in the level of these prices.

Table 4.13 shows that the prices for nonagricultural products rose only modestly before World War I, with most of that rise coming after 1895. Between 1914 and 1918, however, prices increased by almost 50 percent, then leveled off. After rising sharply again in both 1930 and 1931, they fell approximately 30 percent between 1932 and 1935. As before, this behavior loosely follows the long-run prices of manufactured goods in the developed countries and the price of silver. In the United States, for example, prices of manufactured goods fell slowly throughout most of the late nineteenth century, beginning to rise again only just before 1900. They then rose modestly until 1914, at which time the rate of increase quickly accelerated. After a sharp drop with the postwar adjustment in the early 1920s, prices remained roughly constant until the early 1930s, at which time they experienced a modest fall of 10 to 15 percent.

## The Structure of Prices and the Terms of Trade

Drawing on the indices constructed for agricultural and nonagricultural prices, the intersectoral terms of trade can be examined. The terms of trade measures the price of a unit of agricultural output in terms of manufactured goods. A rise in the price of one sector's products relative to the other's is said to show a movement in favor of that sector because it implies an increase in the quantity of goods from the other sector that a unit of its output commands. The terms

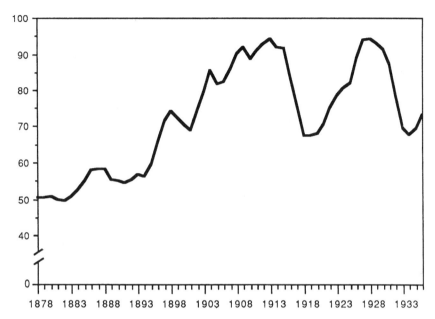

For details see text.

Figure 4.2

Terms of Trade, 1878–1936
(3-year moving average)

of trade are important to this discussion because they influence resource allocation and incomes in the rural economy.

Figure 4.2 graphs a three-year moving average of the terms of trade for the years between 1878 and 1936. Using a three-year moving average helps to remove some of the short-run volatility in the index. For the first few years, the terms of trade remained relatively constant, but beginning in the mid-1880s agricultural prices began a rise relative to nonagricultural prices that continued over the better part of the period. The two major exceptions to this behavior occurred during World War I, when wartime demand and disruptions to international shipping pushed up prices of manufactured goods (in the industrialized countries and in China) while agricultural prices remained at prewar levels and during the early 1930s, when worldwide depression caused agricultural prices to fall relative to nonagricultural prices.[50] Unlike the brief episode during the war, the early 1930s witnessed a sharp decline in the absolute level of agricultural prices as well. Within only four years, the terms at which agriculture traded deteriorated 35 percent.

Figure 4.2 suggests that, except for the war years and early 1930s, prices in the Chinese economy, now heavily influenced by international behavior, moved in favor of agriculture. Not only were agricultural prices rising, but they were rising relative to nonagricultural goods prices. This increase did not occur uniformly over the period, but altogether, and over almost fifty years, the terms of trade rose by as much as 70 to 80 percent.[51] In the early 1930s, however, the farming population saw these gains quickly erode, though the terms of trade still remained higher than they had been half a century earlier. Michelle McAlpin has found roughly similar behavior for India.[52]

## Price Structure, Market Demand, and
## Resource Reallocation

How do increased demand for agricultural products and a changed price structure combine to influence resource allocation, productivity, and the market surplus of a rural economy? Hymer and Resnick have examined this question theoretically in the context of a model that captures some of the essential features of rural China in the late nineteenth and early twentieth centuries.

Their model assumes that autarkic or semi-subsistent farm households allocate their resources (primarily land and labor) between the production of agricultural and nonagricultural goods. Home-produced nonagricultural goods, referred to as "Z" goods, encompass the products of many activities that the household engages in, including the processing of foods and fuels, spinning and weaving of textiles, manufacture and repair of tools and implements, and services such as transport and distribution. Much of this is earmarked for the household's own consumption and could be labeled "home production".

Hymer and Resnick suggest that Z activities do more than absorb the household's relatively low-cost, off-season labor. Rather, any rural economy – even one with a relatively high population density like China's – offers substitution possibilities between Z goods and agricultural output in production. Because farmers can select a variety of crops and agricultural techniques – each differing in labor intensity – they can partially adjust the seasonality of labor requirements and the total amount of labor used in agriculture during the year by changing the composition of their output and their choice of technique.

The model assumes that Z goods are non-traded (or are traded only locally). But farm households do sell agricultural output (F) in order to buy manufactured and processed agricultural goods from the "outside" nonagricultural sector; and they do this at a rate of exchange given by the terms of trade, that is, the price of agricultural goods divided by the price of nonagricultural goods. How the rural sector allocates its resources between agricultural and goods production depends on the terms of trade, to changes in which farm households are assumed to be highly responsive.

Over several decades, market integration and expansion in urban and foreign trade opportunities at terms in agriculture's favor would lead to the following kind of changes in the rural sector. First, farm households will reallocate labor and other resources from the production of Z goods into the more labor-intensive agricultural cultivation. This may take the form of increased multiple-cropping or a shift into cash crops that have higher labor requirement. Second, farm households will supply more food and industrial crops to the nonagricultural sector or export sectors (in other words, agriculture's market surplus will increase) in exchange for manufactured or processed agricultural goods viewed as superior to those produced at home. Farmers consider Z goods "inferior." And third, specialization based on comparative advantage within the agricultural sector will increase, with farm households growing fewer crops while simultaneously increasing the variety and quality of food they consume by importing foods grown and processed elsewhere.

New trade possibilities with the urban and foreign sector and the long-term change in the terms of trade redirect rural economic activity toward the market and away from self-sufficiency. Changing opportunity costs motivate farm households to specialize more fully in agriculture and to use the market to procure manufactured and nonagricultural goods,[53] or even services, that the nonagricultural sector can supply more efficiently.[54] Over time, we would expect many Z-type production activities to decline, with the most inferior goods disappearing the most quickly. The Hymer-Resnick model does not suggest that Z-type activities disappear all at once, but rather that, in the hierarchy of Z-type activities, the more inferior ones will disappear one by one.[55] Unlike the Boserup model, however, this model has demand changes precipitate the intensification of agricultural production, and only secondarily, increased rural population and the size of the rural labor force.[56]

## The Case of Central and East China

The Hymer and Resnick model describes many aspects of the course of development in rural Central and East China. So far, I have documented only the fundamentals: a rise in the terms of trade, the role of new sources of demand, and the accompanying growth in the rural sector's market surplus. Underlying the growth in market surplus were many more changes occurring at the local level.

## Cropping Changes and Cropping Intensity

By all indications, farm households in the region responded favorably to new overseas markets and growing domestic demand by expanding production and marketing of cash crops and grains. Acreage estimates contained in Hsu, for example, show significant increases in cash-crop acreage – in cotton, oilseeds, and tobacco. Buck's data for all of China, reported in Table 4.1, provide additional evidence of these changes for a slightly longer period between 1940–9 and 1929–33. Crops such as cotton, corn, and oilseeds – which offered high yields, were more labor-intensive, but were in great demand either domestically or for export – rose decidedly. In the twenty-seven localities that grew cotton, for example, sown area just about doubled. Similar increases obtained in rapeseed and sesame, while the percentage sown to wheat or rice remained roughly constant. Acreage in coarser grains such as kaoliang (sorghum), barley, and millet, on the other hand, fell between a quarter and a third. Many examples (often only qualitative in nature) testifying to increases in cash-crop production at the local level can be found in Li and Chang.[57]

The cumulative effect of this process on regional agriculture is neatly reflected in data for the 1930s. Tables 4.2 and 4.3 display the cultivated area in each of eight cash crops for the six provinces in the region as well as estimates of total acreage in cash crops measured as a percentage of cultivated area. Rice and wheat were highly commercialized products for many localities, but they are not included in these tables. In the Yangtse region, 33.0 percent of cultivated area was devoted to cash crops, with the percentage as high as 39 percent in the case of Kiangsu, but as low as 27.2 percent in Hunan. Of these cash crops, soybeans, rapeseed, and cotton were the three most important. Adding in the acreage in mulberry trees and tea production would raise the cash-crop percentages slightly. Substantial acreage in parts of the Lower Yangtse was given over to mulberry trees for silk production,[58] exports of which grew roughly

Table 4.1 *Trends in crop acreage between 1904–9 and 1930–3*

| Crop | # Localities Reporting | Percentage of Acreage Sown | | | |
|---|---|---|---|---|---|
| | | 1904–9 | 1914–19 | 1924–9 | 1930–3 |
| *Crops Whose Acreage Increased or Remained the Same* | | | | | |
| Broad beans | 7 | 9 | 9 | 9 | 9 |
| Corn | 22 | 11 | 14 | 16 | 17 |
| Cotton | 27 | 11 | 14 | 18 | 20 |
| Opium | 13 | 14 | 3 | 11 | 20 |
| Peanuts | 18 | 9 | 8 | 11 | 11 |
| Rapeseed | 5 | 15 | 21 | 27 | 28 |
| Rice | 17 | 40 | 41 | 37 | 40 |
| Sesame | 7 | 4 | 8 | 10 | 9 |
| Soybeans | 7 | 8 | 9 | 10 | 8 |
| Sweet potatoes | 18 | 10 | 11 | 12 | 13 |
| Wheat | 29 | 26 | 27 | 27 | 27 |
| *Crops Whose Acreage Decreased* | | | | | |
| Barley | 10 | 24 | 23 | 20 | 19 |
| Indigo | 12 | 10 | 7 | 2 | 0 |
| Kaoliang | 14 | 26 | 23 | 20 | 16 |
| Millet | 15 | 22 | 18 | 17 | 17 |
| Sugarcane | 10 | 7 | 6 | 5 | 6 |

*Source:* Buck, *Land Utilization in China,* p. 317.

2.0 percent per annum between the late 1880s and late 1920s.[59] Further, Hunan, Chekiang, and Hupei were, in that order, the three largest tea producers in China, producing approximately 2 million *picul.*[60] In suburban areas, substantial acreage was in vegetable production to supply the cities, and vegetable farming increased with the growth of the urban population.

Several comparisons can provide insights. First, only 22 percent of cultivated area was in cash crops in the rest of China, or a third lower. If soybeans are excluded – a high percentage of which were grown in Manchuria – the difference is almost one-half. Omitting Manchuria is actually more indicative of the differences that existed between the Yangtse region and the rest of China proper. Even making allowances for differences in the degree of multiple-cropping, we still find marked geographic differences in the degree of cash cropping between Central and East China and other regions of the country.

Table 4.2. *Cultivated area (CA) in cash-crop production 1931–7 (in millions of mou)*

| Province | CA | Sesame | Peanuts | Soybeans | Rapeseed | Cotton | Sugar | Tobacco | Fibers |
|---|---|---|---|---|---|---|---|---|---|
| Kiangsu | 92 | 2.23 | 2.36 | 14.31 | 4.13 | 12.65 | 0.00 | .10 | 0.00 |
| Anhwei | 88 | 3.67 | 2.02 | 10.70 | 6.84 | 3.32 | 0.00 | .57 | .53 |
| Chekiang | 33 | .26 | .33 | 2.86 | 5.70 | 1.88 | .14 | .27 | .12 |
| Hupei | 65 | 2.38 | .96 | 3.17 | 4.62 | 7.19 | 0.00 | .36 | .33 |
| Hunan | 58 | .44 | .72 | 1.34 | 8.40 | 1.93 | .53 | .94 | 1.47 |
| Kiangsi | 43 | 1.48 | .82 | 3.02 | 7.68 | 1.21 | .17 | .24 | .40 |
| Region | 379 | 10.46 | 7.21 | 35.40 | 37.37 | 28.18 | .84 | 2.48 | 2.84 |
| China | 1,471 | 23.21 | 30.89 | 160.57 | 78.20 | 70.03 | 3.10 | 10.58 | 9.40 |

*Source:* Perkins, *Agricultural Development in China*, Appendixes C and D.

Table 4.3. *Degree of cash-cropping by province*

| Province | Area in Cash Crops (in millions of *mou*) | % of Cultivated Area in Cash Crops |
|----------|------------|------------|
| Kiangsu | 35.88 | 39.0% |
| Anhwei | 27.65 | 31.4 |
| Chekiang | 11.56 | 35.0 |
| Hupei | 19.01 | 29.2 |
| Hunan | 15.77 | 27.2 |
| Kiangsi | 15.02 | 34.9 |

*Source:* Perkins, *Agricultural Development in China,* Appendixes C and D.

The second comparison is with contemporary China. For the entire country, and probably for Central and East China, the percentage of sown area in cash crops was noticeably higher in the 1930s than it was forty years later. In 1977, just prior to reforms in the agricultural sector, the percentage of area in all of China in the eight cash crops was only 13.6 percent, or three-quarters of what it averaged in the 1930s.[61] An increase in the degree of multiple-cropping over the last thirty years explains only a small part of this decline; more importantly, total acreage in cash-crop production actually declined and in 1977 was 20 percent lower than it had been in the thirties. No regional estimate can be made for this year. This decline was one cost of a policy of local self-sufficiency in grain production that Nicholas Lardy has recently analyzed.[62] Between 1977 and 1982, acreage in cash crops increased by more than a third in all of China, and the percentage of sown area in cash crops recovered to 18.8 percent. With this growth, for the first time in the post-1949 era, farmland in cash crops exceeded estimated acreage in the same crops during the 1930s. In Central and East China, however, only 16.8 percent of sown area was in cash crops as of 1982 and total cash crop acreage was still 15 percent below that in the 1930s. Only recently has commercialization in the rural sector of the People's Republic of China surpassed the level achieved in the 1930s.

Whether or not the shift into more labor-intensive, more valuable crops after 1890s was accompanied by an increase in the degree of multiple-cropping is difficult to say because data on sown acreage prior to the 1920s and 1930s do not exist. In a recent study, Kang Chao argues that in high probability the multiple-cropping index (MCI) for pre-1949 China peaked at approximately 140 by 1850, and

declined thereafter because the expansion in acreage that followed
was primarily confined to the single-cropping area of Manchuria.[63]
Kang does not present data to substantiate the estimate for the
1850s, but data for the 1930s imply a slightly higher level of
multiple-cropping for China proper than the estimate for 1850.[64]
These estimates, moreover, would not reflect any increased intensity
of land use that may have occurred through increased intercropping.
The margin of error in these data is too great to say definitively
that the MCI increased, but the possibility cannot be ruled out.

## Increasing Specialization

The expanded cultivation of cash crops was typically accompanied
by increasing specialization, the basic outlines of which sometimes
dated back centuries. The specialization is reflected at both the
county and provincial level. Kiangsu and Hupei, for example, were
the two largest cotton producers in Central and East China, but
within each province cotton production was typically confined to a
few key areas particularly well suited for cotton. In Kiangsu, fifty-
one out of the sixty-one *hsien* reported some acreage in cotton.[65]
Cotton acreage in the top ten *hsien*, most of which were situated
along the eastern seaboard, constituted two-thirds of total cotton
acreage in the province, with slightly less than 50 percent of cultivated area in these *hsien* occupied by cotton. For the province as
a whole, 12.7 percent of cultivated area was in cotton. Most important among the producing areas were Tungchou, Taits'ang, Chia-
ting, Changshu, Shanghai, and Kiangyin. In Hupei, cotton acreage
in the ten largest cotton-growing *hsien* accounted for 55 percent of
total provincial cotton acreage, with approximately one-third of the
cultivated area in each *hsien*, or four times the provincial average,
sown to cotton.[66] Most of these counties were located along the Han
and Yangtse rivers. And, finally, in Chekiang cotton production was
highly concentrated in the northeastern part of the province, with
two-thirds of the acreage in just eight *hsien*.

In both Kiangsu and Chekiang, there were also many areas highly
specialized in sericulture, most of them in the Kiangnan area – the
area south of the Lower Yangtse River comprising the southern
prefectures of Kiangsu and the northern prefectures of Chekiang.
To supply the leaves to feed the cocoons, the percentage of cultivated
area in mulberry trees was often very high. County-level data do
not appear to exist for Kiangsu, but for Chekiang Table 4.4 provides
estimates of the percentage of acreage devoted to mulberry in key
sericulture areas.

Table 4.4. *Sericulture in Chekiang*

| County | % of Cultivated Area in Mulberry | % of Households in Sericulture |
|---|---|---|
| Hanghsien | 23.6% | 60.0% |
| Haiyen | 20.0 | 97.5 |
| Chiashan | 11.0 | 49.0 |
| Yuhang | 27.5 | 71.7 |
| Yuchien | 10.0 | 77.5 |
| Wuhsing | 36.0 | 100.0 |
| Changhwa | 10.0 | 97.0 |
| Tonghsiang | 39.0 | 92.0 |
| Pinghu | 19.0 | 80.0 |
| Haining | 45.0 | 100.0 |
| Linhai | 19.0 | 50.0 |
| Changhsing | 27.0 | 88.0 |
| Fuyang | 14.0 | 40.0 |
| Changte | 43.0 | 92.0 |
| Wukang | 22.0 | 70.0 |
| Chiahsing | 24.0 | 10.0 |
| Teching | 48.0 | 99.0 |

*Source:* Ssu-ping Yueh, *Chung-kuo ts'an-ssu,* 1935, pp. 169–70.

Numerous other examples can be provided of localities that by the 1930s were devoting a quarter of total acreage (or in upwards of 35 percent of cultivated area) to a cash crop, especially oil-seed crops. In Kiangsu, almost every *hsien* grew some soybeans, but more than half of the acreage was in the ten largest-producing *hsien*, all located in the north-central part of the province. Approximately 40 percent of the cultivated area in these *hsien* was in soybeans, or almost four times the average for the rest of province. Multiple-cropping here was slightly lower on average, suggesting even greater differences if the sown area was the basis of comparison. Similar concentration characterized soybean production in northern Anhwei along the Yellow River.

Both Kiangsi and Anhwei had substantial acreage in rapeseed and sesame. Rapeseed, a winter crop, was usually sown before a summer crop of rice, and sesame was a spring crop. In Anhwei, sesame production was heavily confined to the northwest, and those *hsien* concentrating in rapeseed were located along the Yangtse. Between 1912 and the late 1920s, shipments of rape through Wuhu

Maritime Customs increased from 30,000 *picul* to over 750,000.[67] Kiangsi devoted more than 20 percent of the cultivated area to these two crops. Hupei, one of China's largest prewar producers of sesame, had almost 2 1/2 million *mou* in the crop, with much of it found in Wuchang, Daye, Puchi, Yanghsin, Chaiyu, and Echeng. Between 1929 and 1931, half of the output was exported through Maritime Customs alone.[68] Hunan was second only to Szechwan as China's producer of rapeseed.

These data suggest how specialization in cash crops was proceeding. It typically involved modifying existing cropping patterns to allow for planting as much as a third of a farm's acreage in one crop. Complete specialization in one crop was rare. Risk aversion and the use of complex cropping rotations to maintain soil fertility and to maximize the intensity of land use mitigated against such behavior.[69]

One consequence of increasing specialization appears to have been that farm households purchased more of their grain requirements from the market. The possibility of doing so doubtless played a pivotal role in facilitating the comparatively high level of specialization. Without these outside supplies of grain, farming would have been much more self-sufficient. Evidence of grain purchases is found in Buck's survey data. For all of China, 21 percent of the calories derived from grain were purchased from the market. In the Yangtse Rice-Wheat Region, the figure was 25 percent, but in the Rice-Tea Region it was 19 percent.[70] These summary measures actually conceal wide differences within the region. Table 4.5 reveals that in a third of forty-one localities surveyed more than 25 percent was obtained from the market. Similar differences can be found in a sample of farm households along the Peking-Hankow Railroad (which ran through Hupei). On average, owner-operator and tenant farms were purchasing 31.5 and 40.85 percent of their grain, with the percentage of total grain consumption purchased in any locality decreasing with average farm size. For these localities with three *mou* or less per family member, 35.3 percent was purchased; this fell to 23.3 percent for localities with three to five *mou* per family member; and for those localities with more than five, only 11 percent was purchased.[71] By comparison, fragmentary data compiled by Lardy suggests that in the first years of the 1950s only about 10 percent of farm household grain consumption was met through market purchases.[72]

No data indicate substantial long-distance trade in grain other than that required to feed the expanding urban population. In other words, most of the grain required to meet these deficits was supplied locally, which I interpret liberally to mean either from the same

Table 4.5. *Percentage of calories from grain
purchased by farm households from the
market*

| Percentage | No. of Localities |
|---|---|
| Less than 10% | 11 |
| 11%–20% | 7 |
| 21%–30% | 11 |
| 31%–40% | 6 |
| 41%–50% | 2 |
| More than 50% | 4 |
| Total no. of localities | 41 |

*Source:* Buck, *Land Utilization in China: Statistical
Volume*, p. 69.

village or not-too-distant areas within the province. It is difficult,
however, to determine the exact source of the grain. The fact that
only a small percentage of a village's grain sales were to other
farmers suggests that much of the grain they bought came from
outside the village.[73] Grain flows of this sort are certainly confirmed
by Buck's marketing data, which show that in the Rice Region rice
was the most important commodity shipped in to the localities surveyed.[74] Soybeans were second. Throughout the early twentieth century, these flows were also apparently increasing.[75] Detailed data
bearing on this question for three villages in North China indicate
a similar role for outside supplies in the case of two of the villages.
These data are provided in Table 4.6.

If local grain deficits were met by outside supplies, then the gains
from commercialization and increasing specialization need not have
been solely confined to areas with immediate access to rail or water
transport. The gains could have been partially diffused to locations
in less-advantaged areas. In those localities, commercialization
would have produced a decline in cash-crop acreage and increased
specialization in grain production.

## Marketing and Trade

With the growth in income from the sale of farm products, rural
households became increasingly dependent on the market for non-

Table 4.6. *Grain balances in three North China villages*

| Village—Crop | Harvested | Sold | Purchased | Consumed | Carry-over |
|---|---|---|---|---|---|
| *Tapeikuan, Pinggu* | | | | | |
| Grains (*shih*) | 1658.35 | 128.56 | 117.67 | 1238.05 | 865.36 |
| Beans (*shih*) | 120.45 | 7.10 | 1.50 | 92.32 | 58.90 |
| Potatoes (*tan*) | 456.80 | 0 | 0 | 451.80 | 40.00 |
| *Chienliangkechuang, Changli* | | | | | |
| Grains (*shih*) | 279.29 | 6.89 | 468.69 | 747.98 | 90.47 |
| Beans (*shih*) | 35.17 | 0.78 | 0 | 26.21 | 9.88 |
| *Fengjun, Michang* | | | | | |
| Grains (*shih*) | 1032.96 | 61.50 | 334.37 | 1071.77 | 372.92 |
| Beans (*shih*) | 20.43 | 0 | 17.02 | 0 | 7.92 |

*Sources:* Minami Manshū Tetsudō Kabushiki Kaisha, Kito Noson Jittai Chosahan, *Dainiji kitō nōson jittai chōsa hōkokusho: tōkeihon, Dai ichiban: Heikoku ken,* Table 12; *Dai sanban: Hōjun ken* Table 12; and *Dai yonban: Shorei ken,* Table 12.

Table 4.7. *Composition of inter-treaty-port trade, 1936*

| Commodity | Value of Trade (in millions of *yuan*) | % of Total |
|---|---|---|
| Cotton textiles | 319.51 | 26.8% |
| Grain | 127.54 | 10.8 |
| Tung oil | 91.70 | 7.8 |
| Tobacco products | 82.87 | 6.8 |
| Cotton | 65.43 | 5.5 |
| Coal | 41.62 | 3.5 |
| Tea | 40.77 | 3.4 |
| Sugar | 38.17 | 3.2 |
| Taro | 30.31 | 2.6 |
| Shelled peanuts | 25.75 | 2.2 |
| Total: top 10 | 863.57 | 71.4% |
| Total: all goods | 1,184.70 | 100.0% |

*Source:* Han, *Chung-kuo pu-chi mao-yi t'ung-chi,* 1936–40, pp. 100-1.

agricultural and processed agricultural goods that they had formerly frequently made themselves or bought locally. Included among these products were yarn, cloth, fuel for heating, cooking oil, matches, sugar, and increasingly, it appears, fertilizer. In a 1935 survey carried out by the National Agriculture Research Bureau, 36 percent of all farm families surveyed in the region reported to have purchased commercial fertilizers (in the form of oil-cakes); and in Hupei and Kiangsu almost one-half did. Eighty percent purchased kerosene.[76] The expenditure data analyzed in the appendix to this chapter show that, when self-supplied consumption is valued at market prices, between 40 and 50 percent of a rural farm household's nonfarming expenditure and a slightly higher percentage of their farm expenditure were in cash.

Detailed data on the intersectoral trade are very limited, but Maritime Customs data provide some insight into its composition and rate of growth. Because much of this trade continued to occur outside Maritime Customs throughout the period, less can be inferred about its absolute level. Table 4.7 provides information on the composition of the inter-treaty-port trade for all treaty ports for 1936. Textiles (yarn and cloth) were the largest item, representing more than a quarter of the inter-treaty-port trade in 1936. Tung oil, tobacco products, and coal are the other major nonagricultural items. Grain, cotton, tea, and sugar were the primary agricultural products

Table 4.8. *Estimated Real Rates of growth in treaty-port trade, 1900–36*

| Item | 1900–14 | 1915–29 | 1900–29 | 1900–36 |
|------|---------|---------|---------|---------|
| Direct imports | 0.005 | 0.061 | 0.014 | 0.012 |
| Direct exports | 0.046 | 0.015 | 0.025 | 0.012 |
| Net foreign imports | 0.008 | 0.067 | 0.023 | n.a. |
| Total exports | 0.039 | 0.045 | 0.042 | 0.036 |
| Inter-treaty-port trade | 0.024 | 0.083 | 0.067 | 0.062 |
| Total trade | 0.025 | 0.053 | 0.034 | n.a. |

*Note:* n.a.—not available.
*Source:* Based on data contained in Chinese Imperial Maritime Customs, *Returns of Trade and Trade Reports,* 1900–36.

shipped through Maritime Customs. Trade in the ten most important goods constituted more than 70 percent of the inter-treaty-port trade. It is perhaps indicative of the changes in the Chinese economy that trade in these same commodities in 1908 represented only 30 percent of the total trade.[77]

Table 4.8 provides estimates of the real rates of growth (rates adjusted for price changes) for key components in the Maritime Customs trade for the treaty ports of Central and East China between 1900 and 1936 and during three subperiods. Because of the confusion over supposed double and triple counting in Maritime Customs data, some brief explanations are in order. First, direct imports and direct exports represent the direct overseas trade of each port. Yet, not all overseas imports were received directly from the country of export; some came as reshipments from other treaty ports, notably Shanghai. Net foreign imports adjusts for this and includes direct overseas imports plus foreign goods received from other treaty ports, less any reexports of foreign goods to foreign countries or other treaty ports. Total exports, on the other hand, are the sum of direct overseas exports plus shipment of goods of local origin to other treaty ports. Inter-treaty-port exports of Chinese goods are the difference between total exports and direct overseas exports. A small amount of double counting occurs in total exports and inter-treaty-port shipments, but data from the 1930s show that reexports as a percentage of inter-treaty-port shipments averaged less than 5 percent of total shipments. Finally, total trade is the sum of total exports plus net foreign imports, and provides an estimate of the total value of trade.

Between 1900 and 1936, total exports adjusted for price changes increased at a fairly impressive annual rate of 3.6 percent. Growth through 1929 was slightly higher at 4.2 percent. With population in the region increasing at less than 1 percent per annum, this implies that exports per capita increased annually at a rate of 3 percent, or by a factor of two and a half.[78] In the 1930s, total exports through Maritime Customs treaty ports in the Yangtse region averaged 650 million *yuan* in current prices, or roughly 6 to 7 percent of regional GDP.[79]

Overseas and inter-treaty-port exports did not make the same contributions throughout the period. Up through 1914, foreign exports were responsible for a major portion of the increased trade through Maritime Customs. Between 1900 and 1914, overseas exports grew almost twice as fast as the inter-treaty-port trade (4.6 percent versus 2.4 percent). The next fifteen-year period presents a sharp contrast. Inter-treaty-port exports accelerated to an annual rate of 8.3 percent, and overseas exports fell to one-third the rate prior to 1914. Overall between 1900 and 1929, inter-treaty-port trade grew two and a half times more rapidly than foreign exports. Furthermore, unlike overseas exports, the inter-treaty-port trade continued to increase through the early 1930s and helped to offset the influence that the sharp drop in overseas demand would have otherwise had on the domestic economy. Inter-treaty-port shipments grew from approximately a quarter of total exports at the turn of the century to almost two-thirds by the 1930s.

Inter-treaty-port trade included the shipments of raw materials and agricultural goods into the treaty ports, as well as the shipment out of Shanghai and Hankow of manufactured and processed goods primarily for domestic consumption. As mentioned, however, domestic consumers also drew heavily on raw materials shipped outside the purview of Maritime Customs. Especially so, comparison of the rates of growth imply that a rapidly expanding domestic market centered in Shanghai and Hankow was largely responsible for the increased volume of regional trade.[80] Growing overseas demand was an early catalyst of the rapid commercialization, but was by no means the primary motive force.

## Extensions

Increasing specialization and exchange occurred not just between the urban and rural sectors, but even within the rural sector – a fact often overlooked. Moreover, this increasingly specialized rural trade complemented the growing rural-urban exchange. Some rural areas specialized in grains or cash crops such as cotton, oilseeds, or tea; some specialized primarily in handicrafts (Z-type goods), and some produced both handicrafts and cash crops.[81] Within localities, households would also specialize. So the period saw increasing exchange among the rural and the urban and the foreign sectors, but also within the rural sector.

Expanding intrarural trade was also related to the growing nonagricultural rural population. With the rapid commercialization of the rural economy, employment opportunities emerged in the nonagricultural sector in industry, in such services as marketing and transportation, and in other capacities as skilled and unskilled labor. Although some of the growth in employment occurred in the urban sector, most of it actually appears to have taken place in nonurban areas. We have no data on employment growth, but the more than doubling (and perhaps tripling) of marketed output in agriculture as well as the rapid growth of trade through Maritime Customs certainly suggest substantial increases in the demand for these services at this level. According to Liu and Yeh, more than 23 million people in the nonagricultural sector were employed in trade and transportation in the 1930s, and in the agricultural sector perhaps as much as an additional 5 to 10 million were employed on a part-time basis.[82] It also seems that employment grew in various kinds of processing industries located in rural areas. To cite just one example, during the late nineteenth and early twentieth centuries, production of oil crops increased substantially. Data for the 1920s and 1930s show that marketing ratios for these crops were high, self-supplied consumption of vegetable oil was low, and processing by industry located in major urban centers represented a relatively small percentage of total processing. These observations suggest that much processing was carried out in larger villages and towns and that it drew on rural labor. The same was true for rice milling.

No doubt new employment opportunities of this kind motivated some individuals to leave agriculture altogether, and for others alternative employments became more important relative to agriculture. Rural households actually spanned a continuum regarding by-employment. Farm household data provided by Buck and the Peking-Hankow Raiload survey show marked differences among localities as well as differences among households within localities.[83] In general, by-employment declined with increasing farm size.[84] Over time, specialization in the sidelines probably became more complete, with an increasing number of individuals leaving agricuture altogether for what they perceived to be more lucrative opportunities. The more than doubling of the nonagricultural population in the region between the 1890s and 1930s supports this interpretation.

The role of intrarural trade cannot be underestimated. In general, increases in the urban-rural trade were supported by an expansion in intrarural trade and by the degree of local specialization. This is perhaps clearest with those localities that specialized in non-grain cash crops and purchased grain on the market. Their ability to increase substantially their production and marketing of cash crops depended on their being able to buy grain on the market. Handicraft cloth producers, for instance, needed both supplies of grain from outlying areas and an expanding market for their cloth. The sale of manufactured yarn to these households would have linked the growth of the modern textile sector to the same factors.

These observations about the relationship between the intrarural and the intersectoral trade point to a shortcoming of looking only at changes in the trade between the urban and the rural sectors as an indicator of the rate at which commercialization and specializatioin were proceeding in the agricultural sector. Associated with any increase in urban-rural trade was an equally important increase in the intrarural trade. Given the influence that the degree of specialization had on productivity, important productivity increases may very well have accompanied what appear to be only modest increases in the urban-rural trade.

## Summary

The last quarter of the nineteenth century marked a critical turning point for agriculture in Central and East China because the region became linked with the outside world. Previous examinations have heavily concentrated on the new international demand for agricultural products such as tea, soybeans, silk, and so forth. Although the expanding export trade made a great difference to some localities in the region, only a small percentage of agricultural output was ever exported overseas. By far the largest percentage of agricultural goods marketed was destined for domestic consumption.

My analysis suggests that the greatest influence the international economy had may well have been exerted through its effect on domestic prices. The change in the structure of domestic prices that followed integration with the international economy was a major contributing factor to the rapid commercialization of agriculture. In this chapter, I have focused only on the role of changes in the terms of trade facing farm households, but price changes actually extended much further. In the next chapter, I examine how changes in the price relationship between raw cotton, yarn, and cloth significantly influenced resource allocation in the handicraft textile sector. This change in the structure of prices, combined with new market opportunities – many of them associated with the region's ongoing urbanization and industrialization – helped redirect rural economic activity toward the market, which in turn promoted increasing specialization and exchange.

By all indications, rural farm households responded very quickly to new trade possibilities. Not only did the region feed an increase in the agricultural population, but it also accommodated a more than doubling of the nonagricultural population while simultaneously increasing the marketing of non-grain crops. The rising income from the sale of this output permitted farm households to increase their consumption of key nonagricultural commodities and some processed agricultural goods. This success is hard to reconcile with the view of others that after the 1890s increases in agricultural production were prevented by a scarcity of land and other factors. In Chapter 5, I reexamine the question of productivity change in agriculture in light of these developments.

APPENDIX TO CHAPTER 4

In a weighted price index for agricultural prices, the price of each commodity is typically weighted by its share in total output. In China, however, a significant portion of farm output was actually consumed by farm households. Because I am concerned with the prices they received for the commodities they sold, I devised a set of weights based on the share of each commodity in total *marketed* output rather than total output. The first step was to calculate the percentage of farm output that was marketed. I drew on Perkins's estimate of farm output for the six provinces of Central and East China and Buck's marketing ratios. These calculations put the value of marketed farm output at 2.00 billion *yuan*, or slightly more than 40 percent of farm output. As I mentioned earlier, the percentage of agricultural output actually marketed was probably higher.

Second, I had to determine the contribution of each crop in total marketed output. Table 4.9 presents general categories: food crops, oil-bearing crops, and so forth. Food crops ranked first by a vast margin. Because some farm output was marketed by absentee landlords who had been paid rent in kind, and because I want to know what happened to prices received by farm households, I have also recalculated the percentage of each crop in total marketed output

Table 4.9. *Marketed output of crops*

| Crop | Marketed Output[a] (in millions of *yuan*) | Percentage | Marketed Output[b] (in millions of *yuan*) | Percentage |
|---|---|---|---|---|
| Food crops | 1,271.82 | 63.6% | 699.78 | 50.6% |
| Soybeans | 86.81 | 4.3 | 78.34 | 5.7 |
| Oil-bearing | 216.21 | 10.8 | 213.06 | 15.4 |
| Plant fibers | 210.86 | 10.6 | 210.86 | 15.3 |
| Other cash crops | 212.85 | 10.7 | 180.06 | 13.0 |
| Total | 1,998.55 | | 1,382.10 | |

[a]Includes output marketed by landlords. [b]Represents only output marketed by farm households.
*Source:* Based on output data contained in Perkins, *Agricultural Development in China*, p. 289, and marketing ratios in Buck, *Land Utilization in China: Statistical Volume*, pp. 227–8.

Table 4.10. *Weights for agricultural price index*

| Commodity | Weight | |
|---|---|---|
| | 1870–1936 | 1913–36 |
| Rice | .50 | .30 |
| Wheat | n.a. | .20 |
| Soybeans | .21 | .06 |
| Cotton | .16 | .16 |
| Sesame | n.a. | .07 |
| Tobacco | .04 | .04 |
| Tea | .06 | .06 |
| Silk | .03 | .03 |
| Peanuts | n.a. | .08 |
| Total: | 1.00 | 1.00 |

*Note:* n.a.—not available.
*Source:* See text.

by farm households only. This effectively reduces the weight of food crops slightly and raises that for remaining crops.

Price information exists for six crops for the years between 1876 and 1912, and there is additional information for three more crops for 1913–36. Indices were constructed using weights reported in Table 4.10 (and based on Table 4.9) and then linked together into one index for agricultural prices for the entire period. More precisely, the annual percentage changes implied by the index for 1876–1912 were used to extend the more comprehensive index back to 1876. It should be pointed out that an index calculated using weights based on shares of total output rather than total marketed output did not differ significantly from the one I report. Table 4.13 displays my index along with the Nankai agricultural price index for 1913–36.

My index obviously has its shortcomings. Above all, the share of each crop in total marketed output changed as time went on because both the composition of farm output and crop-marketing ratios changed. Weights used in the construction of any price index should reflect intertemporal changes of this sort, but I do not have annual production and marketing data and must make do with a set of weights derived from data for the 1930s. The share of non-grain crops in total marketed output was increasing throughout the period, a product of both an increase in their share in total output and an increase in their individual marketing ratios. Insofar as the price

Table 4.11 *Farm household cash expenditure (in percentages)*

| Item | North | East |
|------|-------|------|
| Food | 54.10% | 54.48% |
| of which: | | |
|   supplementary foods/condiments | 29.10 | 31.40 |
|   of which: | | |
|     fish/meat | n.a. | 8.13 |
|     salt | n.a. | 4.86 |
|     cooking oil/soy | n.a. | 9.07 |
|     sugar | n.a. | 2.41 |
|   luxuries | 5.40 | 9.92 |
|   of which: | | |
|     wine | n.a. | 4.64 |
|     tobacco | n.a. | 4.20 |
|     tea | n.a. | .93 |
| Clothing | 7.45 | 8.84 |
| Heating fuels | 11.74 | 5.35 |
| Cultural[a] | n.a. | 5.41[b] |
| Festivals | n.a. | 6.30 |
| Other | 25.02 | 19.62 |
| Total | 100.00 | 100.00 |

[a]Defined to include expenditures on education, medical care, and sanitation.
[b]For Sungkiang, Nantong, and Wuhsi only; for Changshu and Taiyuan, expenditure on medical care amounted to 2.27 percent.
*Note:* n.a.—not available.
*Source:* Minami Manshū Tetsudō Kabushiki Kaisha, Shanhai Jimusho, Chōsashitsu, Kōso-shō Jōjuku-ken nōson jittai chōsahokokusho (Dairen, 1939); Kōso-shō Musha-ken nōson jittai chōsa hōkokusho (Dairen, 1941); Kōso-shō Nantsū-ken nōson jittai chōsa hō ko kusho (Dairen, 1941), Kōso-shō Shōkō-ken nōson jittai chōsa hōkokusho (Dairen, 1940); and Kōso-shō Taisō-ken nōson jittai chōsa hōkokusho (Dairen, 1940).

of non-grain relative to grain crops was either falling or rising, my index would underestimate or overestimate the rate of change in prices. In addition, some localities marketed only two or three crops. In an index constructed on the basis of many commodities, price fluctuations may have averaged out so the index would fail to reveal the magnitude of price swings in any one or two crops marketed in a locality.

Many of the same problems encountered in constructing an index

Table 4.12. *Weights for*
*nonagricultural price index*

| | |
|---|---|
| Cloth | .12 |
| Yarn | .18 |
| Coal | .06 |
| Kerosene | .12 |
| Sugar | .10 |
| Groundnut oil | .20 |
| Iron and steel | .06 |
| Tin | .06 |
| Cigarettes | .10 |
| Total | 1.00 |

*Source:* See text.

for agricultural goods come up when constructing an index for manufactured and nonagricultural goods. The goods may also change in
quality, which the index cannot reflect. This aside, a high percentage, probably 60 percent, of total farm income (including income in
kind) went for food. Nonetheless, with the increasing commercialization of Chinese agriculture, many products that households had
once made themselves or obtained locally were now being obtained
from the market. They included yarn, cloth, heating fuel, cooking
oil, salt, sugar, and even fertilizer. Reflective of this diversity are
the nonagricultural items included in an index for prices paid by
farm households living in Wuchin: soybean oil, rapeseed oil, sesame
oil, sugar, wine, five kinds of candy, eleven kinds of cloth, matches,
native and imported candles, silk, knitting yarn, cotton yarn (fourteen and sixteen count), kerosene, needles, wood oil, umbrellas, soap,
rope, gypsum, cigarettes, and buttons.

In village surveys taken in the 1930s, when self-supplied consumption is valued at market prices, between 40 and 50 percent of
a rural family's nonfarming expenses and a slightly higher percentage of their farm expenditure were in cash.[85] Of the family's
nonfarming cash expenditures, slightly more than half was spent
on food. Table 4.11 summarizes household expenditure data for
North and East China. These data are unique in that they provide
a separate breakdown of cash expenditures and total expenditure,
which would include self-supplied consumption.

Of the expenditure on food, more than one-half (or one-quarter of
total cash expenditure) went for supplementary foods and condi-

Table 4.13. *Agricultural and nonagricultural price data, 1876–1936*

| Year | 1[a] | 2[b] | 3[c] | 4[d] | 5[e] |
|------|------|------|------|------|------|
| 1876 | 30.31 |      | 60.46 |       |       |
| 1877 | 33.14 |      | 66.56 |       |       |
| 1878 | 32.61 |      | 63.26 |       | 50.49 |
| 1879 | 30.83 |      | 61.87 |       | 50.39 |
| 1880 | 31.24 |      | 61.78 |       | 50.65 |
| 1881 | 31.22 |      | 63.12 |       | 49.95 |
| 1882 | 29.64 |      | 60.56 |       | 49.66 |
| 1883 | 30.89 |      | 57.29 |       | 50.77 |
| 1884 | 31.60 |      | 57.69 |       | 52.55 |
| 1885 | 31.49 |      | 55.73 |       | 55.07 |
| 1886 | 35.05 |      | 55.60 |       | 58.11 |
| 1887 | 31.95 |      | 57.81 |       | 58.27 |
| 1888 | 32.65 |      | 58.26 |       | 58.12 |
| 1889 | 32.83 |      | 59.92 |       | 55.37 |
| 1890 | 33.28 |      | 61.66 |       | 54.93 |
| 1891 | 32.93 |      | 59.91 |       | 54.58 |
| 1892 | 31.25 |      | 55.04 |       | 55.24 |
| 1893 | 32.97 |      | 56.17 |       | 56.81 |
| 1894 | 33.61 |      | 62.86 |       | 56.31 |
| 1895 | 40.20 |      | 59.66 |       | 59.85 |
| 1896 | 43.49 |      | 57.70 |       | 65.41 |
| 1897 | 45.99 |      | 63.57 |       | 71.70 |
| 1898 | 49.38 |      | 66.11 |       | 74.14 |
| 1899 | 46.98 |      | 66.90 |       | 72.42 |
| 1900 | 44.85 |      | 67.20 |       | 70.55 |
| 1901 | 48.06 |      | 68.84 |       | 68.93 |
| 1902 | 55.00 |      | 62.42 |       | 74.89 |
| 1903 | 54.84 |      | 67.21 |       | 79.84 |
| 1904 | 58.46 |      | 67.39 |       | 85.49 |
| 1905 | 50.94 |      | 66.30 |       | 81.72 |
| 1906 | 52.86 |      | 63.70 |       | 82.19 |
| 1907 | 62.66 |      | 63.91 |       | 85.95 |
| 1908 | 57.41 |      | 64.19 |       | 90.15 |
| 1909 | 58.25 |      | 65.96 |       | 91.93 |
| 1910 | 61.13 |      | 69.10 |       | 88.74 |
| 1911 | 68.59 |      | 71.00 |       | 91.13 |
| 1912 | 64.35 |      | 69.04 |       | 92.76 |
| 1913 | 62.10 | 61.20 | 66.97 | 71.00 | 94.18 |
| 1914 | 58.25 | 57.83 | 64.67 | 69.78 | 91.86 |
| 1915 | 62.43 | 57.61 | 67.41 | 72.31 | 91.67 |
| 1916 | 58.05 | 60.88 | 83.83 | 75.48 | 83.84 |
| 1917 | 60.98 | 70.39 | 91.73 | 79.83 | 76.11 |
| 1918 | 66.00 | 64.05 | 98.40 | 86.04 | 67.60 |

Table 4.13. (*continued*)

| Year | 1[a] | 2[b] | 3[c] | 4[d] | 5[e] |
|------|-------|--------|--------|--------|-------|
| 1919 | 64.97 | 59.25 | 94.24 | 93.43 | 67.50 |
| 1920 | 69.78 | 77.31 | 102.17 | 97.69 | 68.10 |
| 1921 | 77.68 | 77.69 | 103.88 | 96.90 | 70.67 |
| 1922 | 80.13 | 74.97 | 98.05 | 95.60 | 74.93 |
| 1923 | 81.27 | 81.59 | 102.87 | 98.67 | 78.50 |
| 1924 | 83.55 | 89.03 | 103.33 | 99.31 | 80.53 |
| 1925 | 89.23 | 100.01 | 103.26 | 97.91 | 82.09 |
| 1926 | 100.00 | 100.00 | 100.00 | 100.00 | 89.09 |
| 1927 | 99.73 | 102.51 | 104.64 | 105.35 | 93.91 |
| 1928 | 91.59 | 103.34 | 105.28 | 110.30 | 94.10 |
| 1929 | 99.16 | 106.75 | 102.40 | 114.21 | 93.05 |
| 1930 | 106.03 | 106.82 | 117.55 | 132.09 | 91.34 |
| 1931 | 95.18 | 95.74 | 127.57 | 137.76 | 87.22 |
| 1932 | 87.04 | 89.74 | 122.51 | 131.09 | 78.62 |
| 1933 | 71.81 | 73.03 | 113.11 | 119.49 | 69.71 |
| 1934 | 67.98 | 64.26 | 98.73 | 109.33 | 67.80 |
| 1935 | 76.29 | 81.92 | 99.53 | 110.18 | 69.66 |
| 1936 | 83.76 | 101.93 | 112.19 | 124.07 | 73.39 |

[a]Price index for agricultural goods, six commodities, 1876–1912, nine commodities, 1913–36. [b]Nankai agricultural price index for North China, 1913–36. [c]Price index for nonagricultural goods, four commodities, 1876–1912, nine commodities, 1913–36. [d]Nankai price index for manufactured consumer goods, 1913–36. [e]Three-year moving average of terms of trade, 1878–1936, calculated on the basis of columns 1 and 4.

ments such as salt, cooking oil, sugar, and so forth, and luxuries (tobacco items, wine, and tea). The two other major expenditure items were clothing and heating fuels, which amounted to 15–20 percent of cash expenditure. The remaining expenditures were on housing, ceremonies, entertainment, and so forth.

As in the case of the agricultural price index, I constructed two indices and then linked them together. For the first index, I could draw on the unit values of only four commodities: handicraft cloth, yarn, coal, and sugar. The share of each product in expenditure did not differ radically and so I did not devise a set of weights. For the second index, which incorporates nine items, I derived a set of weights drawing loosely on Table 4.11. The products included are cotton cloth, yarn, kerosene, coal, sugar, cigarettes, groundnut oil, iron, steel, and tin. The weights are as shown in Table 4.12. Lacking a time series on the price of cotton cloth for the entire period between 1913 and 1936, I used the wholesale price in Tientsin. A comparison of the behavior of this series with a similar one for Shanghai for the period 1921–36 and with one for nine types of cloth sold in Wuchin *hsien* between 1910 and 1932 reveals a high degree of similarity and should remove any concern over potential bias. Experimenting with slight modifications of these weights failed to reveal any great sensitivity of the index to the weights selected. This price index is also included in Table 4.13 along with the Nankai index for manufactured consumer goods.

# 5

# Productivity Change and Incomes in the Rural Sector

Rapid commercialization has often been associated with a rising productivity of labor and higher incomes in the farm sector. Late Tokugawa Japan, early Meiji Japan, and the People's Republic of China after 1978 are considered examples,[1] but not late nineteenth and early twentieth-century China. Conventional wisdom for China holds that, with the land under cultivation fixed, net capital formation very low, and farming technology constant, increases in the rural labor force were absorbed into agriculture at falling levels of marginal and average labor productivity.[2] Minor differences aside, this has been the interpretation offered by Dwight Perkins, more recently by Phillip Huang and Kang Chao, and by a host of earlier observers, both Chinese and Western.[3]

I take exception to this long-held view. Although I will not critically examine earlier assessments of such things as cultivated area, capital formation, or farm technology – in other words, those factors that we know greatly affect productivity levels – I will present evidence of rising labor productivity in the agricultural sector. The more than doubling of marketed agricultural surplus and the evidences of increasing specialization and exchange would seem to suggest as much. By necessity, support for my argument is indirect. The poor quality of the output data for agriculture generally precludes calculating such obvious measures of productivity as output per unit of labor.

Time series for real annual wages in agriculture do, however, exist. In a competitive market economy such as China's, in which factors of production were remunerated at levels equal to or near their marginal products, real wages and productivity would have shown high positive correlation over the long run,[4] which permit inferences about productivity change. It is also possible to deduce changes in agricultural labor productivity on the basis of changes in key nonagricultural activity in the rural sector – activity that provided alternative outlets for labor over the course of the year. Finally, because Central-East China remained a net exporter of grain, changes in the size of the nonagricultural population and per capita agricultural consumption permit inferences about labor pro-

ductivity changes. Despite the rather dissimilar methods, the estimates I have obtained about the increase in labor productivity
demonstrate a fair amount of consistency. And associated with
changes in labor productivity, of course, were increases in income
in the rural sector.

The data are not available for Central and East China to pinpoint
exactly when these increases occurred over this forty-to-fifty year
period, but my main interest is to establish that they did. Of course,
an overall labor-productivity increase does not preclude the possibility that some areas in the region may have experienced long
secular declines in productivity or even that the entire region may
have had short reverses. Over the long run and in the aggregate,
however, I believe the overriding tendency during this period of
rapid commercialization was for rural labor productivity to be rising
in central and eastern rural China.

## The Behavior of Real Wages

In rural China, labor could be contracted for on a daily, a monthly,
or annual basis. In the 1930s, approximately one-sixth of agricultural labor was hired.[5] The labor of entirely landless households
made up a very small percentage of hired labor.[6] Typically, households both farmed some land (either owned, rented, or both) and
worked for others. By all indications, competitive markets determined wages paid for seasonal and long-term agricultural workers.
A farmer would hire an additional worker only if he thought the
contribution to output – the worker's marginal product – exceeded
what the farmer had to pay him. On the other hand, a small land-
holder would hire out his own labor (or that of a son) if the income
earned exceeded the value of output obtained by applying the same
amount of labor to his own land. Because a third or more of all farm
households in a village hired out their labor at some point during
the year and at least half as many hired-in at some point, information about wages – opportunity cost of labor – was presumably
very good.[7]

Only a few sources provide comprehensive wage data. In 1889 the
Royal Asiatic Society reported wages paid in 1888 on a daily,
monthly, and annual basis in fifteen localities.[8] Cross-sectional rural
wage data for more than a third of China's two thousand counties
also exist for the early 1930s.[9] Finally, Buck's investigators gathered
annual wage information in the early 1930s for more than a hundred
counties.[10]

## Cross-Sectional Data: The 1880s and 1930s

In 1888 the president of the China Branch of the Royal Asiatic Society invited those of its members familiar with rural economic conditions to submit short reports addressing five areas of inquiry. Fifteen reports were submitted, all by missionaries, and all but a few provide information on the level of rural wages, the terms of employment, and the local price of grain. Although the representativeness of the sample cannot be easily assessed, these data do indicate the level of wages just prior to the rapid acceleration in commercialization.

Wages typically were paid in cash and in kind. For daily labor, in-kind payments were usually a day's food ration. For long-term agricultural workers, in-kind payments were more substantial; in addition to meals, they received clothing, sundries such as wine and tobacco, and in some cases lodging. Drawing on the data in these reports, I have calculated the grain equivalency of the cash component of wages paid agricultural workers.[11] Table 5.1 presents these estimates, with supplementary information that bears on my interpretation of the wage data. With the six observations for annual wages, four for monthly, and seven for daily, the table also includes information on the full cash wage.

Conservatively, the grain equivalent of the cash component of the annual wage was only 5 *picul*; it was less than a *picul* for the monthly wage and roughly 5 to 6 *catty* for daily wage labor (though several more *catty* were paid during peak periods.) To help put this in perspective, an adult male required at a minimum between 3 and 4 *picul* of husked grain per year. At the wage levels noted, an unmarried male agricultural laborer easily supported himself. When at home, often the case for an elder son who hired out, he provided much needed supplementary income for the household. He could not, however, reasonably expect to support a wife, let alone several children, on this income alone.

The wage and productivity level implied by these data are very low, but still substantially higher than the level suggested by Kang Chao's data on monthly wages for the late 1700s and early 1800s. The average monthly cash wage expressed in grain equivalencies for his sample of twenty-one observations taken from the period between 1773 and 1818 was 15 *sheng*, or roughly 20 *catty* (0.20 *picul*).[12] These data, drawn from fifteen provinces, included observations from the provinces of Central and East China except Hunan. The highest wage paid in the sample was 0.45 *picul* (Fukien, 1809); the next highest was 0.30 *picul* (Kwangtung, 1797). Even assuming

Table 5.1. Agricultural wage data, circa 1888

| Wage | | Price of Grain | Wage Grain Equivalency | |
| Full Cash | Cash Component | | Full Cash | Cash Component (in *piculs* of 110 lbs) |
|---|---|---|---|---|
| | | *Annual Wages* | | |
| 1. Laichou *fu*, Shantong: 13 Tls. | 6 Tls. | Millet: 1.00 Tl./100 *catty* of 1.1 lbs. Corn: .80 Tl./100 *catty* of 1.1 lbs. | 14.44[a] | 6.67[a] |
| 2. Yitou *hsien*, Shantong: | 20,000–30,000 cash | 60 cash/*catty* of 1.33 lbs. | | 3.03–4.55 |
| 3. Wuching *hsien*, Chihli: 7 Tls. | | Unknown | | |
| 4. Kuangchi *hsien*, Hupei: | 8,000–10,000 cash[b] | Rice unhusked: Good year, 800–900/*picul*[c] Medium, 1,000/*picul* Bad, 1,400–2,000/*picul* | | 3.20–4.00 |
| 5. Swatow, Kwangtung: $8–14 | | Paddy: $1.25/basket of 80 *catty* of 1.33 lbs.[d] | | 2.56–4.00 |
| 6. Pingyang *fu*, Shansi: | 20,000–30,000 cash[e] | 3000 cash per tan of 160 *catty* of 1.1 lbs. | 10.67–16.00 | |
| | | *Monthly Wages* | | |
| 1. Chinkiang *hsien*, Kiangsu: | 1,700 cash[f] | Rice: 2,870 cash per *picul* of 133.33 lbs | | 49 |

Table 5.1. (*continued*)

| Wage | | Price of Grain | Wage Grain Equivalency | |
| --- | --- | --- | --- | --- |
| Full Cash | Cash Component | | Full Cash | Cash Component (in *piculs* of 110 lbs) |
| 2. Yitou *hsien*, Shantong: | 2,000–3,000 cash | See annual data | | .30–.46 |
| 3. Kweiyang *fu*, Kweichow: | 1,000–1,200 cash | Rice: 2,200–2,800 cash per *tan* of 250 *catty* | | 1.00–1.20 |
| 4. Hangchow, Chekiang: | 2,000–3,000 cash | Rice: 240–320 cash per *tou*[g] | | ~1.10 |
| *Daily Wages* | | | | (in *catty* of 1.1 lbs) |
| 1. Yitou *hsien*, Shantong: | 200–300 cash | See annual data | | 4.00–5.00 |
| 2. Laichou *fu*, Shantong: .06 Tl. | 0.03 Tl.[h] 0.10 Tl.[i] | See annual data | 6.00 | 3.00 |
| 3. Kuangchi *hsien*, Hupei: | 60 cash[j] | See annual data | | ~2.50 |
| 4. Hangchou, Chekiang: | 120–160 cash | See monthly data | | ~6.00 |
| 5. Foodchow, Fukien: | 200 cash[k] | Rice: 1,600 per *picul* of 100 *catty* | | 12.50 |
| | 80 cash[l] | Rice: 1,600 per *picul* of 100 *catty* | | 5.00 |

| | | |
|---|---|---|
| 160 cash[m] | Rice: 1,600 per picul of 100 catty | 10.00 |
| 80 cash[n] | Rice: 1,600 per picul of 100 catty | 5.00 |
| 120 cash[o] | Rice: 1,600 per picul of 100 catty | 7.50 |
| Average: 128 cash | Rice; 1,600 per picul of 100 catty | 8.00 |
| 6. Swatow, Kwangtung:<br>8–10 cents[p] | See annual data | 6.00–7.50 |
| 10–20 cents[q] | See annual data | 7.50–15.00 |
| 30 cents | See annual data | 22.50 |
| 7. Tali *fu*, Yunnan:<br>100 cash[r] | Rice: 300 cash per *tou* of 30 catty | 10.00 |
| 60 cash[s] | Rice: 300 cash per *tou* of 30 catty | 6.00 |

---

[a] I have taken the average, or 0.90 Tl./*picul* of 110 lbs., as the price of grain. I do not know, however, if the prices were for milled or unmilled millet and corn. If unmilled, I have overestimated the wage in its grain equivalency by 20 to 25 percent.

[b] The informer noted: "8,000-10,000 cash is considered good pay. As low as 6,000 cash is paid, but this would be for inferior labor."

[c] In Kuangchi, a *picul* was equal to 12 bushels. A *picul* of unhusked rice, therefore, weighed approximately 75 lbs. Two *catty* of paddy yielded one *catty* of husked rice, implying that a *picul* of rice of 110 lbs. in a good year cost approximately 2,500 cash.

[d] At the prevailing price of paddy, a *picul* of rice of 110 lbs. would have cost $3.13.

Table 5.1. (continued)

e The informer commented: "Shansi has not yet entirely recovered from the great famine in 1877. There are some districts and villages containing from one to twenty families where formerly several tens resided. The best parts of this region have been repeopled from Shantong and Chihli."

f In Chinkiang, it was reported that very often only food and lodging were provided.

g A tou was equal to one-tenth of a tan or picul. The number of catty per the local picul was not provided, however. In calculating the grain equivalency, I have assumed that the picul was the official picul of 133.33 lbs.

h Wage paid at times other than harvest period.

i Wage paid during the harvest period.

j Wage paid in June.

k Wage received for "preparing the ground and planting rice shoots for the first crop."

l Wage received for "weeding and raking between rice plants."

m Wage received for "reaping the first crop."

n Wage received for "preparing the ground and manuring second crop."

o Wage received for "reaping the second crop."

p Wage received by a hired hand.

q Wage received during planting and harvesting periods.

r Wage paid at time of rice transplanting.

s Wage paid at times other than transplanting.

Source: Jamieson, "Tenure of Land in China and the Condition of the Royal Population," pp. 58–143.

that an individual could hire out for all twelve months at the average monthly rate, compensation (excluding as before any income in kind) for the entire year would have amounted to less that 2 1/2 *picul.*

How do these wages compare with the levels of the early 1930s? Table 5.2 presents survey data at the provincial level on the cash component of the wage paid annual farm laborers for 1932. Thomas Wiens's estimates of average provincial grain prices (rice and wheat) are used to convert the cash component into its grain equivalent.[13] With few exceptions, the level of annual wages is substantially higher than that found for the late 1880s. The grain equivalency of the cash component of the annual wage seems to have at least doubled. In Central and East China, the average annual wage exceeded 11 *picul.* The lower than average annual wage level for Hupei may reflect the fact that only rice was used as the numeraire.[14]

What happens to the increase if one includes the in-kind component? In a survey of wages in 153 localities carried out between 1929 and 1933, this component represented slightly more than 50 percent of the total wage compensation.[15] Thus, the in-kind component would increase the grain equivalency of the full cash wage to around 20 to 25 *picul,* or roughly the average wage paid long-term agricultural workers in early Meiji Japan (1868–1912).[16] The few observations that I have for the late 1880s suggest that a similar percentage was paid in kind. In Kuangchi *hsien* (Hupei), the price of rice was 2,500 *cash* per *picul.* At grain consumption levels of 3 to 4 *picul* of husked grain per adult male per year, total expenditure on food would have roughly equaled the cash component of the wage.[17] If other items were included – clothing, tobacco, and so forth – the percentage of the total wage supplied in kind would have again slightly exceeded one-half. The data for Laichou *fu* (Shantong) also suggest that slightly more than half of the wage was received in kind.

If the in-kind component remained the same percentage of the wage over this period, then the growth in the cash component would accurately reflect the percentage increase in the total wage. But, if the in-kind component declined with time, then the growth in the cash wage would exaggerate the rate of increase. Even allowing for the possibility that in the late 1880s the in-kind component constituted upwards of two-thirds the total wages and fell to slightly more than one-half by the 1930s, the total annual wage still increased 60 to 70 percent.

Monthly wage change over this forty-year period also suggests substantial real growth. Table 5.3 contains two estimates of the monthly wage paid during the agricultural season and an estimate of the off-season monthly wage, all for 1932. I have also calculated

Table 5.2. *Annual wage data, 1932*

| Province | Cash Wage | | | Price of Major Grain | Grain Equivalency (in *piculs* of 110 lbs.) |
|---|---|---|---|---|---|
| | I | II | III | | |
| Shantong | n.a. | 56.78 | 45.81 | 3.70 (Wheat) | 13.86 |
| Hopei | n.a. | 55.00 | 43.89 | 5.10 (W) | 9.10 |
| Shansi | n.a. | 48.69 | 40.22 | 4.65 (W) | 9.56 |
| Shensi | n.a. | 37.27 | 32.57 | 3.95 (W) | 8.84 |
| Honan | n.a. | 27.73 | 24.71 | 5.50 (W) | 4.77 |
| Kiangsu | 51.30 | 45.16 | 35.35 | 6.60 (Rice) | 9.60 |
| | | | | 3.50 (W) | |
| Chekiang | n.a. | 65.11 | 57.98 | 4.95 (R) | 12.43 |
| Anhwei | n.a. | 45.00 | 39.85 | 3.50 (R) | 12.12 |
| Kiangsi | n.a. | 60.71 | 57.52 | 4.65 (R) | 12.71 |
| Hupei | n.a. | 31.54 | 34.08 | 4.25 (R) | 7.72 |
| Hunan | 48.48 | 47.27 | 38.26 | 3.60 (R) | 12.40 |

| | | | | |
|---|---|---|---|---|
| Fujian | n.a. | 64.00 | 72.30 | 5.65 (R) | 12.06 |
| Kwangtung | n.a. | 62.67 | 69.03 | 6.20 (R) | 10.62 |
| Yunnan | n.a. | 36.92 | 43.41 | 3.45 (R) | 11.64 |
| Kweichow | n.a. | 33.12 | 28.82 | 3.45 (R) | 8.98 |
| Szechwan | n.a. | 25.85 | 23.09 | 5.80 (R) | 4.21 |
| Kwangsi | n.a. | 40.61 | 48.98 | 6.30 (R) | 7.11 |

*Note*: n.a.—not available. In Kiangsu, both rice and wheat served as major food grains. For the purpose of calculating a grain equivalency, therefore, I have used an average of these prices. The average price of wheat in Kiangsu in 1935 was 3.70 per *picul*. Shanghai wheat prices were used to link 1935 and 1932 average prices. Wheat also played a similar role in Anhwei and Hupei. The average price of wheat in Anhwei in 1932 was almost the same as the price of rice, so no bias is introduced in using only rice prices. Data on average rice and wheat prices in Hupei for 1932 have not been found, but in 1935 average wheat prices were almost 40 percent lower than average rice prices.

*Sources*: Annual wage series I: *Chung-kuo shih-yeh chih: Chiang-su sheng* and *Chung-kuo shih-yeh chih: Hunan sheng*; series II: Ch'en, *Ko-sheng nung-kung ku-yung ku-yung hsi-kuan chi hsu-kung chuang-kuang*; series III: "Ko-sheng nung-kung kung-tzu t'ung-chi," pp. 99–106; grain price data: Wiens, "The Microeconomics of Peasant Economy: China, 1920–1940," p. 471.

Table 5.3. *Monthly wage data, 1932*

| Province | Cash Wage | | | Price of Major Grain | Grain Equivalency (in *piculs* of 110 lbs.) | |
|---|---|---|---|---|---|---|
| | I | II | III | | A | B |
| Shantong | 3.53 | 8.50 | 9.90 | 3.70 (W) | 1.85 | 2.49 |
| Hopei | 3.23 | 7.26 | 7.57 | 5.10 (W) | 1.16 | 1.45 |
| Shansi | 3.13 | 5.87 | 5.84 | 4.65 (W) | 1.07 | 1.26 |
| Shensi | 2.53 | 5.74 | 6.57 | 3.95 (W) | 1.18 | 1.56 |
| Honan | 1.82 | 3.72 | 4.20 | 5.50 (W) | 0.62 | 0.72 |
| Kiangsu | 3.51 | 7.09 | 7.95 | 6.60 (R) | | |
| | | | | 3.50 (W) | 1.17 | 1.49 |
| Chekiang | 6.31 | 9.83 | 10.19 | 4.95 (R) | 1.75 | 2.02 |
| Anhwei | 3.32 | 6.41 | 6.84 | 3.50 (R) | 1.43 | 1.77 |
| Kiangsi | 5.13 | 8.85 | 8.56 | 4.65 (R) | 1.64 | 1.87 |
| Hupei | 3.54 | 5.92 | 5.00 | 4.25 (R) | 1.21 | 1.27 |
| Hunan | 3.57 | 5.92 | 5.40 | 3.60 (R) | 1.41 | 1.57 |
| fukien | 7.45 | 11.63 | 8.60 | 5.65 (R) | 1.81 | 1.79 |
| Kwangtung | 6.78 | 12.77 | 9.20 | 6.20 (R) | 1.74 | 1.77 |
| Yunnan | 3.83 | 5.92 | 6.26 | 3.45 (R) | 1.51 | 1.77 |
| Kweichow | 3.20 | 5.09 | 6.69 | 3.45 (R) | 1.29 | 1.71 |
| Szechwan | 2.01 | 3.18 | 3.43 | 5.80 (R) | 0.48 | 0.57 |
| Kwangsi | 4.96 | 7.54 | 5.62 | 6.30 (R) | 1.06 | 1.04 |

*Note:* Cash wage I is the wage paid during the off-season, and cash wage II is the wage paid during the farming season. Both are from *T'ung-chi yueh-pao* 13 (Sept.-Oct. 1933), p. 100. Cash wage III is an alternative estimate of the monthly wage presumably paid during the farming season from Ch'en, *Ko-sheng nung-kung ku-yung hsi-kuan chi hsu-kung chuang-kuang*, Table 9. The grain price data are the same used in Table 5.2. Grain equivalency A is a weighted average of I and II assuming that the agricultural season lasted eight months, and grain equivalency B is an average of II and III.

116

a weighted monthly wage under the assumption that the agricultural season lasted eight months. Even including Kwangsi, Szechwan, and Honan, the weighted monthly cash wage commutes to 1.33 *picul* and the cash wage paid during the agricultural season to over 1.5 *picul*. For Central and East China, monthly wages were approximately 10 percent higher. It is reassuring to find that average wages in Chekiang and Kweichow in the 1930s were also markedly higher than they were in the 1880s in Hangchow (Chekiang) and Kweiyang *fu* (Kweichow). Tables 5.1 and 5.2 suggest that wage levels in these two localities may well have been in the upper tail of the wage distribution in the late 1880s.

Because of seasonal differentials, daily wage data are much more difficult to interpret. Not only did daily wages differ during the farming and off season, but even during the farming season itself. In Foochow (Fukien), the wage paid for planting the first crop of rice was two and a half times the wage paid for weeding, raking, and manuring. The data for the 1930s provide estimates of the average wage paid during the cropping season, but not whether premiums were possibly paid at a certain time in the farming season. With this in mind, daily farm wages for the 1930s are presented in Table 5.4. The average daily wage was approximately 8.5 *catty*, and a half *catty* lower for Central and East China, with the lowest wages in Honan and Szechwan. This compares favorably with an average wage of approximately 6 *catty* in the 1880s. A higher overall average daily wage (9.3 *catty*) was also paid in Fukien in the 1930s than in Foochow of the late 1880s. Table 5.4 offers some indication that daily wages rose, but by a smaller percentage than found for either monthly or annual wages.[18]

## Time Series Data

Buck's agricultural survey is the other primary source on rural wages. His investigators gathered information on cash farm wages between 1901 and 1933 for long-term agricultural laborers in almost a hundred counties. Series were constructed for each locality on the basis of information provided by three well-informed villagers and reported in the form of indices with 1926 equal to 100. In all, there are observations on twenty-nine localities in Central and East China: three in Kiangsu, eleven in Chekiang, four in Anhwei, five in Kiangsi, four in Hupei, and two in Hunan.

I have deflated each series by my long-term index for agricultural prices to obtain indices for real wages for each locality. The use of the same deflator can be justified for this exercise by the relatively

Table 5.4. *Daily wage data, 1932*

| Province | Cash Wage[a] | | Price of Major Grain | Grain Equivalency (in *catty* of 1.1 lbs.) |
|---|---|---|---|---|
| | I | II | | |
| Shantong | 0.56 | 0.62 | 3.70 (W) | 15.9 |
| Hopei | 0.40 | 0.41 | 5.10 (W) | 7.9 |
| Shansi | 0.27 | 0.29 | 4.65 (W) | 6.0 |
| Shensi | 0.34 | 0.31 | 3.95 (W) | 8.2 |
| Honan | 0.24 | 0.23 | 5.50 (W) | 4.3 |
| Kiangsu | 0.35 | 0.36 | 6.60 (R) | |
| | | | 3.50 (W) | 7.1 |
| Chekiang | 0.40 | 0.45 | 4.95 (R) | 8.6 |
| Anhwei | 0.30 | 0.31 | 3.50 (R) | 8.7 |
| Kiangsi | 0.37 | 0.44 | 4.65 (R) | 8.7 |
| Hupei | 0.25 | 0.43 | 4.25 (R) | 8.0 |
| Hunan | 0.21 | 0.26 | 3.60 (R) | 6.0 |
| Fujian | 0.48 | 0.57 | 5.65 (R) | 9.3 |
| Kwangtung | 0.45 | 0.65 | 6.20 (R) | 8.9 |
| Yunnan | 0.26 | 0.30 | 3.45 (R) | 8.1 |
| Kweichow | 0.25 | 0.35 | 3.45 (R) | 8.7 |
| Szechwan | 0.18 | 0.20 | 5.80 (R) | 3.3 |
| Kwangsi | 0.28 | 0.35 | 6.30 (R) | 5.0 |

[a]Cash wage I and II are both for the farming season.
*Sources:* Cash wage I: *T'ung-chi yueh-pao* 13 (Sept.-Oct. 1933), p. 100; cash wage II: Ch'en, *Ko-sheng nung-kung ku-yung hsi-kuan chi hsu-kung chuang-kuang,* p. 9.

high degree of market integration among these localities by this period. Regressing the natural log of each series on time provides an estimate of the rate of growth of real wages.[19]

There are a number of obvious weaknesses in these series: They are based on recollection and reflect the behavior of the cash component of the wage only. Moreover, these localities probably tended to be more commercialized than the average. If this high level of commercialization in the 1930s simply reflects a faster rate of commercialization over the preceding forty years, then the rate of growth implied by these wage series may also be higher than other rural areas in the region experienced.[20]

With these shortcomings in mind, I report the estimated rate of growth of real wages for each locality in Table 5.5.[21] Clearly, real wages tended to rise. Only eight of the twenty-nine localities offer evidence of negative or zero growth. Three of these localities were located in Hupei. In the remaining twenty-one localities, real wages were increasing at an annual average rate of approximately 2 percent. For all twenty-nine localities, the average rate of growth was 0.9 percent. Excluding as outliers those localities for which real wages were rising or falling by more than 4 percent, the average rate of growth was slightly more than 1 percent.

Over a forty-year period, a 1-percent annual increase translates into a 50-percent increase in real wages; a 2-percent increase, on the other hand, becomes an increase of 120 percent. The growth in real wages implied by Buck's data is certainly of the same order of magnitude as that suggested by the cross-sectional data for the late 1880s and early 1930s. These data provide convincing proof that real wages and productivity rose over this period. Does other evidence for productivity increase in the rural sector exist? What about nonagricultural activity?

## Productivity in Nonagricultural Activity

Farm households allocated part of their labor to an expanding number of income-earning nonagricultural activities. They also devoted substantial time to "home production" for their own consumption. Buck's data for the early 1930s suggest that farm households in East-Central China allocated 83 percent of their labor-time (exclusive of home production) to agriculture and the remainder to nonagricultural activities.[22] For many localities as well as individual households, the percentage was even higher.[23]

The amount of labor a household allocated to farming was partially based on how much land its members owned, how much land they could rent, their ability to hire out as seasonal or annual workers, and so forth. More generally, however, they divided their labor between agricultural and a host of nonagricultural activities with the intention of maximizing total household income. This action required that the household equate the returns to labor in these alternative uses at the margin.[24] So long as there were differences, households would reallocate their resources between them. In a rural economy with many markets, highly mobile resources, and few barriers to entry, differences in the returns to labor would be arbitraged away. In other words, systematic differences in the productivity and returns to labor in alternative uses could not persist for long.[25] If agricultural wages were rising in rural China, we would expect to observe a rising return to labor in the nonagricultural activities that provided alternative outlets for a household's labor.

Table 5.5. *Rates of growth of real wages, 1906–33*

| Province | Locality | Rate of Growth | Years Covered |
|----------|----------|----------------|---------------|
| Kiangsu | Wuhsi | .023 | 1907–1932 |
| | Yencheng | .006 | 1918–1930 |
| | Wuchin | − .002 | 1908–1933 |
| Chekiang | Kashing | .015 | 1906–1930 |
| | Teching | .014 | 1906–1930 |
| | Shunan | .021 | 1906–1930 |
| | Tungyang | .018 | 1906–1930 |
| | Yuyao | .020 | 1907–1931 |
| | Fenghwa | .042 | 1907–1931 |
| | Tangki | .011 | 1907–1931 |
| | Tunglu(1) | .003 | 1907–1931 |
| | Tunglu(2) | .000 | 1907–1931 |
| | Linhai | .013 | 1908–1932 |
| | Yungkia | .004 | 1908–1932 |
| Anhwei | Tingyuan | .045 | 1905–1929 |
| | Liuan | .030 | 1908–1932 |
| | Wuhu | .005 | 1908–1932 |
| | Fengyang | .025 | 1908–1932 |
| Kiangsi | Kaoan | .045 | 1907–1932 |
| | Fouliang | .020 | 1908–1932 |
| | Tuchang | .016 | 1908–1932 |
| | Nanchang | .026 | 1908–1933 |
| | Pengtse | − .015 | 1916–1933 |
| Hupei | Tsaoyang | − .026 | 1907–1931 |
| | Yunmeng | .003 | 1907–1931 |
| | Anlu | − .052 | 1908–1930 |
| | Yingcheng | − .057 | 1917–1931 |
| Hunan | Yiyang | .020 | 1909–1933 |
| | Changte | − .002 | 1909–1933 |

*Note:* Indexes for nominal wages for each locality appear in Buck, *Land Utilization in China: Statistical Volume*, pp. 159–62. I have deflated each series by my index for agricultural prices for the purpose of estimating growth rates.
*Source:* See text.

Some scholars take exception to the view that the market equalized the returns to labor in various activities. They contend that nonagricultural activities in rural China were confined to the off season and absorbed labor only at rates of remuneration substantially below that in agriculture at other times of the year. This particular veiwpoint has often been expressed about handicraft textiles, perhaps the most important sideline in late nineteenth and early twentieth-century rural China.[26] Kang Chao, in fact, has attributed the sector's ability to compete with output from the manufacturing sector throughout the early twentieth century to the fact that there was a growing surplus of labor in the countryside to draw on.[27] Although in some cases the limited opportunities in the agricultural sector may have "compelled" farm households to work at handicraft textiles, in the 1930s the return to adult labor in handicraft textiles appears to have been very similar to that in agriculture. Second, the returns to labor in this sideline rose significantly throughout the late nineteenth and early twentieth centuries, much as it had in agriculture. A 1939 survey carried out in Nantong *hsien* (Kiangsu) supports the first assertion.[28]

Throughout the Ch'ing, Nantong had been a major handicraft textile center and continued to be so in the early twentieth century. Of the 94 households surveyed in 1939, some 54 engaged in textiles as a sideline. Handicraft cloth production, which went on all year long,[29] drew almost solely on the labor of adult men and women.[30] In addition to producing handicraft textiles and farming small amounts of their own or rented land, households in Nantong carried on other activities: 38 households had members working off their farms as day laborers in agriculture for an average of 75 days per year; 3 households had a member hiring out as an annual laborer in agriculture and 1 household had a member hired out for half the year; 27 households had a member working in industry on an annual or semiannual basis in either the nearby market town or Shanghai; and 19 households had a member working in a sideline other than textiles on a part-time basis for an average of 85 days.[31]

The survey did not measure the returns to labor in handicraft textiles, but one can do so using other information provided. In a ten-hour day, an individual could weave between sixty and eighty square feet of cloth or could spin half a pound of yarn. Dividing these estimates into the total amount of cloth and yarn produced by the households surveyed, total labor input would have been approximately 4,000 days, or slightly less than 80 days per household. Value-added in this sector in the 1930s averaged roughly 20 percent of the total value of output, implying a return to labor of 0.40 *yuan* per day.[32] By comparison, the return to labor in other subsidiary activities averaged 0.37 *yuan* a day. The average cash wage in agriculture was 0.26 *yuan*. With the value of income in kind typically between 40 and 50 percent of the total daily wage, the total agricultural wage would have been between 0.45 and 0.50 *yuan*. A female agricultural worker hiring herself out could expect to earn only 60 to 70 percent of this. In Nantong, therefore, marked differences do not show up in returns to the same labor used in various economic activities.

Interestingly, data from North China suggest a similar interpretation. In Ting *hsien* (Hopei), weaving was done primarily by adult women and remunerated labor in upwards of 0.40 *yuan* per ten-hour day.[33] This wage was slightly higher than that (including income in kind) quoted for second- or third-class agricultural laborers during the busy season, but less than the wage paid a first-class day laborer, who could expect to earn 0.30 to 0.40 *yuan* per day, plus food (making a cash total of 0.50 to 0.60) daily during the busy season. The daily wage in 1930 for cotton ginning and batting, primarily a male occupation, was 0.45 *yuan*.

Although limited, these data do support the view that the returns to labor in agriculture and sidelines were probably tied to each other. Moreover, it may not have been only areas like Nantong where this held true. But to demonstrate that labor productivity in handicraft textiles rose as much as it did in agriculture requires estimates of the returns to labor in this sideline over the period. Value-added per unit of labor applied to handicrafts provides such a measure. To calculate this, one must first obtain estimates of handicraft output, total value-added, and labor input.

## Output of Handicraft Textiles

Handicraft textile industry in rural China during the late nineteenth and early twentieth centuries has been a subject of great interest. Many scholars have argued that beginning in the 1880s imported manufactured yarn and cloth seriously undermined the handicraft sector.[34] This decline was just one of the high costs that foreign trade imposed upon China. Later work by Myers, Feuerwerker, Reynolds, Chao, and Kraus, however, suggests that the costs might have been minimal.[35]

Table 5.6 draws on earlier work by Feuerwerker, Chao, and others to estimate handicraft yarn and cloth output for 1871–80, 1901–10, and 1931–6. The assumptions and calculations underlying these estimates are discussed in more detail in Table 5.11. The final estimates may be off by as much as plus or minus 10 percent, but even so offer a fairly accurate picture of the change that occurred in the handicraft sector.[36]

At first, as has been argued, a great decline occurred in the pro-

Table 5.6. *Handicraft textile output, 1871–1936 (in millions)*

| Item | 1871–80 | 1901–10 | 1931–6 |
|---|---|---|---|
| Yarn (bales)[a] | 1,289 | 809 | 903 |
| Cloth (sq. yds.) | 1,434 | 2,013 | 2,480 |

[a]A bale was equal to 420 pounds.
*Source:* For details on the derivation of these estimates, see Table 5.11.

duction of handicraft yarn. I estimate that between the 1870s and 1900s handicraft yarn production fell by more than 35 percent, as imported, and later domestically manufactured, factory yarn replaced handicraft yarn produced in the countryside. Between 1871–80 and 1901–10, average yarn imports increased from less than 100,000 Maritime Customs *picul* to almost 2 1/2 million, and manufactured yarn production in China increased from zero to over 1 million Maritime Customs *picul*.[37] In the early twentieth century, when domestic factory yarn production experienced rapid growth, Table 5.6 indicates a modest increase in handicraft yarn production. Although I do not rule out this possibility, I am inclined to believe that handicraft production remained constant or maybe even fell. If I had assumed in the calculations that per capita consumption of cotton for other than yarn production rose rather than remained constant, an assumption consistent with the view that incomes were rising over the period, handicraft yarn production in the mid–1930s would have been roughly the same as it was thirty years earlier.

Although handicraft yarn production declined, handicraft cloth production grew substantially. Between 1871–80 and 1931–6, handicraft cloth production increased approximately 80 percent, or at an annual rate of 1 percent. The data in Table 5.7 actually suggest a lower rate of growth in the latter half of this sixty-year period than in the first half, but these estimates are also sensitive to assumptions I have made regarding the noncloth consumption of cotton yarn, which I assumed increased over time from 3 percent of total output in 1871–80, to 6 percent in 1901–10, to 9 percent in 1931–6.[38] If I had allowed the percentage of yarn for noncloth consumption to remain constant (which would still allow an increase in per capita consumption for other uses), the rate of growth of handicraft cloth production would have accelerated slightly.

What explains the changing composition of output in the handicraft textile sector? Before the importation of manufactured yarn, the textile industry was vertically integrated through the individual households. Because households sold only a very small amount of handicraft yarn, household cloth production was limited simply by the amount of yarn the household could spin. Chung-p'ing Yen has figured that it took between three and four hours of spinning to produce yarn for one hour of weaving.[39] This same productivity differential is implied in data Cheng-ming Wu compiled from various Ch'ing gazetteers.[40] Yarn imports and domestically manufactured yarn eliminated this constraint and permitted farm households to do more weaving. Even households that did not grow cotton could weave. By most indications, the degree of specialization in handicraft production increased.

Change in the price structure sheds additional light on the reallocation of resources within the handicraft textile sector. After the 1870s, the price of yarn fell relative to the price of cotton, and the price of yarn remained roughly constant relative to the price of cloth.[41] Cotton and labor were the two major inputs in handicraft yarn production. Capital costs were marginal. The decline in the price of yarn relative to cotton suggests that the return to labor fell in handicraft yarn production over this period. In other words, relatively inexpensive yarn from overseas substantially reduced the profitability of handicraft yarn production. At the same time, per unit value-added in cloth production appears to have remained roughly the same. Consequently, households reduced the time spent spinning and shifted over to weaving.

## Value-Added and Labor Input

Drawing on the output estimates and estimates of per unit value-added for yarn and cloth, Table 5.7 presents estimates of total value-added in handicraft yarn and cloth output for the three periods. Value-added in yarn was 7.73 *yuan* per *picul*, or 18.4 percent of the market price of hand-spun yarn. For cloth, it was 1.52 *yuan* per bolt, or 21.7 percent of the average price of native cloth.[42] Despite the substantial decline in handicraft yarn production, the estimates imply that total value-added in the industry was still higher in the early 1900s than in the 1870s because handicraft cloth production increased. In the early twentieth century, overall value-added in the sector grew as handicraft cloth output expanded. These estimates support the view that in the aggregate the costs to rural China of overseas yarn imports were minor.

Because of the changes in the price structure, however, using the same estimates for unit value-added in all three periods is hard to

Table 5.7. *Value-added in handicraft textiles, 1871–1936 (in millions of 1933* yuan*)*

| Years | Yarn | Cloth | Total |
|---|---|---|---|
| 1871–1880 | 38 (57)[a] | 54 | 92 (111)[a] |
| 1901–1910 | 24 | 76 | 100 |
| 1931–1936 | 27 | 94 | 121 |

[a]Calculated under the assumption that per unit value-added in spinning was 50 percent higher than it was in the 1930s.
*Source:* See text.

justify. Fragmentary price data suggest that value-added (measured as a percentage of the price of yarn and cloth) in spinning declined throughout the late 1800s but remained roughly constant or slightly rose in weaving. After the turn of the century, the price ratios among cotton, yarn, and cloth remained more or less constant (except for immediately after World War I), implying similar value-added measures in percentage terms. Applying the same estimates of per unit value-added in the 1930s to output in the 1870s would bias downward the value-added estimates in constant prices for the earlier period. The problem is not so serious when using the same estimates for the 1900s and mid–1930s because relative prices for the two periods are similar.

To adjust for these changes, I assume that per unit value-added in yarn production was 50 percent higher in the 1870s than in the early twentieth century.[43] This may have been partially offset by a lower per unit value-added in cloth in the 1870s, but I made no adjustments along these lines because of data limitations. Under the assumption that per unit value-added in spinning was 50 percent higher in the 1870s, total value-added in handicraft yarn production (in 1930s prices) would have been 57 million *yuan* (rather than 38), and value-added in the entire handicraft textile sector almost 111 million *yuan*. Over the next thirty years, though households were reallocating time from spinning to weaving (in which value-added per unit did not decline), total value-added still declined 10 to 15 percent to 100 million *yuan*. Throughout the early twentieth century, total value-added rose and by the 1930s had surpassed the levels of the 1870s and 1880s by at least 10 to 15 percent. Value-added in the handicraft textile sector certainly did not decline over this sixty-year period, and it probably rose. Moreover, much of the

short-run disruption (lost income) that the increased use of manufactured yarn may have caused in the late 1880s was offset by an
increase in cloth production.

But what about labor input? Although value-added in the handicraft textile sector probably increased, the total amount of time
rural households allocated to this activity declined significantly between the 1870s and 1930s. Two key forces contributed to this decline: the reallocation of labor from spinning to weaving and
technological change in weaving. Although technological change has
long been recognized, its implications for labor input and value-
added per unit of labor have not.

After 1900, several new looms were introduced, among them an
"improved" wooden loom, the iron-gear loom, and the Jacquard
loom.[44] I have not uncovered productivity information on the Jacquard looms, but the improved wooden loom permitted a household
to produce two times and the iron-gear loom four times the amount
of cloth it could produce in a day using the traditional wooden loom.[45]
Evidence is again fragmentary, but the new technology appears to
have been rapidly disseminated throughout China.[46] Gamble cites
data for a village in Ting *hsien* (Hopei province), in which the number of "improved" wooden looms and iron-gear looms increased from
only 7 percent of the total to 80 percent over a twenty-year period,
during which the total number of looms fell by 15 percent.[47] In
Kaoyang, Hopei province, traditional looms were replaced by the
new iron-gear looms within four to five years. One source asserts
that more than 50 percent of total handicraft cloth production in
the province as a whole in the late 1920s came from iron-gear
looms.[48] Although the improved wooden looms were not much more
expensive than the traditional looms (approximately 10 to 15 *yuan*),
the iron-gear and Jacquard looms cost five to six times as much.[49]

The output totals of Table 5.6 permit us to estimate the total
number of days that farm households allocated to handicraft textiles
for these three periods and also to estimate labor productivity in the
two activities. The most frequently cited estimate of output per ten-
hour day in handicraft spinning is Chung-p'ing Yen's four *liang* per
day.[50] Because a *liang* equaled fifty grams, slightly less than half a
pound of yarn could be spun in one day. Gamble says that in Ting
*hsien* in the 1930s approximately a half a *catty* could be spun in a
day.[51] The more recent compilation of estimates by Cheng-ming Wu
suggests spinners averaged between five and six *liang* of yarn.[52] I
will assume that spinners averaged half to two-thirds of a pound
per day.

Feuerwerker's estimates for cloth production suggest that weavers could weave 36 square feet (a piece 10 yards by 12 inches) or one-tenth of a bolt (40 square yards or 360 square feet) on the typical old-style loom in a ten-hour day.[53] Gamble's survey of Ting *hsien* suggests that up to a third more could be woven daily on the same kind of loom.[54] I have assumed that 40 square feet, or one-ninth of a bolt, could be woven per day using the traditional loom. The improved wooden loom would have increased productivity to 80 square feet (a piece approximately 2 feet by 40 feet), and as much as 120 to 160 square feet could be woven on the iron-gear loom.

Although productivity in spinning remained roughly constant over the entire period, output per labor day in weaving rose throughout the early twentieth century as people began to use the newer looms. In calculating labor days allocated to handicraft textiles, I have assumed 40 square feet of cloth per day in the two earlier periods. For the mid–1930s, I have used three alternative estimates: 60, 80, and 100 square feet per day. Calculating labor input on the basis of these three alternatives allows us to relate labor input to productivity increase, or increased productivity in weaving of 50, 100, and 150 percent, respectively. Given the relatively low cost of the improved wooden loom and the anecdotal evidence regarding its dissemination, there is good reason to believe that productivity in weaving at least doubled in the early twentieth century.

Table 5.8 estimates the total number of days allocated to handicraft textiles for these three periods. Between the 1870s and the 1900s, labor input declined 15 to 20 percent. Spinning went down almost double this, but about a third of spinning labor was reallocated to weaving. Labor input in handicraft textiles probably continued to decline through the first three decades of the twentieth century. Any increase in labor input that may have resulted from the very modest increase in yarn production was more than offset by the decrease in labor input related to the increase in productivity in weaving. Over the thirty-year period from 1900 to 1930, labor input may have declined an additional 10 to 15 percent, implying a total reduction of 25 to 30 percent in the amount of labor allocated to handicraft textiles between the 1870s and 1930s.

The estimated rise in total value-added and the decline in labor input can only mean that the return to labor in handicraft textiles rose. More precisely, my estimates suggest that the value of a labor day rose between 40 and 50 percent, from 0.098 to 0.142 *yuan* (assuming that two-thirds of a pound of yarn could be spun a day and that productivity in weaving doubled) or .077 to .126 *yuan* (assuming that half a pound of yarn could be spun per day and labor productivity doubled).[55] This increase simply reflects the increase in labor

Table 5.8. *Labor input in handicraft textiles, 1871–1936 (in millions of days)*

| Type of Textile | 1871–80 | 1901–10 | 1931–6 |
|---|---|---|---|
| *Yarn* | | | |
| 1. @ ⅔ lb./day | 810 | 510 | 570 |
| 2. @ ½ lb./day | 1,100 | 680 | 760 |
| *Cloth* | | | |
| 3. @ 40 sq. ft./day | 325 | 455 | |
| 4. @ 60 sq. ft./day | | | 370 |
| 5. @ 80 sq. ft./day | | | 280 |
| 6. @ 100 sq. ft./day | | | 225 |
| *Total: yarn and cloth* | | | |
| 1. and 3. | 1,135 | 965 | |
| 2. and 3. | 1,435 | 1,135 | |
| 1. and 4. | | | 940 |
| 1. and 5. | | | 850 |
| 1. and 6. | | | 790 |
| 2. and 4. | | | 1,130 |
| 2. and 5. | | | 1,040 |
| 2. and 6. | | | 985 |

*Source:* See text.

productivity associated with the reallocation of labor from spinning into weaving and the technological change in weaving itself. For labor input to have declined at the same time the returns to labor rose suggests that the productivity and returns to labor in other activities must have risen also.

Even so, the value of a labor day in handicraft textiles in the 1930s was substantially lower than the average daily wage paid in agriculture during that decade.[56] Does this contradict my earlier remarks regarding the relationship between productivity and returns to labor in subsidiary activity and agriculture? Not at all. Males occasionally worked in handicraft textiles, but spinning and weaving remained primarily a female activity. In agriculture, adult females typically earned 60 to 70 percent of male wages, so the relevant opportunity cost approximates a similar percentage of the daily wage in agriculture. Moreover, if Ting *hsien* and several other counties are representative, much of the spinning was done by children and elderly adults. Girls would not begin weaving until they

Table 5.9. *Value of a labor day in handicraft textiles, 1871 – 1936*

| Years | Assumptions | | Value-Added per Day |
|---|---|---|---|
| | Spinning | Weaving | |
| 1871 – 1880 | ½ lb./day | 40 sq. ft./day | 0.077 |
| | ⅔ lb./day | 40 sq. ft./day | 0.098 |
| 1901 – 1910 | ½ lb./day | 40 sq. ft./day | 0.088 |
| 1901 – 1910 | ⅔ lb./day | 40 sq. ft./day | 0.104 |
| 1931 – 1936 | ½ lb./day | 60 sq. ft./day | 0.107 |
| | ½ lb./day | 80 sq. ft./day | 0.116 |
| | ½ lb./day | 100 sq. ft./day | 0.123 |
| | ⅔ lb./day | 60 sq. ft./day | 0.129 |
| | ⅔ lb./day | 80 sq. ft./day | 0.142 |
| | ⅔ lb./day | 100 sq. ft./day | 0.152 |

*Source:* See text.

were sixteen and seventeen, and they would not produce salable cloth until they had six months of experience.[57] Adult women appeared to spin far less time than the aggregate labor data in Table 5.9 suggests, which in turn implies a higher average daily wage for adult women from this sideline. According to Table 5.9, some 65 to 70 percent of labor went to spinning and the remainder to weaving. If the largest proportion of women's time went to weaving, the daily wage would have been approximately 0.25 *yuan*. Finally, in most localities producing handicraft textiles, spinning had all but disappeared and weaving depended on manufactured yarn. In such localities, the increase in the returns to labor would have been greater than in Table 5.9.

In Central and East China, much of the cotton grown went to the rapidly expanding manufacturing textile industry. Most of the yarn required to weave the 25 to 30 million bolts of handicraft cloth probably came from mills in Kiangsu, and to a lesser extent Hupei.[58] In Nantong, less than 15 percent of the yarn used was self-supplied, and only between one-fifth and one-sixth of labor went to spinning.

These considerations suggest that the return to adult female labor was not out of line with wages in agriculture. Lest there be any concern that agricultural wages cannot be used as a basis for assessing the opportunity cost of adult females, one need only remember that adult women supplied approximately one-seventh of family labor to farming. The increased return to labor in the textile sector suggested by my calculations is also consistent with the wage gains implied by Buck's for long-term agricultural workers. Along with increased productivity in the farm sector, handicraft textile productivity also rose.

## Indirect Estimates of Changes in Labor Productivity

In general, increases in agricultural output can arise from both increases in the labor force in agriculture and increases in labor productivity or output per worker. Algebraically, this is captured by the following equation:

$$Q_t - Q_{t-1} = (L_t - L_{t-1})*(Q/L)_{t-1} + L_t*[(Q/L)_t - (Q/L)_{t-1}] \qquad (1)$$

where $Q_t$ is the level of output at time t, $L_t$ is the level of labor input at time t, and so forth. Dividing both sides by $Q_t$ and with some algebra, equation 1 becomes:

$$\%\triangle Q = \%\triangle L + (L_t/L_{t-1})*[\%\triangle(Q/L)] \qquad (2)$$

where the percentage change in output ($\%\triangle Q$) is equal to ($Q_t - Q_{t-1})/Q_{t-1}$, and $L_t/L_{t-1}$ is the ratio of the agricultural labor force in time t to that in time $t-1$. With further manipulation, the percentage change in labor productivity between period t and period $t-1$ is equal to:

$$\%\triangle(Q/L) = L_{t-1}/L_t*(\%\triangle Q - \%\triangle L) \qquad (3)$$

Equation (3) is an identity and relates the percentage change in labor productivity to: the percentage change in output, the percentage change in the labor force in agriculture, and the ratio of the number of individuals engaged in agriculture in period $(t - 1)$ to that in period t.

Dwight Perkins suggests that between 1893 and 1933 the population in the region increased from 129.2 million to 163.2 million, or 26.3 percent.[59] Over the same period, the nonagricultural population grew from roughly 16 percent of the entire population to 28 percent.[60] In 1893 the nonagricultural population would have been 20.7 million and the agricultural population 108.5. By 1933, these two segments of the population would have grown to 45.7 and 117.50 million, respectively. Assuming that labor-force participation rates in the agricultural sector remained roughly constant over this forty-year period, these data imply a percentage increase in the agricultural labor force of 8.3 percent, that is, $(117.5 - 108.5)/108.5$, and a value of .92 for $L_{1893}/L_{1933}$.

If we knew how rapidly output grew between the 1890s and the 1930s, we could easily estimate the percentage change in average labor productivity, but this information does not exist. I believe, however, that previous estimates have seriously underestimated the growth rate of agricultural output over this period. I first assume that agricultural output grew at least as rapidly as population or that per capita agricultural consumption remained constant. Perkins and Liu and Yeh have assumed that for China between 1914 and 1936.[61] This assumption also concurs with my earlier analysis of agricultural marketing and crop selection and the behavior of wages for long-term agricultural workers. Not only did Central-East China remain a net grain exporter of grain, but the production of non-grain crops also increased. At the same time, the real wages paid for long-term agricultural workers did not fall; indeed, they appear to have risen substantially. The wage rise effectively precludes the possibility that the region remained a net exporter of grain and increased its cash cropping by reducing the consumption levels of the rural society's poorest members. To assume that agricultural output grew at least as rapidly as population is not to assume "too much."

In order for per capita agricultural output to have remained constant over this period, output would have had to increase at least 26.3 percent, the estimated population growth. This translates into an annual rate of growth of almost 0.6 percent. Equation (3) calculates the percentage change in labor productivity that is consistent with a growth in agricultural output of 26.3 percent and the estimates for the agricultural labor force. Assuming that the agricultural labor force grew by 8.3 percent, the output per worker had to increase 16.5 percent over this forty-year period.

The estimate of labor productivity change implied by this method clearly depends on assumptions about the rate of growth of the nonagricultural population and changes in per capita agricultural consumption. The faster the growth rate of the nonagricultural population, the more rapidly labor productivity had to increase to maintain constant per capita agricultural consumption. Table 5.10 presents these calculations for three alternative estimates of the nonagricultural labor force in the early 1890s: 14 percent, 16 percent, and 18 percent. If the nonagricultural share of the population in 1893 was only one-half of that in 1933, a 19.4-percent increase in labor productivity had to occur, whereas a nonagricultural population of 18.0 percent in 1893 implied a 13.1-percent increase.

If per capita agricultural consumption remained constant, these calculations suggest that labor productivity in agriculture very

Table 5.10. *Changes in the nonagricultural population and implied rates of productivity change, 1893 and 1933*

| Year | Nonagricultural Population | Agricultural Population |
|------|---------------------------|------------------------|
| *Assuming Nonagricultural Population = 14.0% in 1893* | | |
| 1893 | 18.1 | 111.1 |
| 1933 | 45.7 | 117.5 |

$\%\triangle L_A$ = 5.8%; $L_{A,1893}/L_{A,1933}$ = .95; $\%\triangle(Q/L)_A$ = .95[26.3-5.8] = 19.4%

| | | |
|------|---------------------------|------------------------|
| *Assuming Nonagricultural Population = 16.0 in 1893* | | |
| 1893 | 20.7 | 108.5 |
| 1933 | 45.7 | 117.5 |

$\%\triangle L_A$ = 8.3%; $L_{A,1893}/L_{A,1933}$ = .92; $\%\triangle(Q/L)_A$ = .92[26.2-8.3] = 16.5%

| | | |
|------|---------------------------|------------------------|
| *Assuming Nonagricultural Population = 18.0% in 1893* | | |
| 1893 | 23.3 | 105.9 |
| 1933 | 45.7 | 117.5 |

$\%\triangle L_A$ = 11.6; $L_{A,1893}/L_{A,1933}$ = .90; $\%\triangle(Q/L)_A$ = .90[26.2-11.6] = 13.1%

*Source:* See text.

likely rose. But the increases implied by my calculations are substantially lower than those suggested by the wage data or productivity estimates presented earlier.[62] Given that the percentage of the population defined as nonagricultural at most doubled, any increase in labor productivity above 19.4 precent must be the product of a growth in agricultural output in excess of the rate of population increase.

Under the assumption that the nonagricultural population in the region grew from 16 percent to 28 percent, how rapidly would agricultural output have had to increase in order for average labor productivity to have risen 40 percent, 50 percent, or as high as 60 percent?[63] Equation (3) again shows that output would have had to increase 52 percent, or at an annual rate of 1.05 percent, in order for productivity to have risen by 40 percent. But a 50-percent increase in productivity would have required a 63-percent increase in output, or an annual increase of 1.21 percent. Finally, a 60-percent increase in labor productivity is consistent with an increase in output of 74 percent, or an annual increase of 1.41 percent. If the nonagricultural population doubled in percentage terms, slightly smaller increases would have been required; on the other hand, if the total population grew faster than 0.6 percent per annum, slightly larger increases would be implied.

With information on the income and price elasticity of demand for agricultural goods, the growth in incomes consistent with such increases in output can be calculated. I do not have estimates for China, but the income elasticity of demand for agricultural goods for Meiji Japan was around 0.70.[64] This implies that for every 10-percent increase in per capita incomes, expenditure on agricultural products rises by 7 percent. The price elasticity of demand, on the other hand, is negative and in low-income countries much more inelastic than the income elasticity. Japanese experience suggests an estimate of $-0.35$, implying a decline in consumption of agricultural goods of 3.5 percent for every 10 percent rise in the relative price of agricultural goods. Assuming that population grew between 1893 and 1933 from 129.2 million to 163.2, a 52-percent increase in output would imply a 20-percent rise in per capita agricultural consumption; a 63-percent increase would infer a 29-percent increase; and, finally, a 74-percent increase would suggest an increase of 38 percent. Between the mid–1890s and 1930s, on the other hand, the relative price of agricultural goods rose roughly 30 percent. Given the parameter estimates for the income and price elasticity of demand, increases in per capita agricultural consumption suggested above (20, 29, and 38 percent, respectively) would have required increases in per capita incomes of 44 percent, 56 percent, and 69 percent, respectively,[65] or annual growth in per capita incomes of 0.92 percent, 1.12 percent, and 1.32 percent. Obviously, the larger (smaller) the income (price) elasticity of demand, the smaller the coresponding increases in income.

Are such increases reasonable? Drawing on some of the same wage data I have used, Thomas Rawski came to his "preferred" estimates of 25 to 28 percent for changes in per capita incomes for all China during the period between 1914–18 and 1931–6.[66] An increase in per capita incomes of 44 percent and a rise in labor productivity in agriculture of 40 percent for the period between the 1890s and 1930s can easily be reconciled with his estimates. In fact, even slightly higher increases would not be totally unexpected. Moreover, slightly higher increases would also be consistent with the 55-percent rise in per capita cloth consumption implied by my textile estimates (see Table 5.11).

## Summary

Scholars have long considered the late nineteenth and early twentieth centuries to be a period of declining productivity during which

Chinese agriculture failed to absorb increases in labor at existing levels of average productivity. Much subsequent analysis in the West, taking this as a given, has concerned itself with why this failure occurred. This in turn led to a preoccupation with distributive questions, both as a potential explanation for the low rates of growth in output, and because the consequences of inequality are always much more severe when incomes are declining. My analysis should go far in erasing these preconceptions regarding the capabilities of Chinese agriculture.

Even allowing for the fact that localities did not benefit equally from the commercialization process, my analysis points to substantial increases in the aggregate in average agricultural labor productivity. Rising real wages for long-term agricultural workers are one such indicator, as are my estimates of labor productivity in handicraft textiles. Given the competitive nature of rural markets, rising real wages can only be reconciled with rising productivity. It is especially interesting to note that in the handicraft textile sector not only did the return to labor rise but also total labor input declined. Had handicrafts been a sector only absorbing surplus labor, we would have expected the opposite: rising labor input and declining returns. This behavior also suggests that alternative outlets existed for a household's labor that offered rates of return as high or higher than those in handicrafts. Finally, because East-Central China remained a net exporter of agricultural produce, rising productivity can also be inferred from the small but important shift in the composition of the labor force, and the unlikelihood that per capita consumption of agriculture output fell.

The rising productivity, increased per capita consumption of cloth, and rise in the terms of trade in agriculture's favor can only mean that incomes in the rural sector were rising throughout much of the period. This certainly provides some empirical content for the observations of 90 percent of Buck's local informants, who reported that the standard of living had risen in recent years.[67] Insofar as incomes were rising, the question naturally arises as to how the benefits of this growth were distributed.

Table 5.11. *Derivation of handicraft textile output estimates, 1871–1936*

| Item | | 1871–80 | 1901–10 | 1931–6 |
|------|--|--------:|--------:|-------:|
| 1. | Domestic cotton output (millions of lbs.) | 933 | 1,067 | 1,920 |
| 2. | Net cotton imports (millions of lbs.) | 19 | −91 | 209 |
| 3. | Population (millions) | 350 | 415 | 505 |
| 4. | Non-yarn consumption of cotton (millions of lbs.) | 350 | 415 | 505 |
| 5. | Cotton for yarn production (millions of lbs.) | 602 | 561 | 1,624 |
| 6. | Total yarn output (thousands of bales) | 1,289 | 1,201 | 3,478 |
| 7. | Manufactured yarn (thousands of bales) | 0 | 392 | 2,575 |
| 8. | Handicraft yarn output (thousands of bales) | 1,289 | 809 | 903 |
| 9. | Net yarn imports (thousands of bales) | 31 | 750 | −112 |
| 10. | Total supply of yarn (thousands of bales) | 1,320 | 1,951 | 3,366 |
| 11. | Yarn for cloth consumption (thousands of bales) | 1,280 | 1,834 | 3,030 |
| 12. | Yarn consumption, manufactured cloth (thousands of bales) | 0 | 37 | 816 |
| 13. | Yarn consumption, handicraft cloth (thousands of bales) | 1,280 | 1,797 | 2,214 |
| 14. | Manufactured cloth output (million sq. yds.) | 0 | 56 | 1,249 |
| 15. | Handicraft cloth output (million sq. yds.) | 1,434 | 2,013 | 2,480 |
| 16. | Net cloth imports (million sq. yds.) | 376 | 654 | 330 |
| 17. | Total supply of cloth (million sq. yds.) | 1,810 | 2,723 | 4,059 |
| 18. | Per capita cloth consumption | 5.17 | 6.56 | 8.04 |

*Documentation for Estimates*

1. Domestic cotton output: 1871–80, 7 million Maritime Customs *picul*, Feuerwerker, "Handicraft and Manufactured Cotton Textiles in China,

135

1871–1910," p. 365; 1901–10, 8 million Maritime Customs *picul*, Note 34, Chapter 3; 1931–6, based on estimates in Perkins, *Agricultural Development in China*, p. 283, Chao, *The Development of Cotton Textile Production in China*, p. 224, and Kraus, "Cotton and Cotton Goods in China, 1918–1936," p. 31, with a slight adjustment for the fact that much of the exceptionally high level of output in 1936 (almost 20 million *picul*) would not have been used until 1937.

2. Net cotton imports: 1871–80 and 1901–10, Hsiao, *China's Foreign Trade Statistics,* pp. 38–9 and 85–6; 1931–6, Kraus, "Cotton and Cotton Goods in China, 1918–1936, pp. 51–2.

3. Population: 1870–80 and 1931–6 are based on Perkins's estimates for 1873 and 1933. The estimate for 1901–10 has been interpolated. Perkins, *Agricultural Development in China,* p. 212.

4. Non-yarn consumption of cotton: following Feuerwerker, "Handicraft and Manufactured Cotton Textiles in China, 1871–1910," p. 353, I have assumed approximately a pound of cotton per capita primarily for wadding.

5. Cotton for yarn production: (1) − (2) − (4).

6. Total yarn output: cotton for yarn consumption divided by 467 lbs., the cotton input requirements per bale of yarn. The latter estimate is provided by Tzu-chien Wang and Chen-chung Wang, *Ch'i-sheng hua-shang sha-ch'ang tiao-ch'a pao-kao* (Shanghai, 1935), p. 34.

7. Machine-spun yarn: Naosuke Takamura; *Kindai Nihon boseigyō to Chūgoku* (Tokyo, 1982), p. 98.

8. Handicraft yarn production: (6) − (7).

9. Net yarn imports: 1871–80 and 1901–10, Hsiao, *China's Foreign Trade Statistics,* pp. 38–39 and 85–86; 1931–6, Kraus, "Cotton and Cotton Goods in China," Table 3.9.

10. Total supply of yarn for domestic use: (7) + (8) − (9).

11. Yarn for cloth consumption: Chung-p'ing Yen assumed in his estimates of yarn and cloth output for the 1930s that 15 percent of manufactured yarn was used for other than weaving. This is consistent with estimates for the early 1950s which show that approximately 10 percent of total yarn (handicraft plus factory) output went for such uses, and the fact that slightly more than two-thirds of yarn was manufactured. According to Feuerwerker, citing George Anderson, *Cotton Goods in China* (Washington, 1911), pp. 25–6, in 1900 a much lower percentage of total yarn production went for these uses than it did in 1930. Consistent with these observations, I have assumed that the percentage of yarn for other than weaving rose from 3 percent of (10) in 1871–80, to 6 percent in 1901–10, to 9 percent in 1931–6.

12. Yarn consumption, manufactured cloth: (14) multiplied by the amount of yarn required to produce one unit of cloth. On the basis of data

Table 5.11. (*continued*)

provided by Kang Chao and Feuerwerker, it took approximately 0.0262 bale of yarn to produce one bolt of manufactured cloth. This implies that slightly more than thirty-eight bolts of machine-woven cloth could be produced from a bale of yarn.

13. Yarn consumption, handicraft cloth: (11) − (12).

14. Manufactured cloth output: Takamura, *Kindai Nihon boseigyō to Chūgoku,* p. 98.

15. Handicraft cloth output: (13) divided by 0.0357 bales, the amount of yarn (in bales) needed to produce one bolt of handicraft cloth. Handicraft cloth required more yarn per bolt than manufactured cloth because of its heavier weight.

16. Net cloth imports: 1871–80 and 1901–10, Feuerwerker, "Handicraft and Manufactured Cotton Textiles in China," pp. 359–60; 1931–6, Kraus, "Cotton and Cotton Goods in China," Table V.2.

17. Total supply of cloth: (14) + (15) + (16).

18. Per capita consumption of cloth: (17) divided by (3).

# 6

# The Distributive Consequences of Commercialization

Popular perceptions are that, even if per capita output remained constant, the well-being of most Chinese rural farm households deteriorated badly during the late nineteenth and early twentieth centuries. This decline has been variously linked to rapid commercialization of the rural sector and associated with increasing land concentration, rising tenancy, increasing landlessness, and ultimately greater disparity in income distribution in the Chinese countryside.[1] Like many of the other assertions about the period, however, this decline in well-being has never been empirically substantiated.

The distribution of landownership greatly influences rural income distribution, especially when economic activity is not particularly diversified and households depend almost entirely on farming for income. Tenancy allows for slightly more equal access to land, but the fact remains that the richest households own the most land, the poorest are landless, and inequality in income has a high positive correlation with unequal land distribution. For rural China, a high degree of inequality of landownership has been interpreted to mean an equally high degree of income inequality.

I believe that, rather than widening income differentials at the local levels, accelerated commercialization in the Yangtse region (and other parts of China for that matter) probably helped to narrow them.[2] By increasing the demand for labor both on and off the farm and by generating new off-farm opportunities, commercialization significantly increased the returns to labor in the rural sector. And, in doing so, commercialization reduced the influence that land distribution had on rural income distribution, perhaps even reducing inequality.

Data limitations prevent me from using conventional measures of income inequality such as the Gini coefficient to compare the degree of income inequality in the 1890s with that in the 1930s. A number of other factors, however, lead me to believe that rural income inequality probably declined over this forty-five-year period. First of all, nothing indicates that landownership became more concentrated.

## Distribution of Land Ownership

During the late nineteenth and early twentieth centuries, commercialization is thought to have exacerbated the inequality of landownership in several ways.[3] The argument goes that producing for the market introduced new risks. Small farm households faced a highly cyclical demand for cash crops and had to buy grain on the market; at times, they had to borrow to cover capital requirements associated with cash cropping. Sudden shifts in the market or a less-than-average crop could be devastating, forcing small farm households to mortgage or sell land to repay debts and cover immediate consumption expenditures. Meanwhile, landlords, urban entrepreneurs, and capitalists invested the enormous amounts of capital they had earned in commercial-related activities in land, buying up the parcels the small households had to sell. Over time, the number of owner-operators declined, tenantry and landless-laboring households rose, and the inequality of landholdings became much more severe.

What is actually known about land distribution in rural China? For the early 1930s, the summary report of the National Land Commission provides the best information on the size distribution of own landholdings in rural China. A total of 1,745,344 rural households residing in 163 counties in 16 provinces were surveyed.[4] Of these, 450,343 households, or approximately a quarter of those sampled, owned no land. The landless group included tenant households, households that earned a living as annual farm workers, and households that were engaged in nonagricultural pursuits. I have combined information from the summary report in Table 6.1 to reconstruct the distribution of own landholdings for the 1.75 million rural households surveyed. These data imply a very high degree of concentration of own landholdings in rural China. The top 1 percent owned 18.54 percent of the land; the top 5 percent owned 38.72 percent; and the top 10 percent owned 53.37 percent. By contrast, slightly more than a quarter were landless, and an additional quarter owned less than 5 *mou*. The holdings of those owning less than 5 *mou* constituted only 6.21 percent of all land. The Gini coefficient, a frequently used measure of inequality, is 0.72.[5] Because landholdings and family size were positively correlated, a per capita (rather than per household) measure of inequality would probably be slightly smaller. Even so, Table 6.1 confirms what others have long argued about the inequality of landownership in rural China.

In a number of respects, however, the data as presented in Table 6.1 need to be qualified. The data exclude the holdings of absentee

Table 6.1 *Distribution of own landholdings for rural households,
1930s*

| Size of Holdings (in *mou*) | Average Size (in *mou*) | Percentage of Households | Percentage of Land |
|---|---|---|---|
| Landless | — | 25.80% | 0.00% |
| 0–5 | 2.65 | 26.42 | 6.21 |
| 5–10 | 7.23 | 17.80 | 11.42 |
| 10–15 | 12.25 | 9.77 | 10.63 |
| 15–20 | 17.42 | 5.93 | 9.17 |
| 20–30 | 24.33 | 6.10 | 13.17 |
| 30–50 | 38.01 | 4.60 | 15.54 |
| 50–70 | 58.59 | 1.61 | 8.38 |
| 70–100 | 82.61 | 0.98 | 7.16 |
| 100–150 | 120.21 | 0.54 | 5.71 |
| 150–200 | 171.97 | 0.18 | 2.76 |
| 200–300 | 240.95 | 0.15 | 3.17 |
| 300–500 | 378.40 | 0.08 | 2.63 |
| 500–1000 | 671.87 | 0.01 | 2.30 |
| 1,000 + | 1,752.60 | 0.01 | 1.75 |

*Source:* T'u-ti wei-yuan hui, *Ch'uan-kuo t'u-ti tiao-ch'a pao-kao kang-yao,*
p. 32.

landlords and publicly or officially owned lands, which other data
in the summary report show amounted to about 4,538,164 *mou*.[6]
This represents 18.76 percent of total cultivated holdings, or 61.5
percent of all rented land. Approximately 30 percent of the farmland
in China was rented out, and in the Yangtse region the percentage
was nearer to 45 percent.[7] Depending on the distribution of the
landholdings of absentee landlords, overall concentration of landownership was probably even higher than that suggested by the
data for rural households alone.

On the other hand, Table 6.1 makes no allowances for the dual
ownership of some land.[8] In China, landowners frequently contracted with households to reclaim new lands in exchange for long-
term tenancy rights. The rents would be fixed for long periods of
time, sometimes even in perpetuity. These rights, frequently referred to as "top-soil" rights (as contrasted with the original landowner's "sub-soil" rights) or rights of permanent tenancy (*yung-
t'ien*), could be sold or mortgaged by the tenant.[9] The rights were

also inheritable. Land reclamation was not the only way that top-soil rights were acquired. A landlord would sell or mortgage them to raise capital. Regardless of how they were acquired, the system conferred on the tenant property rights very similar to those usually associated with land ownership. Although estimates differ, the institution of permanent tenancy appears to have been very prevalent in parts of Central and East China; according to the National Land Commission, 41 percent of the land contracts in Kiangsu, 30 percent in Chekiang, and 44 percent in Anhwei were of this type.[10] If many smallholders enjoyed these rights, the landholding distribution would be more equal than Table 6.1 suggests.

I do not have data at either the national or provincial level on the size distribution of own landholdings for the 1880s or 1890s. Despite the relatively high degree of inequality for the 1930s, however, other data for the period fail to support the changes that some scholars have postulated accompanied a growing inequality of landowner-ship. For both 1912 and 1931–6, for example, information on the breakdown of Chinese farm households between owner-operators, part-owners (owner-tenants), and tenants was collected. The data for Central and East China are reproduced in Table 6.2. Over this twenty-five year period, commercialization proceeded very rapidly. Even with the sharp contraction in overseas demand for products such as silk in the early 1930s, and the simultaneous decline in agriculture's terms of trade, there are few indications that the incidence of tenancy was rising. Tenant farms as a percentage of total farm families remained roughly 30 percent, and owners and part-owners made up the majority. In Central and East China, two out of every five households remained tenants.[11]

What about landless, farm-laborer households, that is, households which owned no land and earned income primarily as long-term agricultural laborers. Did their numbers increase while the percentage of households in the owned or tenant categories remained the same? Again, my data are limited to the 1930s; nonetheless, these estimates suggest an exceptionally low number of such households. Of the 1.75 million households the National Land Commission surveyed in 1934, only 1.57 percent were so classified, and in the Yangtse region the percentage was even less: in Kiangsu, 0.60 percent; Chekiang, 2.03 percent; Anhwei, 0.58 percent; Kiangsi, 0.42 percent; Hunan, 0.844 percent; and Hupei, 0.56 percent.[12] The percentage of households that had a least one member hiring out on an annual basis was much higher, but a majority of these households actually owned or rented in significant amounts of land.[13] The view

Table 6.2. *Classification of farm households by type, 1912 and 1931–6 (in percentages)*

| Province | No. of hsien | Tenant | | | Owner | | | Owner-tenant | | |
|---|---|---|---|---|---|---|---|---|---|---|
| | | 1912 | 1931–6 | 1936 | 1912 | 1931–6 | 1936 | 1912 | 1931–6 | 1936 |
| Kiangsu | 48 | 31% | 33% | 30% | 45% | 41% | 45% | 24% | 26% | 25% |
| Chekiang | 45 | 41 | 47 | 47 | 27 | 21 | 20 | 32 | 32 | 33 |
| Anhwei | 42 | 43 | 44 | 42 | 38 | 34 | 35 | 19 | 22 | 23 |
| Kiangsi | 24 | 41 | 41 | 40 | 29 | 27 | 27 | 30 | 32 | 33 |
| Hupei | 28 | 38 | 40 | 41 | 34 | 31 | 33 | 28 | 29 | 26 |
| Hunan | 39 | 48 | 48 | 50 | 29 | 27 | 22 | 23 | 30 | 28 |

*Source: Nung-ch'ing pao-kao, vol. 5, 12 (December 15, 1937), p. 330.*

that an increasing number of households subsisted almost entirely on the income they earned as annual farm workers appears to rest on a misreading of the data.[14]

Are these data on the extent of tenancy and the number of landless laborers contradicted by other data pointing to an increasing concentration of landholdings? Drawing on Ch'ing land records for individual households and on data for the 1930s, Kang Chao persuasively argues that there was not a group of landlords rapidly accumulating an increasing percentage of landholdings and renting it out. In most counties, the leading landlord owned less than a 1,000 *mou*, and frequently much less.[15] Moreover, the rate of accumulation was typically very slow (averaging less than a *mou* a year in most cases) and was usually interrupted after a generation or so by the custom of *fen-chia*.[16] Fragmentary data suggest that the percentage of land rented in the 1880s was nearly the same as in the 1930s.[17]

For a few localities, the land distribution in the 1930s can be compared with that at the turn of the century and in some cases even earlier.[18] These data reveal no higher degree of land concentration in the 1930s than in earlier periods. This is not to say that land distribution remained constant throughout the entire period or that some small landholders did not lose their land through the mechanism others have described, but very complicated processes relating to landownership were at work that are only now beginning to be examined.[19] The overwhelming evidence, nonetheless, is that land ownership did not become more concentrated.

Finally, because slightly less than half of all land in Central and East China was rented out, access to land was actually more equitable among rural households than the distribution of landownership would suggest. Tables 6.3 and 6.4 offer information on the size distribution of farms for all of rural China and for the six Yangtse provinces.[20]

Several points can be made. First, most farms in Central and East China were between five and thirty *mou*, so the size distribution of farms looks very much the way it did in early Meiji Japan.[21] Second, differences in land endowments were partially equalized through the rental market. If we compare Tables 6.1 and 6.3, the degree of concentration in the size distribution of cultivated farms at the national level is not nearly as great as that found for own landownership. At the provincial level, because a much higher percentage of land was rented out in Central and Eastern China than it was in the aggregate, these equalizing tendencies would have been even more pronounced. Assuming that all size categories of farms rented the same percentage of land, households farming less than thirty

Table 6.3. *Size distribution of cultivated holdings, 1930s*

| Size (in *mou*) | Percentage of Households[a] | Percentage of Land[b] |
|---|---|---|
| Less than 5 | 26.69% | 4.1% |
| 5–10 | 25.94 | 11.9 |
| 10–15 | 15.59 | 12.0 |
| 15–20 | 9.67 | 10.4 |
| 20–30 | 9.97 | 15.3 |
| 30–50 | 7.24 | 17.8 |
| 50–70 | 2.36 | 8.7 |
| 70–100 | 1.38 | 7.2 |
| 100–150 | 0.72 | 5.5 |
| 150–200 | 0.20 | 2.1 |
| 200–300 | 0.14 | 2.1 |
| 300–500 | 0.06 | 1.5 |
| More than 500 | 0.03 | 1.4 |

[a]To arrive at an estimate of the percentage of households in each size category at the national level, the Summary Report of the National Land Commission calculated arithmetical averages using the provincial data. I have computed weighted averages using as weights the number of households surveyed in each province as a percentage of the total number of households surveyed.
[b]The survey did not provide the mean size farm in each category. In order to estimate the percentage of land farmed by each size category, I have used the mid-points of each interval as an estimate and assumed that farms in the largest size category averaged 750 *mou*. This procedure leads to a slight overestimate of total acreage of 3 percent, but should not introduce any serious bias into the distribution.
*Source:* Tu-ti wei-yuan hui, *Ch'uan-kuo t'u-ti tiao-ch'a pao-kao kang-yao*, p. 26.

*mou* in Central and East China would have cultivated two-thirds of all acreage, or roughly twice what they owned.[22] This has potential implications for income distribution inasmuch as through land rental households received a higher percentage of total output than they did as wage laborers because they captured the returns to their managerial inputs and supervisory capacity, and were compensated for either partially or totally bearing output uncertainty.

## Farm Household Behavior

The rapid commercialization of the rural sector generated new opportunities both on and off the farm. Not only were new cash crops

Table 6.4. *Size distribution of cultivated holdings by province, 1930s*

| Size | Kiangsu | | Chekiang | | Anhwei | |
|---|---|---|---|---|---|---|
| (in *mou*) | % Hshlds | % Land | % Hshlds | % Land | % Hshlds | % Land |
| 0–5 | 23.67% | 3.83% | 37.20% | 8.81% | 23.39% | 3.40% |
| 5–10 | 28.59 | 13.87 | 29.80 | 21.17 | 23.72 | 10.39 |
| 10–15 | 17.48 | 14.14 | 14.70 | 17.41 | 15.51 | 11.32 |
| 15–20 | 10.48 | 11.87 | 7.03 | 11.66 | 10.66 | 10.89 |
| 20–30 | 10.19 | 16.48 | 6.11 | 14.77 | 11.99 | 17.50 |
| 30–50 | 5.78 | 14.96 | 3.45 | 13.07 | 9.61 | 22.40 |
| 50–70 | 1.52 | 5.90 | .94 | 5.35 | 3.07 | 10.75 |
| 70–100 | .98 | 5.31 | .47 | 3.78 | 1.41 | 6.99 |
| 100–150 | .90 | 7.28 | .20 | 2.36 | .59 | 4.31 |
| 150–200 | .19 | 2.15 | .05 | .83 | .10 | 1.02 |
| 200–300 | .16 | 2.59 | .03 | .71 | .03 | .44 |
| 300–500 | .05 | 1.30 | .01 | .37 | .01 | .24 |
| 500+ | .01 | .32 | .02 | .08 | .10 | .30 |
| | | | | | | |
| *Hsien* surveyed | 12 | | 15 | | 12 | |
| Households | 218,149 | | 116,212 | | 107,343 | |
| % land rented | 42.43 | | 51.31 | | 47.80 | |
| % of households classified as landless laborers | 0.60 | | 2.03 | | 0.58 | |

Table 6.4. (continued)

| Size | Hupei | | Hunan | | Kiangsi | |
|---|---|---|---|---|---|---|
| (in mou) | % Hshlds | % Land | % Hshlds | % Land | % Hshlds | % Land |
| 0–5 | 31.11 | 6.39 | 30.79 | 5.31 | 33.48 | 7.47 |
| 5–10 | 29.32 | 18.05 | 25.70 | 13.30 | 20.76 | 13.91 |
| 10–15 | 15.44 | 15.86 | 15.36 | 13.25 | 20.46 | 22.85 |
| 15–20 | 8.43 | 12.11 | 8.81 | 10.74 | 11.53 | 17.66 |
| 20–30 | 8.16 | 16.75 | 9.21 | 15.89 | 9.56 | 21.34 |
| 30–50 | 5.50 | 18.07 | 6.27 | 17.30 | 3.72 | 13.29 |
| 50–70 | 1.39 | 6.84 | 2.04 | 8.44 | .31 | 1.94 |
| 70–100 | .44 | 3.10 | 1.03 | 6.05 | .15 | 1.14 |
| 100–150 | .16 | 1.61 | .48 | 4.14 | .03 | .34 |
| 150–200 | .02 | .28 | .14 | 1.69 | .004 | .06 |
| 200–300 | .01 | .21 | .11 | 1.90 | | |
| 300–500 | .01 | .32 | .06 | 1.66 | | |
| 500+ | .01 | .41 | .01 | .35 | | |
| | | | | | | |
| Hsien surveyed | 11 | | 14 | | 5 | |
| Households | 106,546 | | 240,211 | | 23,697 | |
| % land rented | 27.89 | | 47.80 | | 45.10 | |
| % of household classified as landless laborers | 0.56 | | 0.84 | | 0.42 | |

Source: T'u-ti wei-yuan hui, Ch'uan-kuo t'u-ti tiao-ch'a pao-kao kang-yao, p. 26.

and cropping systems more labor-intensive, but the demand for many kinds of auxiliary services related to marketing and distribution increased as well. Although access to land was only partially equalized through land rental, how much any one farm household benefited from these opportunities still depended for the most part on the decisions it and other households made with respect to the crops it grew, how much to market, and how to allocate resources (especially labor) more generally.

Drawing on farm-level survey data for the early twentieth century, Phillip Huang has recently argued that fundamental differences in farm household behavior and efficiency in the commercialized areas of the North China plain gave rise to wide differences among farms in the returns to commercialization.[23] He contrasts the behavior of small family farms that relied primarily on their own labor with that of the larger and more profitable managerial farms that hired in much of the labor they required. Differences between these two basic types of farms were reflected in such areas of decision making as crop selection, input use, and marketing, and were the product of local market imperfections, most notably those in the rural labor market.

Interpretations such as Huang's actually draw much support from the growing research on rural market structure in present-day low-income countries. Albert Berry and William Cline, in the most frequently cited work on the subject, have argued that the systematic differences that exist among farm households in resource allocation and efficiency in these countries result from the same kinds of market imperfections that many earlier observers have argued were endemic to rural China before the turn of the century and on through the Republican period.[24]

Huang's work excluded, however, the consensus now emerging is that markets in the late nineteenth and early twentieth centuries worked reasonably well and were relatively free from the kinds of distortions so common to other low-income countries.[25] Implied in this view is that farm household behavior should have differed only modestly. Even allowing for differences in risk aversion, farm households of all sizes should have been making similar decisions about crops and inputs and should, therefore, have been equally efficient and profitable.[26] In other words, it is only when imperfect markets confer market power on a few that the possibility that differences in endowments of land and other assets among households will give rise to differences in input use, crops, and so forth, exists. Does Huang's work overturn this consensus? Or were his results perhaps unique to North China or peculiar to his data?

Huang relies very heavily on one survey: a sample of fourteen households in Michang village (Fengrun county, Hopei province) in 1937 (the year the Japanese invaded China). Many of the same households were surveyed in 1938 and 1939. Similar surveys were also taken in 1939 in Matsun village (Huolu county, Hopei) and in Wukuan (Changte county, Honan) just inside the Honan-Hopei border. Huang decided not to use these additional data.

Drawing on all five surveys and on data compiled by John Buck in a number of major farm surveys carried out in the 1920s and 1930s for both North China and Central and East China, I will show that observed farm household behavior was not inconsistent with revisionist views on rural market structure. Although farm households in commercialized areas often differed greatly in the contribution of women and children to farm work and in the amount of time devoted to nonagricultural subsidiary activities, they still made remarkably similar decisions regarding crop selection, input use, marketing, and so forth, and were equally efficient in resource allocation.

## Data from North China

I begin the examination of farm household decision making by drawing on the expanded data set for North China.[27] From numerous vantage points, these data suggest an underlying similarity, rather than difference, in farm household decision making among size groups. Tables 6.5 and 6.6 show the percentage of area sown to major crops and marketing ratios (the percentage of total farm output marketed) for each farm category in the three villages. In general, the figures suggest only modest differences among farm groups. Although in Wukuan smaller farm households sowed a slightly higher percentage to millet and wheat (the two major food grains) and less to cotton, farms under fifteen *mou* (a *mou* is equal to one-sixth of an acre or one-fifteenth of an hectare) still devoted almost half their land to cotton. On the other hand, the percentage of farm output marketed rose slowly with farm size, the largest farms marketing an average of 15 to 20 percent more of their total output than the smallest. Even so, farms under fifteen *mou* still produced heavily for the market and sold about half of their output.

Table 6.7 presents additional information on cropping intensity (as measured by the multiple-cropping index, MCI) and gross farm output per unit of cultivated area for each of five farm-size categories in these villages. Two points are noteworthy. First, the largest farms do not appear to have used their land as intensively as smaller ones.

Table 6.5. *Cropping percentages by farm size*

| Village | Cotton | Millet | Wheat | Sorghum | Corn | Beans |
|---|---|---|---|---|---|---|
| *Michang* | | | | | | |
| Above 50 *mou*[a] | 44.9% | 0 | 5.3% | 28.4% | 8.5% | 0 |
| 25–50 | 41.4 | 0 | 7.3 | 27.4 | 7.3 | 0 |
| 15–25 | 45.8 | 0 | 7.4 | 25.9 | 14.5 | 0 |
| Below 15 | 45.0 | 0 | 11.3 | 23.3 | 11.7 | 0 |
| *Matsun* | | | | | | |
| Above 50 *mou* | 29.4 | 29.3% | 19.9 | 0 | 0 | 8.0% |
| 25–50 | 21.0 | 27.8 | 23.0 | 0 | 0 | 8.5 |
| 15–25 | 21.7 | 31.7 | 24.7 | 0 | 0 | 7.9 |
| Below 15 | 26.5 | 24.5 | 16.3 | 0 | 0 | 6.6 |
| *Wukuan* | | | | | | |
| Above 50 *mou* | 67.8 | 14.0 | 9.8 | 0 | 0 | 0 |
| 25–50 | 56.3 | 21.5 | 20.1 | 0 | 0 | 0 |
| 15–25 | 46.2 | 25.3 | 22.2 | 0 | 0 | 0 |
| Below 15 | 44.3 | 29.9 | 20.5 | 0 | 0 | 0 |

[a]One *mou* is equal to one-sixth of an acre or one-fifteenth of a hectare.
*Sources: Hokushi keizai shiryō no. 36,* Table 3; *Hokushi keizai shiryō no. 25,*
Table 3; *Hokushi keizai shiryō, no. 32,* Table 3. See Note 68, Chapter 6, for
full citation.

Nonetheless, the difference between them amounts to less than 10
percent, and the differences between the remaining catgories are
small and seemingly random. Second, unlike what is commonly
found today in low-income countries, the three villages fail to show
any systematic relationship between farm size and land productivity, particularly any tendency for land productivity to decline with
increasing farm size. Interestingly, when the data for Wukuan (in
1940 prices) are deflated and pooled with Michang and Matsun (both
in 1939 prices) to calculate averages for each size category in the
aggregate, most of the local differences average out.[28]

Given that similarity, it is no surprise to find no major differences
in net profits per unit of cultivated area among farm households
either.[29] In some cases, small farm households actually outperformed
their larger counterparts (see Table 6.8, which reports farm size and
total net profits). Yet, there are a number of reasons why these
calculations may actually favor larger farms, one of which has important implications for the econometric analysis of farm household
behavior that follows.

Table 6.6. *Percentage of farm output marketed by farm size (in* mou*)ᵃ*

|  | Farm Size Class | | | | |
| Village | 0–15 | 15–25 | 25–50 | Over 50 | Average |
| Michang | 49.0% | 60.2% | 58.3% | 65.4% | 62.5% |
| Matsun | 36.8 | 43.0 | 41.5 | 56.2 | 45.3 |
| Wukuan | 59.0 | 60.1 | 68.2 | 75.5 | 64.6 |

ᵃOne *mou* is equal to one-sixth of an acre or one-fifteenth of a hectare.
*Sources: Hokushi keizai shiryō no. 36,* Table 9; *Hokushi keizai shiryō no. 25,* Table 9; *Hokushi keizai shiryō no. 32,* Table 9. See Note 68, chapter 6, for full citation.

In order to estimate net profits, surveyors had to assign a value to family labor. The 1937 survey multiplied the average daily wage rate paid to hired labor by the number of days that the household labored on the family farm. The calculations in Table 6.8 employ the same convention. Evaluating family labor in this manner can be justified, however, only insofar as labor is homogeneous. If it is not, labor days supplied by the family must first be adjusted to reflect differences in the age or sex of laboring members and in the number of hours actually worked and then adjusted for any qualitative differences between family and wage labor. Although surveys do this nowadays, it was not done in 1937. In addition, on smaller farms, women and children appear to have contributed more to farming labor.[30] For these reasons, reported labor days probably exaggerate differences in labor use among farms and lower the profitability estimates for smaller farms.

Buck's investigation of almost 3,000 farm households in the early 1920s supports this view.[31] He expressed labor days supplied in terms of an adult-male equivalency and found the difference in labor-use intensity between the smallest and largest of farms to be only 10 to 15 percent and sometimes even less. By comparison, the 1937–40 data frequently suggest differences in excess of 50 percent. Table 6.9 reproduces Buck's data along with the percentage of hired-in labor for each locality.

In addition, although the Japanese survey assigns a value to family labor and deducts it from farm revenue, it does not give similar consideration to the opportunity cost of capital tied up in land, fixtures, and inventories. Smaller farms rented a higher percentage of

Table 6.7. *Output per unit of cultivated acreage by farm size (in* yuan*)*

| Acreage | Average Farm Size | MCI[a] | Gross Farm Output/*Mou*[b] |
|---|---|---|---|
| *Michang (1939)* | | | |
| Up to 15 *mou* | 11.8 | 105 | 39.98 |
| 15–25 | 18.7 | 106 | 33.68 |
| 25–50 | 41.3 | 108 | 39.96 |
| 50–100 | 65.6 | 110 | 56.30 |
| Above 100 | 137.2 | 101 | 47.76 |
| *Matsun (1939)* | | | |
| Up to 15 | 11.9 | 129 | 28.31 |
| 15–25 | 21.3 | 118 | 33.50 |
| 25–50 | 36.3 | 138 | 40.57 |
| 50–100 | 69.6 | 127 | 37.96 |
| Above 100 | 115.2 | 114 | 26.59 |
| *Wukuan (1940)* | | | |
| Up to 15 | 10.6 | 135 | 93.30 |
| 15–25 | 19.4 | 133 | 67.14 |
| 25–50 | 35.7 | 129 | 54.85 |
| 50–100 | 59.5 | 122 | 76.45 |
| *All 3 villages* | | | |
| Up to 15 | | | 39.13 |
| 15–25 | | | 34.20 |
| 25–50 | | | 36.44 |
| 50–100 | | | 44.82 |
| Over 100 | | | 37.14 |

[a]The multiple-cropping index (MCI) is the ratio of sown area to cultivated area multiplied by 100.
[b]One *mou* is equal to one-sixth of an acre or one-fifteenth of a hectare.
*Sources: Hokushi keizai shiryō no. 36,* Tables 3 and 13; *Hokushi keizai shiryō no. 25,* Tables 3 and 12; *Hokushi keizai shiryō no. 32,* Tables 3 and 13. See Note 68, Chapter 6, for full citation.

their land and their rental payments are deducted from farm revenue. Comparisons that fail to deduct the opportunity costs of larger farms may very well overestimate their profitability. Table 6.10, which estimates the opportunity cost of capital tied up just in land and recalculates profits for farming households in Matsun, bears out this argument.

Table 6.8. Additional net profit calculations (*in yuan*)

| Farm No.[a] | Michang 1938 Size[b] | Net Profits | Michang 1939 Size | Net Profits | Matsun 1939 Size | Net Profits | Wukuan 1940 Size | Net Profits |
|---|---|---|---|---|---|---|---|---|
| 1 | 134 | 1,089 | 145 | 2,405 | 115 | 867 | 60 | 760 |
| 2 | 68 | 437 | 129 | 3,216 | 87 | 956 | 45 | 397 |
| 3 | 67 | 471 | 78 | 1,535 | 52 | 129 | 44 | 286 |
| 4 | 66 | 504 | 72 | 2,260 | 43 | 604 | 28 | 89 |
| 5 | 60 | 212 | 60 | 927 | 41 | 533 | 25 | 85 |
| 6 | 47 | 158 | 53 | 1,425 | 41 | 607 | 23 | 221 |
| 7 | 42 | 201 | 49 | 701 | 30 | 243 | 22 | 138 |
| 8 | 41 | 293 | 47 | 705 | 28 | 420 | 20 | 99 |
| 9 | 38 | 226 | 41 | 531 | 24 | 116 | 19 | 229 |
| 10 | 35 | 224 | 38 | 642 | 24 | 232 | 19 | 249 |
| 11 | 34 | 158 | 38 | 694 | 24 | 229 | 18 | 129 |
| 12 | 33 | 198 | 34 | 665 | 21 | 155 | 18 | 80 |
| 13 | 22 | 58 | 24 | 458 | 18 | 150 | 16 | 190 |
| 14 | 20 | 57 | 20 | 46 | 18 | 84 | 14 | 127 |
| 15 | 16 | 40 | 16 | 256 | 14 | 105 | 12 | 373 |
| 16 | 15 | 182 | 15 | 263 | 14 | 56 | 12 | 202 |
| 17 | 11 | 97 | 15 | 262 | 13 | 248 | 12 | 223 |
| 18 | 8 | 16 | 13 | 45 | 13 | 129 | 8 | 29 |
| 19 | — | — | 10 | −43 | 11 | 145 | 6 | 123 |
| 20 | — | — | — | — | 8 | 18 | — | — |

[a]The numbering of farms does not correspond to the original numbering in the surveys.

[b]Farm size is expressed in *mou*; one *mou* is equal to one-sixth of an acre or one-fifteenth of a hectare.

*Note:* In these calculations, family labor has been valued at the prevailing market wage rate in each locality. Net profits have also been deflated by the Nankai price index.

*Source:* See Note 68, Chapter 6, for full citation.

Table 6.9. *Adjusted labor input per mou by size of farm (measured in days/mou)*[a]

| County | S[b] | MS | M | ML | L | AVG | Labor Hired[c] (percentage) |
|---|---|---|---|---|---|---|---|
| *North China* | | | | | | | |
| Hwaiyuan, Anhwei | 6.38 | 5.81 | 5.57 | 5.96 | 5.39 | 5.36 | 21.3% |
| Su, Anhwei | 6.93 | n.a. | 5.73 | n.a. | 4.54 | 4.94 | 25.3 |
| Pinghsiang, Chihli | 4.91 | n.a. | 4.45 | n.a. | 4.37 | 4.45 | 14.3 |
| Yenshan, Chihli, 1922 | 6.55 | 6.26 | 6.22 | n.a. | 6.09 | 6.19 | 7.0 |
| Yenshan, Chihli, 1923 | 6.01 | n.a. | 5.75 | n.a. | 5.49 | 5.61 | 14.6 |
| Sincheng, Honan | 5.92 | 5.57 | n.a. | 5.54 | 5.36 | 5.51 | 6.9 |
| Kaifeng, Honan | 3.98 | 4.13 | n.a. | 4.04 | 3.98 | 4.03 | 27.7 |
| Wuhsiang, Shansi | 5.77 | 5.44 | 4.24 | 5.24 | 5.07 | 5.20 | 29.0 |
| Wutai, Shansi | 4.89 | 4.83 | 4.86 | 4.82 | 4.79 | 4.83 | 26.5 |
| *East/Central China* | | | | | | | |
| Laian, Anhwei, 1921 | 8.67 | 7.40 | n.a. | 7.23 | 6.65 | 7.16 | 18.0 |
| Laian, Anhwei, 1922 | 10.62 | n.a. | 7.73 | n.a. | 7.07 | 7.70 | 9.0 |
| Wuhu, Anhwei | 10.66 | 10.70 | n.a. | 10.84 | 11.06 | 10.90 | 15.5 |
| Chinhai, Chekiang | 13.09 | n.a. | 12.72 | n.a. | 12.31 | 12.60 | 31.8 |
| Lienkiang, Fukien | 10.39 | n.a. | 11.16 | n.a. | 9.33 | 9.83 | 4.7 |
| Kiangning, Kiangsu | 14.64 | 9.49 | n.a. | 9.46 | 9.24 | 9.78 | 34.1 |
| Kiangning, Kiangsu | 11.59 | 11.01 | 10.60 | 11.16 | 10.95 | 10.97 | 11.0 |
| Wuchin, Kiangsu | 9.58 | 9.92 | 9.96 | 9.93 | 9.55 | 9.85 | 36.9 |

[a]One *mou* is equal to one-sixth of an acre or one-fifteenth of a hectare.
[b]S represents small, MS medium-small, M medium, ML medium-large, L large, and AVG average.
[c]Hired labor is measured by wages paid as a percentage of total labor costs.
*Note:* n.a.—not available.
*Source:* Buck, *Chinese Farm Economy.*

Table 6.10. *Revised profit calculations for Matsun (in* yuan*)*

| Farm No. | Size (in *mou*)[a] | Net Profits[b] | Capital in Land[c] | Economic Profits[d] |
|---|---|---|---|---|
| 1 | 115 | 1,587 | 20,216 | −30 |
| 2 | 87 | 1,750 | 12,955 | 714 |
| 3 | 52 | 1,669 | 5,070 | 1,263 |
| 4 | 43 | 1,105 | 3,814 | 800 |
| 5 | 41 | 976 | 4,865 | 587 |
| 6 | 41 | 1,111 | 6,600 | 583 |
| 7 | 30 | 444 | 1,200 | 348 |
| 8 | 28 | 768 | 4,516 | 407 |
| 9 | 24 | 213 | 3,860 | −96 |
| 10 | 24 | 420 | 890 | 354 |
| 11 | 24 | 420 | 1,550 | 296 |
| 12 | 21 | 285 | 1,800 | 141 |
| 13 | 18 | 275 | 4,390 | −76 |
| 14 | 18 | 154 | 80 | 148 |
| 15 | 14 | 193 | 120 | 183 |
| 16 | 14 | 103 | 120 | 73 |
| 17 | 13 | 388 | 2,100 | 220 |
| 18 | 13 | 236 | 1,150 | 144 |
| 19 | 11 | 259 | 1,500 | 139 |
| 20 | 8 | 33 | 330 | 7 |

[a]One *mou* is equal to one-sixth of an acre or one-fifteenth of a hectare.
[b]Net profits are the undeflated totals from Table 4.2.
[c]Capital in land is the value of the land owned by the household.
[d]Economic profits are net profits less the opportunity cost of the capital tied up in land; an interest rate of 8 percent was used to calculate opportunity cost.
*Source:* See Note 68, Chapter 6, for full citation.

## Consistency with Buck's Data

Ninety observations at the farm level is obviously too small a sample to generalize about the extent of similarity in farm household behavior and decision making in North China, let alone all of China. Yet, the data John Buck compiled on almost 3,000 farm households in the early 1920s, and on almost 17,000 farms in over 175 countries between 1929 and 1933, though not nearly as detailed, suggest a similar interpretation.

Using the data contained in the latter survey, I have calculated the grain equivalent per hectare for each size category of farm in the eight regions of China.[32] These estimates, presented in Table 6.11, show that in seven out of the eight regions farm size and land productivity were also not systematically related. The one exception was the Southwestern Rice Area. Other data compiled in the same survey on the percentage of farmland in productive use, yields, and cropping intensity are consistent with the productivity data; as before, they reveal only minor differences between size categories. The Yangtse Rice-Wheat and the Rice-Tea Regions, which encompass most of Central and East China, are no exceptions.[33] How can this similarity be explained?

## Rural Factor Markets

The economic development literature has increasingly paid attention to the influence of rural market structure on farm household decision making and agricultural productivity. In general, if factor markets in the countryside operate effectively, households with landholdings too small to absorb the supply of family labor should be able to hire out some of their labor or rent additional land to help offset this constraint. When land and labor markets function imperfectly, however, these same households must use their land more intensively by applying more labor and other inputs per unit of land.[34] This phenomenon explains the tendency for land productivity to decline with increasing farm size in most low-income countries.[35]

By all indications, factor markets in localities such as those surveyed in North China and in the commercialized areas of rural Central and East China were well established, competitive, and effectively used by all households to offset any imbalances they faced in resource endowment. In North China, for example, approximately 25 percent of the land was rented, 15 to 20 percent of farm work was done by hired labor, and one out of three households had at least one family member hiring out as either a seasonal or annual laborer. In Central and East China, the contribution of hired labor was about the same, but 45 percent of the land was rented in. Because commercialization usually meant better information about the market, more economic opportunities, new sources of credit, and so forth, the likelihood of an individual possessing substantial market power in these areas was actually much less than elsewhere.

Data from the Mantetsu surveys provide insights into the operation of the three major factor markets (land, labor, and draft animals). For the labor market, investigators not only obtained information on the number of days members supplied to the family

Table 6.11. *Relationship between land productivity and farm size by region*

| Region | Farm Size[a] | | | | |
|---|---|---|---|---|---|
| | S | M | ML | L | VL |
| *Spring Wheat* | | | | | |
| Average size (in hectares) | 1.12 | 2.16 | 3.44 | 5.72 | 7.70 |
| Grain equivalent per hectare (kgs.) | 393 | 508 | 448 | 414 | 553 |
| Percent of farm in productive use | 88.7 | 89.4 | 89.8 | 94.5 | 91.0 |
| Multiple-cropping index | 107 | 110 | 108 | 100 | 107 |
| Yield index | 99.7 | 100.8 | 96.8 | 91.5 | 101.3 |
| *Winter-Wheat Kaoliang* | | | | | |
| Average size (in hectares) | .67 | 1.35 | 2.36 | 3.69 | 8.12 |
| Grain equivalent per hectare | 1,377 | 1,369 | 1,290 | 1,314 | 1,100 |
| Percent of farm in productive use | 89.9 | 92.0 | 93.2 | 93.7 | 93.7 |
| Multiple-cropping index | 123 | 118 | 119 | 118 | 117 |
| Yield index | 99.6 | 99.5 | 98.9 | 98.3 | 101.5 |
| *Winter-Wheat Millet* | | | | | |
| Average size (in hectares) | .60 | 1.18 | 1.97 | 2.87 | 4.57 |
| Grain equivalent per hectare | 1,230 | 1,061 | 1,078 | 1,013 | 1,016 |
| Percent of farm in productive use | 90.1 | 92.5 | 93.6 | 94.4 | 94.7 |
| Multiple-cropping index | 143 | 143 | 139 | 139 | 139 |
| Yield index | 101.5 | 98.8 | 99.2 | 98.6 | 96.2 |
| *Yangtse Rice-Wheat* | | | | | |
| Average size (in hectares) | .56 | 1.14 | 2.18 | 2.61 | 4.88 |
| Grain equivalent per hectare | 2,140 | 1,985 | 1,756 | 2,218 | 1,832 |
| Percent of farm in productive use | 90.1 | 91.8 | 93.5 | 93.2 | 94.3 |
| Multiple-cropping index | 169 | 166 | 163 | 166 | 153 |
| Yield index | 99.4 | 97.7 | 99.5 | 100.3 | 102.8 |
| *Rice-Tea* | | | | | |
| Average size (in hectares) | .39 | .76 | 1.29 | 1.78 | 1.78 |
| Grain equivalent per hectare | 2,656 | 2,590 | 2,623 | 2,533 | 2,600 |
| Percent of farm in productive use | 92.4 | 93.6 | 94.1 | 94.4 | 94.6 |
| Multiple-cropping index | 175 | 170 | 169 | 165 | 163 |
| Yield index | 100.3 | 99.7 | 101.0 | 98.1 | 100.3 |
| *Szechwan Rice* | | | | | |
| Average size (in hectares) | .49 | .94 | 1.62 | 2.54 | 3.62 |
| Grain equivalent per hectare | 1,944 | 2,432 | 2,655 | 2,417 | 3,373 |
| Percent of farm in productive use | 85.0 | 89.7 | 90.9 | 92.5 | 93.9 |
| Multiple-cropping index | 175 | 172 | 167 | 164 | 162 |
| Yield index | 97.1 | 99.1 | 100.4 | 100.8 | 99.6 |

Table 6.11 (continued)

| Region | S | M | ML | L | VL |
|---|---|---|---|---|---|
| | | | Farm Size[a] | | |
| *Double-Cropping* | | | | | |
| Average size (in hectares) | .42 | .74 | 1.15 | 1.65 | 2.99 |
| Grain equivalent per hectare | 3,021 | 2,808 | 3,276 | 3,181 | 2,741 |
| Percent of farm in productive use | 89.4 | 91.8 | 92.7 | 93.5 | 94.0 |
| Multiple-cropping index | 175 | 178 | 177 | 178 | 171 |
| Yield index | 98.4 | 98.4 | 102.2 | 97.5 | 101.0 |
| *Southwestern Rice* | | | | | |
| Average size (in hectares) | .38 | .82 | 1.37 | 2.07 | 4.08 |
| Grain equivalent per hectare | 4,650 | 4,076 | 3,818 | 3,212 | 2,811 |
| Percent of farm in productive use | 87.3 | 88.2 | 88.1 | 84.9 | 82.9 |
| Multiple-cropping index | 153 | 153 | 151 | 144 | 137 |
| Yield index | 105.1 | 100.8 | 98.9 | 96.4 | 97.1 |

[a]S represents small, M medium, ML medium large, L large, and VL very large.
*Source:* Buck, *Land Utilization in China: Statistical Volume,* pp. 65, 289–91, 295–7, and 302.

farm, but also the number of days hired in, the number of days hired out, and the daily wage paid by each farm household for hired labor. These data appear in Table 6.12 for Matsun for 1939. Farm households in Matsun often participated both as buyers and sellers of labor, with all but a few households hiring labor at some point during the year. Surveys for the other two villages reflect the same phenomena. This participation would have contributed to a farm household's overall awareness of the opportunity cost of their labor and aided them in allocating their time in the interests of maximizing their income.[36] The small farmer does not ask, "Do I work one more day on my small plot?" but "Do I work one more day for myself or for someone else?" Rational small farmers would hire themselves out until the marginal returns for all alternatives were equivalent. Table 6.12 also reveals great similarity in the wages paid by farm households. As might be expected, however, those households that hired labor only at peak periods paid a higher average daily wage rate.

Hiring out was not the only way that households tried to offset the constraint they faced because their landholdings were too small

Table 6.12. *Labor supply, Matsun, 1939*

| Farm No. | Size (in *mou*) | Days Supplied by Family on Farm | Days Hired In | Wage[a] (in *yuan*) | Days Family Hired Out |
|---|---|---|---|---|---|
| 1 | 115 | 146 | 1,046 | .70 | 2 |
| 2 | 87 | 272 | 513 | .69 | 14 |
| 3 | 52 | 428 | 112 | .65 | 114 |
| 4 | 43 | 444 | 9 | .96 | 93 |
| 5 | 41 | 346 | 305 | .69 | 16 |
| 6 | 41 | 328 | 30 | .76 | 24 |
| 7 | 30 | 328 | 27 | .62 | 32 |
| 8 | 28 | 284 | 44 | .53 | 29 |
| 9 | 24 | 276 | 59 | .63 | 69 |
| 10 | 24 | 263 | 29 | .97 | 34 |
| 11 | 24 | 446 | 16 | .78 | 35 |
| 12 | 21 | 345 | 20 | .89 | 144 |
| 13 | 18 | 251 | 68 | .67 | 41 |
| 14 | 18 | 261 | 32 | .85 | 65 |
| 15 | 14 | 173 | 7 | 1.49 | 292 |
| 16 | 14 | 249 | 6 | .93 | 214 |
| 17 | 13 | 253 | 29 | .55 | 13 |
| 18 | 13 | 140 | 0 | — | 0 |
| 19 | 11 | 20 | 119 | .97 | 0 |
| 20 | 8 | 144 | 0 | — | 95 |

[a]The wage paid is the average daily wage, including the value of payment in kind.
*Source: Hokushi keizai shihyō no. 32,* Tables 3, 14, and 39. See Note 68, chapter 6, for full citation.

for their labor supply. Alongside the labor market existed a rental market for land. Tenancy was less common in North China than in the south, but households still rented approximately 25 percent of their land. Buck's data suggest that each size category of farm rented the same percentage of land, but for two of the three localities I examined the percentage of rented land declined with increasing farm size (see Table 6.13).

It is hard to ascertain how imperfect the land rental market was. Some insight is gained by comparing land rental per *mou* with farm size. If rental rates decreased with farm size, it would suggest that the implicit price of land was lower for larger farms than for smaller farms. Because of their size, larger farms may

Table 6.13. *Percentage of land rented in by farm size (in* mou*)*[a]

| Village | Less than 15 | 15–25 | 25–50 | 50–100 | More than 100 |
|---------|-------------|-------|-------|--------|---------------|
| Michang | 88.9% | 61.3% | 38.1% | 11.9% | 0.0% |
| Matsun | 65.0 | 39.9 | 24.7 | 10.4 | 0.0 |
| Wukuan | 12.6 | 29.6 | 26.6 | 0.0 | — |

[a]One *mou* equals one-sixth of an acre or one-fifteenth of a hectare.
*Sources: Hokushi keizai shiryō no. 36,* Table 3; *Hokushi keizai shiryō no. 25,*
Table 3: *Hokushi keizai shiryō no. 32,* Table 3. See Note 68, chapter 6, for
full citation.

have been able to command better terms from landlords. Such a
difference would have encouraged greater land use (relative to
other factors) by these farms and contributed to lower levels of
land productivity on them. Regressions of land rental per *mou* on
farm size, however, failed to reveal any relationship. Given that
land quality or tenancy arrangement could not be controlled,
these results are not conclusive, but they are consistent with the
hypothesis of competitive factor markets.

Finally, a relatively efficient market for draft animals operated
in these villages. Small farms that did not own such animals could
easily rent one, and farms that owned one often hired out both their
own labor services and that of the animal. This market helped to
eliminate the natural indivisibility of an asset like a draft animal
and equalize its use among farms. The operation of this market helps
explain why there was no greater use of animal power on managerial
(farms larger than 100 *mou*) and rich peasant farms than on small
family farms.[37]

By all indications, then, markets in these localities functioned
reasonably well. Their operation helped to assure that farm households of all sizes faced the same vector of prices for the inputs they
used and for the output they sold. This, in turn, produced great
similarity among them in decision making and presumably in efficiency of resource use. I now test to see if such was indeed the case.

### A Formal Test for Differences in Economic Efficiency among Farms

Differences in relative economic efficiency among groups of farms
can be analyzed more rigorously through the use of the profit func-

tion. When the profit function is estimated along with the input demand functions for the variable inputs, this technique not only allows us to test whether farms are profit maximizers, but also to apportion any differences that might exist in relative economic efficiency among them between price and technical efficiency, which the literature defines as the components of economic efficiency.[38]

If a farm equates the marginal product of each variable input to its marginal cost, it is considered absolutely price efficient and profit maximization is implied. Differences in price efficiency among groups of farms, therefore, are related to differences in the ability of each group to implement this calculus of profit maximization. Technical efficiency, on the other hand, relates to differences among farms in the quantity of output produced from a given set of measured inputs. Environmental factors, managerial ability and other nonmeasurable fixed inputs can all contribute to differences in technical efficiency.

Here I test for any differences in relative economic efficiency between two basic kinds of farms in North China: those larger and those smaller than thirty *mou*.[39] Equation (1) presents the profit function consistent with a Cobb-Douglas production function and relates profits for each farm to the prices for the two variable inputs (labor and draft animals), to capital services, and to the amount of land under cultivation. Equations (2) and (3), on the other hand, are the derived demand equations for the two variable inputs, assuming a Cobb-Douglas profit function.

$$\ln \pi = a_0 + a_1 {*} \ln W + a_2 {*} \ln R + b_1 {*} \ln K \qquad (1)$$
$$+ b_2 {*} \ln A + d_1 {*} D_L + e_1$$

$$-WX_1/P = a_1{}^S {*} D_S + a_1{}^L {*} D_L + e_2 \qquad (2)$$

$$-RX_2/P = a_2{}^S {*} D_S + a_2{}^L {*} D_L + e_3 \qquad (3)$$

where $\pi$ is variable profit per farm (total current value minus total current variable cost), $a_0$ is the intercept of the profit equation, $D_L$ is the dummy for farms larger than thirty *mou*, $D_S$ is the dummy for those smaller, W is the daily wage rate for both family and hired labor, R is the imputed daily rental fee for draft animal use, K is capital services, A is cultivated area, and $X_1$ and $X_2$ are total labor input and animal input measured in days.[40] Labor input includes both family and hired labor. $WX_1$ and $RX_2$ are the total value of labor and draft-animal input. All variables expressed in value terms have been deflated for pooling purposes. The $a_i$ and $b_i$ are the coefficients to be estimated; S and L are superscripts for small and large farms. Equations (1) through (3) constitute Model I. (For Model II, see below.)

Before estimation it is necessary to impute a value for family labor so that the total value of labor input, $WX_1$, and the average daily rate, $W$, can be calculated for each farm.[41] Some cases justify the use of the prevailing market wage rate for hired labor; more often, however, a lower rate is required because the value of a labor day of an adult male who worked on his own farm appears to have been less than that of an adult male who hired out, and the value of a labor day supplied by women and children on a family farm was less than that of their adult male counterpart.[42] Ignoring these differences and evaluating each day of self-supplied labor at the prevailing market wage rate leads to an overestimation of labor input on some farms and so would possibly bias comparisons among households.

The remedy is either to impute values that are less than the prevailing market wage rate to the various kinds of family labor or to adjust the reported number of days the family worked on their land before evaluating it at the prevailing market wage rate. If we had information on the exact composition of family labor, such adjustments would be rather easy, but unfortunately the surveys do not report the actual number of days supplied by women and children and adult males to the family farm; the data provide only total family labor input. Without this additional information, the only kind of adjustment that I can make is to value self-supplied labor at the same rate for all farms. On the basis of data compiled by Buck, I have selected a value equal to 85 percent of the prevailing market wage rate.[43] I must point out, however, that using the same weight for all size farms will still lead me to overestimate the wage bill and average daily wage rate for farm labor on those farms that relied more heavily on women and children (smaller farms) relative to those on which the contribution was smaller (larger farms).[44] This, in turn, will bias our econometric estimates of $d_1$, the coefficient on the dummy for larger farms, and the absolute value of $a_1^S$ upwards.

Column $I_A$ of Table 6.14 presents the results of estimating the unrestricted version of Model I using Zellner's minimum distance estimator. Standard errors are in parentheses. I used Zellner's method because of the likely correlation of the error terms between equations and because it provides more efficient estimates than regression applied separately to the equations.[45] All the coefficients have the expected signs; on both the wage rate and the draft-animal rental rate, the signs are negative, but they are positive on capital services and cultivated area, the two fixed factors. Moreover, the

Table 6.14. *Parameter estimates for Models I and II*

| Parameter | Model I | | | Model II | | |
|---|---|---|---|---|---|---|
| | $I_A$ | $I_B$ | $I_C$ | $II_A$ | $II_B$ | $II_C$ |
| $a_0$ | 1.712 | 1.691 | 1.593 | 1.700 | 1.676 | 1.590 |
| | (0.272) | (0.250) | (0.143) | (0.287) | (0.264) | (0.146) |
| $d_1$ | 0.360 | 0.139 | 0.097 | 0.358 | 0.138 | 0.103 |
| | (0.153) | (0.109) | (0.061) | (0.153) | (0.110) | (0.622) |
| $d_2$ | | | | 0.015 | 0.011 | 0.014 |
| | | | | (0.027) | (0.027) | (0.026) |
| $a_1$ | −0.474 | −0.551 | −0.553 | −0.463 | −0.549 | −0.551 |
| | (0.107) | (0.062) | (0.061) | (0.103) | (0.062) | (0.062) |
| $a_2$ | −0.253 | −0.167 | −0.167 | −0.253 | −0.167 | −0.167 |
| | (0.107) | (0.020) | (0.020) | (0.108) | (0.020) | (0.020) |
| $b_1$ | 0.111 | 0.118 | 0.121 | 0.108 | 0.117 | 0.120 |
| | (0.058) | (0.058) | (0.058) | (0.059) | (0.059) | (0.058) |
| $b_2$ | 0.843 | 0.848 | | 0.851 | 0.854 | |
| | (0.087) | (0.087) | | (0.088) | (0.088) | |
| $a_1^S$ | −0.706 | | | −0.706 | | |
| | (0.104) | | | (0.104) | | |
| $a_1^L$ | −0.438 | | | −0.438 | | |
| | (0.111) | | | (0.111) | | |
| $a_2^S$ | −0.193 | | | −0.195 | | |
| | (0.029) | | | (0.029) | | |
| $a_2^L$ | −0.135 | | | −0.135 | | |
| | (0.031) | | | (0.031) | | |

*Note:* Standard errors are in parentheses. $I_A$ is the unrestricted version of Model I. $I_B$ incorporates the restrictions that $a_1 = a_1^S = a_1^L$ and $a_2 = a_2^S = a_2^L$. $I_C$ incorporates the additional restriction $b_1 + b_2 = 1$. Analogous definitions hold for Model II.
*Source:* See text.

standard errors for both $a_1$ and $a_2$ are small and their $t$-statistics high.[46]

In order to determine whether the two groups showed differences in economic efficiency, and if so, the basis for such differences, I examine a set of five hypotheses using likelihood ratio tests.[47] Equations (1) through (3) were estimated in unconstrained form and then reestimated with the constraint(s) implied by each null hypothesis imposed. The null hypotheses are tested using a likelihood ratio statistic $[-2(\ln_c - \ln_u)]$, where $\ln_c$ is the log of the likelihood function of the constrained system of equations and $\ln_u$ that of the unconstrained system. The test statistic is distributed chi-squared with degrees of freedom equal to the number of restrictions imposed. If the calculated value of the test statistic is greater than the critical value of the chi-square for the appropriate number of degrees of freedom, the null hypothesis can be rejected. The hypotheses are presented in Table 6.15 and the actual test results in Table 6.16.

Consider the hypothesis of equal relative economic efficiency. With no differences in relative economic efficiency, profits for the two groups of farms would be the same at all observed prices of the variable inputs, given the distribution of the fixed factors. In terms of equation (1), this implies $d_1$, the coefficient on the dummy for larger farms, equal to zero. With a calculated value of 5.78 for the test statistic, the null hypothesis of equal relative economic efficiency can easily be rejected at the 5-percent level and almost at the 1-percent level. The positive value for $d_1$ indicates that larger farms were more economically efficient than smaller ones.

At first examination, this result might seem consistent with existing interpretations. We need to know, however, the basis for the superior economic efficiency of larger farms. Were small farms not maximizing profits and thus less price efficient, or were they less efficient technically, or maybe both? Hypothesis tests (2) through (5) are the key to answering these questions. In test (2), I consider the absolute price efficiency of small farms with respect to labor and draft-animal use. In other words, did small farms maximize profits by equating the marginal product of labor and draft animal to their respective market costs? In test (3), I do the same thing for larger farms. Rejecting hypothesis (2) or (3) would imply that one or both groups of farms were not making decisions on the basis of profit maximization. The next two hypothesis tests examine whether or not the two groups were equally price efficient with respect to labor and draft-animal use. Test (4) is for equal relative price efficiency, and test (5) is for equal absolute price efficiency. The relative test is weaker than the absolute one and tests only whether the two groups of farms equate the marginal products of the variable inputs to their market costs to the same degree. Rejecting (4) or (5) would imply important differences in price efficiency between the two groups of farms.

Table 6.16 shows that for each group of farms the hypothesis of absolute price efficiency for labor and draft-animal use (hypotheses 2 and 3) cannot be rejected (even at the 10 percent level). Neither

Table 6.15. *The Hypotheses*

| Test No. | Testing for: | Hypothesis test |
|---|---|---|
| 1 | Equal relative economic efficiency | H: $d_1 = 0$ |
| 2 | Absolute price efficiency for labor and draft-animal use for farms less than 30 *mou* | H: $a_1^S = a_1$ and $a_2^S = a_2$ |
| 3 | Absolute price efficiency for labor and draft-animal use for farms larger than 30 *mou* | H: $a_1^L = a_1$ and $a_2^L = a_2$ |
| 4 | Equal relative price efficiency for labor and draft animals | H: $a_1^S = a_1^L$ and $a_2^S = a_2^L$ |
| 5 | Equal absolute price efficiency for labor and draft animals | H: $a_1 = a_1^S = a_1^L$ and $a_2 = a_2^S = a_2^L$ |
| 6 | Returns to scale | H: $b_1 + b_2 = 1$ |
| 7 | Effect of tenancy on economic efficiency | H: $d_2 = 0$ |

*Source:* See text.

Table 6.16. *Hypotheses test results*

| Null Hypothesis | Computed Test Values | | Critical Values | |
|---|---|---|---|---|
| | Model | Model II | 0.10 | 0.01 |
| 1. $d_1 = 0$ | 5.780 | 5.334 | 2.705 | 6.635 |
| 2. $a_1^S = a_1$ and $a_2^S = a_2$ | 2.588 | 2.752 | 4.605 | 9.210 |
| 3. $a_1^L = a_1$ and $a_2^L = a_2$ | 1.046 | 1.050 | 4.605 | 9.210 |
| 4. $a_1^S = a_1^L$ and $a_2^S = a_2^L$ | 3.728 | 3.810 | 4.605 | 9.210 |
| 5. $a_1 = a_1^S = a_1^L$ and $a_2 = a_2^S = a_2^L$ | 5.066 | 5.238 | 7.779 | 13.277 |
| 6. $b_1 + b_2 = 1$ | 0.418 | 0.300 | 2.705 | 6.635 |
| 7. $d_2 = 0$ | — | 0.312 | 2.705 | 6.635 |

*Source:* See text.

of the two remaining hypotheses regarding equal absolute and equal relative price efficiency among the two groups can be rejected either, which is not unexpected given the results of the previous two tests.

What can we conclude on the basis of these results? Failure to reject a null hypothesis does not necessarily imply that it is true. Any such conclusion regarding the null is usually best postponed until more is known about the power of the test (in other words, the probability of a type-II error).[48] For this material, determining the power of the test is not only computationally difficult, but is further handicapped by the lack of meaningful alternative hypotheses. Nonetheless, the fact that I failed to reject at the 10-percent level the hypothesis of absolute price efficiency for each group of farms separately, and the hypotheses of equal absolute and relative price efficiency, suggests an underlying similarity in behavior between the two groups of farms and leads me to believe that they were equally successful in maximizing profits through the rational allocation of labor and draft-animal power to their farms. Both large and small farms apparently applied inputs only to the point where their marginal products were equal to their market costs. Smoothly working markets facilitated this kind of behavior and made the two groups of farm households equally aware of the opportunity costs of their inputs. The test results, then, are consistent with the view that farm size did not systematically affect how farm households were allocating resources to agriculture.[49]

If farms of different sizes allocated their resources with equal efficiency, any greater relative economic efficiency on the part of

Table 6.17. *Input elasticities and estimates of relative economic efficiency*

| Item | Model I | | Model II | |
| --- | --- | --- | --- | --- |
| | $I_B$ | $I_C$ | $II_B$ | $II_C$ |
| *Input Elasticities* | | | | |
| Labor | 0.321 | 0.321 | 0.320 | 0.320 |
| Draft animal | 0.097 | 0.097 | 0.097 | 0.097 |
| Land | 0.493 | 0.511 | 0.498 | 0.513 |
| Fixed capital | 0.069 | 0.071 | 0.068 | 0.070 |
| Summation of coefficients | 0.980 | 1.000 | 0.983 | 1.000 |
| *Estimates of Relative Economic Efficiency* | | | | |
| Large/small | 1.085 | 1.058 | 1.084 | 1.062 |

*Note:* $I_B$ and $II_B$ are based on estimates with the first set of restrictions imposed, and $I_C$ and $II_C$ include the additional restriction of constant returns to scale.
*Source:* See text.

larger farms had to be the product of superior technical efficiency. Following a procedure outlined by Pan Yotopoulos and Lawrence Lau and using the results from the restricted estimation (see the estimates in columns IB and IC of Table 6.14), I have quantified differences in economic efficiency between these two groups of farms.[50]

Table 6.17 provides measures of relative economic efficiency along with the estimates of the input elasticities obtained indirectly from the profit function.[51] The calculations suggest that farms over thirty *mou* were between 6 and 9 percent more efficient than their smaller counterparts. Alternatively, controlling for differences in fixed inputs and factor prices, profits on larger farms were 6 to 9 percent higher. Because of the nature of the bias in my estimate of $d_1$, these percentages can probably be taken as an upper bound of any differences that may have existed; actual differences were probably less.

As small as the differences may be, a number of factors may explain the superior economic efficiency of larger farms, including increasing returns to scale, qualitative differences in inputs not successfully captured in our estimation, and, finally, tenancy. Of the three, the first can be quickly ruled out. The results of test (6) (Tables

Table 6.18. *Average farm and parcel size (in hectares)*

|            | Size  |       |       | Average Parcel Size |      |      |
|------------|-------|-------|-------|--------|------|------|
|            | China | WWK[a] | WWM[b] | China  | WWK  | WWM  |
| VC[c]      | 0.50  | 0.81  | 0.34  | 0.21   | 0.29 | 0.13 |
| S          | 0.58  | 0.67  | 0.60  | 0.21   | 0.22 | 0.19 |
| M          | 1.15  | 1.35  | 1.18  | 0.29   | 0.29 | 0.25 |
| ML         | 1.99  | 2.36  | 1.97  | 0.39   | 0.39 | 0.31 |
| L          | 2.90  | 3.69  | 2.87  | 0.53   | 0.47 | 0.37 |
| VL         | 5.27  | 8.12  | 4.57  | 0.71   | 0.58 | 0.42 |
| VVL        | 8.89  | 10.31 | 5.72  | 0.82   | 0.54 | 0.48 |
| VVVL       | 9.46  | 14.12 | 7.50  | 1.29   | 0.68 | 0.67 |
| Avg        | 1.69  | 2.25  | 1.71  | —      | —    | —    |

[a]WWK is Winter Wheat-Kaoliang.
[b]WWM is Winter Wheat-Millet.
[c]VS represents very small, S small, M medium, and so forth.
*Source:* Buck, *Land Utilization in China: Statistical Volume,* pp. 291–2 and 63–4.

6.15 and 6.16) suggest no basis for increasing or decreasing returns to scale in agriculture.[52]

My tests did not adjust the land input for any qualitative differences. No systematic relationship appears to have held between the average price of land (a measure of land quality) and farm size: land fragmentation would probably pose a more serious problem for smaller farms, however, than it did for the larger ones. Family farm households rarely cultivated contiguous land parcels. The typical household farmed an average of five to six parcels, with the farthest parcel often up to a kilometer from the farmstead. Land fragmentation certainly hindered the rational use of land, capital, and other inputs.[53]

Table 6.18 reports Buck's data on average farm size and average parcel size for all of China and two subregions: Winter Wheat-Millet (WWM) and Winter Wheat-Kaoliang (WWK). (Matsun and Wukuan were both located in WWM and Michang in WWK.) Larger farms typically cultivated parcels twice the size of smaller farms households. Thus, land fragmentation may have imposed relatively higher costs on smaller farms and contributed to their slightly lower technical efficiency.

Finally, differences in the percentage of land rented may have contributed to differences in economic efficiency. Buck found that the percentage of land rented did not differ greatly by farm size. But, in the localities I examined, smaller farms typically rented a higher percentage of the land they farmed. Wukuan represents a slight exception, with farms of less than fifteen *mou* renting less land than farms in the next two size categories. If tenancy was negatively correlated with economic efficiency and smaller farms rented a higher percentage of their lands, larger farms may seem more economically efficient when tenancy is not properly taken into account.

Theoretically, the influence of tenancy on farm efficiency still remains ambiguous.[54] But the China literature takes it almost as a given that existing tenancy arrangements imposed substantial disincentives and inefficiencies. The problem reportedly became even more severe during the late 1930s and early 1940s, a period marked by wartime inflation. Those localities where rents were paid in cash generally reported rental contracts of one year, rather than the customary five to ten years.

The influence of tenancy on economic efficiency can be tested for, nonetheless, by following the methodology first outlined by Ronald Trosper.[55] Letting T be the percentage of land that is rented, the appropriate model becomes:

$$\ln \pi = a_0 + a_1 * \ln W + a_2 * \ln R + b_1 * \ln K \qquad (4)$$
$$+ b_2 * \ln A + d_1 * D_L + d_2 * T + e_4$$

and equations (2) and (3). Hereafter, equations (2), (3), and (4) will be referred to as Model II. The influence of tenancy on economic efficiency can now be examined by a hypothesis test on the coefficient $d_2$.[56]

Table 6.14 provides the parameter estimates for Model II, with and without restrictions. Hypothesis tests for differences in relative economic efficiency and for the separate influence of tenancy on overall economic efficiency – test (7) – are carried out in Table 6.16.[57] In general, the incorporation of tenancy into the model results in few changes. The parameter estimates for the two models are very similar, and the outcomes of tests (1) through (6) are the same as before. The coefficient on $d_2$ is very small, and test (7) shows that we cannot reject the hypothesis that it is equal to zero. In other words, these results suggest that tenancy failed to exert any influence, positive or negative, on economic efficiency in the farm sector. This leaves land fragmentation as the only factor of the three that might have contributed to the marginally superior technical efficiency of larger farms.

## Summary: Farm Household Behavior

The farm-level survey data for North China helps explain why there is no tendency for land productivity to decline with increasing farm size. By all indications, factor markets for land, labor, and draft animals were well established and relatively free from the kinds of distortions commonly reported in other low-income countries. Households of all sizes used the markets effectively; it was not uncommon, for example, for a farm household to be simultaneously renting in land, hiring out labor, and hiring draft-animal services either in or out. In Central and East China, hired labor played an equally important role in farming and an even higher percentage of land was rented in. It is a good bet that the wide similarity exhibited among households in Buck's more aggregate data for the region is a product of the same kind of market structure. In light of these results, it is hard to sustain the view that there were systematic differences between farm households in commercialized areas of rural China.

## Reinterpreting the Influence of Commercialization on Income Distribution

Even without time-series data on income distribution, there is much that can be inferred about evolving income differences between households in the rural sector. By all indications, land distribution did not become more concentrated. Moreover, farms of all sizes seem to have taken equal advantage of the opportunities offered by cash cropping and market expansion. These observations are important in two respects. First, they preclude increasing land concentration as a source of growing income inequality in the rural sector. Second, they suggest that more general arguments linking commercialization with growing income inequality do not fit China's rural sector particularly well.

Because land distribution did not become more concentrated and decision making in agriculture was very similar among farm households, income distribution in the rural sector depended heavily on the relative returns to the various factors of production in agriculture (most importantly land and labor) and the contribution of agriculture to total rural incomes. If the contribution of agriculture to total rural incomes remained constant, but the return to land rose relative to that for labor, landowners would capture an increasing percentage of total income and income differentials between the landed and landless would widen. This does not appear to have happened in the commercialized areas of the Yangtse.

In Chapter 5, I analyzed the behavior of the returns to labor in farming between the 1890s and the 1930s from three alternative perspectives: wages paid long-term agricultural workers; the returns to labor in handicraft textiles, which provided an alternative outlet for labor; and productivity changes consistent with shifts in the sectoral composition of the labor force and reasonable assumptions regarding per capita consumption of agricultural output. All three point to substantial increases in the productivity and returns to labor in farming. Who did this benefit? Obviously, rising real rural wages substantially benefited households that owned only small amounts of land, rented in land, and hired out their labor.[58] In other words, they benefited households in the bottom third or even half of the distribution. But did they gain relative to larger landowners?

Here we lack information on land rents. If land rents remained the same percentage of output, land and labor would have shared equally the increase in incomes associated with rising farm output.[59] If the share going to land rose or fell, land would have captured either an increasing or decreasing percentage of output. It is in the former case that income distribution would worsen, even if the absolute level of incomes of the poorest strata were rising.

Data on land rents are seriously inadequate. On the basis of several centuries of yield data, Perkins observed that land rents consistently amounted to about half the yield of the main summer crop, and in areas of double-cropping a similar percentage of the second crop.[60] According to Niida, during the Ming and Ch'ing share contracts in areas of double-cropping typically specified rents of 60 percent of the first crop and 40 percent of the second.[61] Presumably fixed rental contracts convert to a similar percentage of output.

By contrast, data for the early twentieth century suggest that in areas of double-cropping significantly less than 50 percent of output was paid in rent. Table 6.19 provides provincial estimates of stipulated and actual rental payments measured as a percentage of the harvest. In Central and East China, the unweighted averages of stipulated and actual rents were 42.30 and 34.69 percent, respectively.[62] A similarly low percentage of output was paid in the form of rents in several southern provinces, but in the north (Hopei, Shantong, and Honan) approximately half of the output went to the landowner. Table 6.20 provides additional information on stipulated rents for contracts in which the tenant provided seed, fertilizer, and

Table 6.19. *Rents measured as a percentage of output (I)*

| Province | No. of hsien | No. of Households | Stipulated Rent | Actual Rent |
|---|---|---|---|---|
| Kiangsu | 12 | 158 | 37.44% | 36.26% |
| Chekiang | 15 | 249 | 45.30 | 35.25 |
| Anhwei | 10 | 189 | 34.18 | 30.77 |
| Kiangsi | 3 | 32 | 48.73 | 41.11 |
| Hupei | 6 | 48 | 46.65 | 35.09 |
| Hunan | 10 | 164 | 41.67 | 29.61 |
| Fukien | 10 | 143 | 37.42 | 37.42 |
| Kwangsi | 8 | 17 | 35.48 | 35.48 |
| Hopei | 20 | 287 | 54.21 | 53.67 |
| Honan | 11 | 156 | 47.40 | 47.27 |
| Shantong | 16 | 207 | 49.95 | 49.82 |

*Source:* T'u-ti wei-yuan hui, *Ch'uan-kuo t'u-ti tiao-ch'a pao-kao kang-yao,* Table 30.

Table 6.20. *Rents measured as a percentage of output (II) (seed, fertilizer, and draft-animal services supplied by tenant)*

| Province | No. of Observations | Mean | Median | Mode |
|---|---|---|---|---|
| Kiangsu | 478 | 40.26% | 40.37% | 39.88% |
| Chekiang | 523 | 42.44 | 40.95 | 35.08 |
| Anhwei | 393 | 40.36 | 40.00 | 39.76 |
| Kiangsi | 188 | 42.63 | 36.50 | 30.10 |
| Hupei | 240 | 38.62 | 38.28 | 39.73 |
| Hunan | 303 | 44.22 | 45.78 | 50.54 |

*Source:* Chen, *Chung-kuo k'o-sheng te ti-tsu,* Table 34.

draft-animal services. The mean stipulated rent was 41.42 percent of the harvest and the mode, at 39.18, slightly lower. These data also reveal higher rental rates in the north.

If earlier in the nineteenth century rents in the Yangtse region amounted to about half of output, and the relative contributions made by the landlord and tenant in the form of seed, fertilizer, and draft-animal services did not change too much subsequently, the data for the 1930s point to a rising relative return to labor. In other words, an increasing percentage of output was going to labor – a development that most favored those households poorly endowed in terms of land.

In addition, households with less land also benefited significantly from the growth of nonagricultural activity in the rural sector: sericulture in Kiangsu and Chekiang; handicraft textile production in Kiangsu and Hupei using new improved looms; refining of edible (soybeans and rapeseed, for example) and inedible (tung) oil as a sideline and by small handicraft factories in market towns; production of egg products such as dried yolks and albumen, overseas exports of which grew from only 1–2 million *yuan* at the turn of the century to over 50 million *yuan* by 1930; and marketing and transportation services that employed thousands.[63] For a majority of sidelines, the relatively modest capital requirements posed no serious barrier to entry. For smaller farms, by-employments were much more important. The percentage of income earned from sidelines declined with increasing farm size. On average, the smallest of farms in Buck's survey derived 20 to 25 percent of income from off-farm sources, as opposed to 6–8 percent on larger farms. In Chapter 4, I noted that many households appear to have left agriculture altogether.

The combination of a rising return to labor and the growth in off-farm opportunities associated with the growing commercialization and diversification of the rural sector extended benefits to most, if not all, rural households. There is no reason to believe that a small number of larger landowning households monopolized these gains; in fact, households owning less than ten to fifteen *mou* probably profited the most (in relative terms).

I believe the equalizing tendencies of these forces on incomes are reflected in Table 6.21, which reports the Gini coefficients for the cultivated holdings of all rural households and the Gini for incomes of all rural households. Recall that for all of rural China the Gini for own landholdings was 0.72. By contrast, the degree of inequality of cultivated holdings was much less. In the aggregate, it was 0.615 and for the region it was 0.554[64] The high in Central and East China was 0.601 in Hunan, and the low was 0.525 in Hupei. The degree of income inequality was much lower still. For the entire region, it was 0.425, and at the provincial level usually less. The low was 0.339 in Kiangsi, and the high was 0.473 in Anhwei. Because household incomes were positively correlated with family size, per capita measures would probably reveal even lower degrees of inequality.[65]

Table 6.21 *Gini coefficients for land and income distribution, 1930s*

| Province | Cultivated Holdings All Rural Households | Incomes All Rural Households |
|---|---|---|
| Kiangsu | 0.570 | 0.430 |
| Chekiang | 0.569 | 0.412 |
| Anhwei | 0.538 | 0.473 |
| Kiangsi | 0.530 | 0.339 |
| Hupei | 0.525 | 0.428 |
| Hunan | 0.601 | 0.393 |
| Pooled | 0.554 | 0.425 |

*Source:* Calculated using data contained in T'u-ti wei-yuan hui, *Ch'uan-kuo t'u-ti tiao-ch'a pao-kao kang-yao*, pp. 26 and 49.

It cannot be inferred from these estimates that income differentials in the rural sector were declining or, for that matter, remaining the same. Yet, when these estimates are looked at in a comparative perspective, they reveal a low-to-moderate degree of inequality in Yangtse's rural sector compared to other low-income countries and one very similar to that found in other Asian economies. Michael Todoro, for example, has classified low-income countries with Gini's between 0.40 and 0.50 as having moderate inequality.[66] Using this criterion, Anhwei would fall into the middle of the category; Kiangsu, Chekiang, and Hunan would fall into the low end; and Kiangsi and Hupei would be considered as having low inequality. In Table 6.22, Gini coefficients are presented for the distribution of rural household incomes for six Asian countries in the 1960s and 1970s. Only in the case of Taiwan, which benefited significantly from land reform, do we find a markedly lower degree of rural income inequality than that estimated for the region for the 1930s.[67] If income inequality was worsening over this period, it would imply that by international standards China in the 1890s had an exceptionally low degree of inequality.

Yet, the data I have presented on land distribution, the behavior of real wages, and so forth simply do not support such an assertion. It is much more likely that income differentials remained the same or narrowed slightly. Rising real wages, a growth in off-farm opportunities, and new nonagricultural sources of incomes all helped to reduce the role of landownership in income distribution. I believe the successively lower measures of inequality for landownership,

Table 6.22. *Gini coefficients for rural household incomes in Asia*

| Country | Years | Coefficient |
|---------|-------|-------------|
| Philippines | 1961 | 0.397 |
|  | 1965 | 0.423 |
|  | 1971 | 0.462 |
| Thailand | 1962/63 | 0.361 |
|  | 1968/69 | 0.381 |
|  | 1971/73 | 0.466 |
| Malaysia | 1957 | 0.421 |
|  | 1970 | 0.464 |
| Taiwan | 1972 | 0.344 |
|  | 1975 | 0.363 |
| Singapore | 1966 | 0.447 |
|  | 1975 | 0.436 |
| India | 1961/62 | 0.410 |
|  | 1964/65 | 0.350 |
|  | 1967/68 | 0.460 |
|  | 1968/69 | 0.430 |

*Sources:* For all countries except India: Harry Oshima and Toshiyuki Mizoguchi, eds., *Income Distribution by Sectors and Overtime in East and Southeast Asian Countries* (Quezon City, Philippines, and Tokyo, Japan, 1978); for India: I. K. Bhatty, "Inequality and Poverty in Rural India."

cultivated area, and incomes reveal the equalizing tendencies these forces had between the 1890s and 1930s.

APPENDIX TO CHAPTER 6

The village surveys for North China used in this chapter were carried out by the Japanese South Manchurian Railroad (Minami Manshu Tetsudo Kabushiki Kaisha, or Mantetsu) between 1937 and 1940.[68] One or more of these surveys has been used before by Myers and Dietrich, Wiens, and Huang.[69] The Mantetsu collected from ninety farm households data relating to family size, the age and sex of family members, family expenditure and income (including income in kind), value of farm assets, and value of farm output and inputs (both those supplied by the farm as well as those obtained from the market). Labor input supplied by the family household or

Table 6.23. *Distribution of farms by size and type*

**Michang**

| Type | Size (in mou) | | | | | | | | | | Total | Avg. Size | % of Households |
|---|---|---|---|---|---|---|---|---|---|---|---|---|---|
| | 150–100 | | 100–50 | | 50–25 | | 25–10 | | Under 10 | | | | |
| | No. | Avg. | No. | Avg. | No. | Avg. | No. | Avg. | No. | Avg. | | | |
| Owner | 3 | 124.2 | 13 | 62.5 | 4 | 34.5 | 7 | 19.0 | 6 | 3.3 | 33 | 44.8 | 33.7 |
| Owner/tenant | 1 | 118.0 | 1 | 56.2 | 14 | 38.0 | 15 | 16.2 | 5 | 5.4 | 36 | 27.1 | 36.7 |
| Tenant | 0 | — | 0 | — | 4 | 37.0 | 15 | 15.0 | 10 | 5.9 | 29 | 14.9 | 29.6 |
| Average | 4 | 122.7 | 14 | 62.0 | 22 | 37.2 | 37 | 16.2 | 21 | 5.0 | 98 | 29.4 | — |

Percentage of land rented: 27.2%

**Matsun**

| Type | Size (in mou) | | | | | | | | | | Total | Avg. Size | % of Households |
|---|---|---|---|---|---|---|---|---|---|---|---|---|---|
| | 150–100 | | 100–50 | | 50–30 | | 30–10 | | Under 10 | | | | |
| | No. | Avg. | No. | Avg. | No. | Avg. | No. | Avg. | No. | Avg. | | | |
| Owner | 3 | 109.3 | 8 | 70.3 | 12 | 37.3 | 49 | 16.3 | 62 | 4.6 | 134 | 18.1 | 55.6 |
| Owner/tenant | 0 | — | 5 | 59.4 | 12 | 38.5 | 38 | 16.3 | 25 | 6.2 | 80 | 19.2 | 33.2 |
| Tenant | 0 | — | 1 | 70.0 | 0 | — | 8 | 13.3 | 18 | 4.4 | 27 | 9.4 | 11.2 |
| Average | 3 | 109.3 | 14 | 66.4 | 24 | 37.9 | 95 | 16.0 | 95 | 5.5 | 241 | 17.5 | 100.0 |

Percentage of land rented: 24.2%

# Table 6.23. (*continued*)

*Wukuan*

| | | Distribution by Size | | | | |
|---|---|---|---|---|---|---|
| 200–100 | 100–50 | 50–25 | 25–15 | Under 15 | Total | Avg. Size |
| 3 | 4 | 8 | 14 | 116 | 145 | 13.6 |

| Distribution by Type | | |
|---|---|---|
| Number | Average Size | Percentage |
| Owners | 116 | 12.7 | 80.0% |
| Owner/tenant | 18 | 22.9 | 12.4 |
| Tenants | 11 | 8.2 | 7.6 |

Percentage of land rented: 18.3%

*Note:* For Michang and Matsun, farm households were grouped jointly by size and type; for Wukuan, they were grouped separately.

*Sources:* Michang: *Hokushi keizai shihyō no. 36*, pp. 151–5; Matsun: *Hokushi, keizai shihyō no. 32*, pp. 82–7; Wukuan: *Hokushi keizai shihyō no. 25*, pp. 87–9.

hired-in and draft-animal use were enumerated in days and evaluated at market prices.

After compiling village-wide information on all types of farms (that is, owner, owner/tenant, and tenant) and farm size, the Mantetsu selected approximately twenty farm households from each village for more detailed investigation. To ensure a representative cross-section, the survey examined many farm households with more than 30 *mou* as well as many renting land. Table 6.23 provides the distribution of farms by their size and type for each of the three localities. Population densities differed among the three, with the average farm size being 29.4 *mou* in Michang, but only 17.5 and 13.4 *mou* in Matsun and Wukuan. For all three villages, average farm size was 18.7 *mou*.[70]

The distributions of households by farm size in Matsun and Wukuang are very similar, with 80 to 90 percent of all farms falling in the two smallest categories. Less than a quarter of the land was rented in either of these localities, with pure tenants making up about 5 percent of village households. In Michang, only slightly more land was rented, but 30 percent of households were pure tenants. Moreover, approximately 40 percent of all farms in Michang exceeded 25 *mou*.

All three villages devoted an unusually high percentage of cultivated area to cash crops. It Matsun, 59.0 percent of the sown area was planted in cotton; in Michang and Wukuan, the figures were 33.8 percent and 26.4 percent. Market dependency occurred because each locality was serviced by a major railroad line: Michang was located near the Peking-Mukden Railroad; Matsun was at the intersection of the Peking-Hankow and Lung-hai Railroad; and Wukuan was also on the Peking-Hankow Railroad. Michang and Matsun marketed about two-thirds of farm output; Wukuan marketed slightly less than one-half (as compared to about 35 or 40 percent of the farm output for all of China).

# 7

# Conclusion

Much of the analysis of the late nineteenth and early twentieth-century Chinese economy has been concerned with explaining the reasons for and the consequences of the agricultural sector's inability to accommodate very modest population growth. With the exception of Manchuria, existing data strongly suggest that per capita agricultural output declined over this period. This failure has been attributed to a variety of institutional and technological constraints that many believe were not eliminated until after the Communists came to power in 1949. Commercialization only exacerbated these difficulties and was itself a source of expanding rural poverty and widening income differentials among rural households.

In the case of Central and East China, this study demonstrates that these interpretations are seriously flawed. Between the 1890s and 1930s, agricultural output in Central and East China increased more than two times the estimated rate of population growth of 0.6 percent per annum, only modestly below the rates of output growth achieved in Japanese agriculture over the same period.[1] This not only enabled the agricultural sector to accommodate a more than doubling of the nonagricultural population and an increased demand for cash crops, but would have also allowed for higher levels of consumption by the farm population. By all indications, the benefits of this growth were rather evenly distributed and not concentrated in the hands of a small segment of rural society.

Underlying this growth was the rapid commercialization of the agricultural sector in the region and for that matter in many other parts of China. Beginning in the mid-to-late nineteenth century, developments in transportation and communications acted as powerful forces integrating China at both the national and international level. For farm households and handicraft producers alike, this ultimately meant access to new markets, both domestic and international, new sources of inputs, and new technologies; for the economy more generally, expanded opportunities for increasing specialization and exchange.

Over two hundred years ago, Adam Smith called attention to the returns to division of labor and specialization. Although the precise sources of output growth cannot be quantified, increased productivity in resource use resulting from increasing specialization no doubt play a prominent role. There are many evidences of this in the rural sector. In agriculture, farm households devoted an increasing percentage of their acreage to cotton and other cash crops in response to growing demand of the domestic manufacturing industry. In handicraft textiles, on the other hand, yarn imports and domestically manufactured yarn permitted households to do more weaving and to take advantage of the higher returns offered by new looms imported from Japan (and later manufactured domestically) and Europe. Rising real wages are just one reflection of the rising productivity.

What made much of this possible were relatively well-working product and factor markets. Many previous analyses have tended to view markets in rural China as highly uncompetitive and a source of exploitation. In the commercialized areas of rural China, this description now does not seem very fitting. Markets in land, land, and to a lesser extent capital enabled households to offset imbalances they faced in resource endowment and contributed to a high degree of efficiency in resource use, while product markets effectively conveyed to rural farm households the relative profitability of a host of farm and off-farm activities. Although the accelerated commercialization of agriculture introduced new uncertainties into the rural sector, in the long run this was more than offset by the gains that this redirection of economic activity toward the market offered.

Although increasing specialization and exchange was the source of much of the growth in agriculture during this period, it obviously could not be counted on as a continued source of growth. In the future, much of the increase in output would have to come through higher rates of capital formation, the introduction of new higher-yielding varieties, and the increased use of modern inputs such as commercial fertilizers. There is now concern that post-reform agriculture may be facing similar problems as it exhausts the returns to increasing specialization.

Yet, there are many indications that foundations were being laid (or already existed) for just this sort of growth. By the 1930s, more than 40 percent of all farm households in Central and East China were using commercial fertilizers; there was growing financial intermediation by Shanghai-based banks in rural areas that was beginning to provide farm households access to new sources of credit; and there was more than ten years of accumulated experimental work on new higher-yielding varieties of rice and other crops. It is a frequently forgotten fact that much of the seed improvement of the 1950s (a major contributing factor to increased output) was based on this earlier work.[2] With increased public investment in agriculture, an end to the political disruptions of the economy, and perhaps other modest reforms, agriculture as it existed in the 1930s probably could have been expected to achieve rates of growth comparable to, if not higher than, those found for the preceding forty years.

# Notes

### Chapter 1. Introduction

1. Although the reinstitution of the family as the basic decision-making unit in agriculture has been the hallmark of these reforms, equally important changes have taken place in marketing and pricing policies. Because they all occurred at once, it is very difficult to isolate the influence of any one change.

2. Between 1978 and 1984, agricultural output (in constant prices) increased at an annual rate of 7 percent. By all indications, output in the rural nonagricultural sector increased even faster. Although there are official survey data on rural incomes for this period, they involve a number of problems that prevent our estimating from them the rate of growth of real per capita incomes. These problems are discussed in Nicholas Lardy, "Consumption and Living Standards in China, 1978–1983," *China Quarterly* 100 (1984), pp. 849–65. Data on agricultural output are taken from *Chung-kuo t'ung-chi nien-chien* (Peking, 1985).

3. See, for example, Ho-fa Feng, ed. *Chung-kuo nung-tsun ching-chi tzu-liao* (Shanghai, 1935), 2 volumes; Han-seng Chen, *The Present Agrarian Problem in China* (Shanghai, 1933), and *Industrial Capital and Chinese Peasants: A Study of Chinese Tobacco Cultivation* (Shanghai, 1939); and Wen-chih Li and You-yi Chang, eds., *Chung-kuo chin-tai nung-yeh-shih tzu-liao*, 3 vols. (Beijing, 1957). Ramon Myers, *The Chinese Peasant Economy: Agricultural Development in Hopei and Shantung, 1890–1949* (Cambridge, 1970), provides an introduction and excellent summary of some of this literature. Myers himself takes a slightly more optimistic view about commercialization, but goes no further than to argue that it allowed the rural economy of North China to support an expansion in population at living standards equivalent to those of the 1880s and 1890s.

4. Many of the same views have been expressed in the context of nineteenth-century India. See, for example, Bipan Chandra, "Reinterpretation of 19th Century Indian Economic History," *Indian Economic and Social History Review* 5, 1 (March 1968), especially pp. 50–1.

5. Albert Feuerwerker, "Handicraft and Manufactured Cotton Textiles in China, 1871–1910," *Journal of Economic History* 30 (1970), pp. 338–78.

6. Dwight Perkins, *Agricultural Development in China, 1368–1968* (Chicago, 1969).

7. Seventy-five percent of the increase in cultivated area between 1893 and 1933 was in Manchuria.

8. R. H. Tawney, *Land and Labor in China* (London, 1932), p. 102.

9. G. B. Cressey, *China's Geographical Foundation* (New York, 1934).

10. See, for example, Han-sheng Chuan and Richard Kraus, *Mid-Ch'ing Rice Markets* (Cambridge, 1975), and Evelyn Rawksi, *Agricultural Change and the Peasant Economy of South China* (Cambridge, 1972).

11. Perkins, *Agricultural Development in China*, pp. 212, 236, and Appendixes C and D.

12. In light of the drop-off in rice shipments to southern markets, Chuan and Kraus, *Mid-Ch'ing Rice Markets*, actually suggest the possibility that the Yangtse was less commercialized in the 1920s and 1930s than it was two hundred years earlier.

13. As will be obvious throughout the course of the book, some of the observations and arguments that are made about Central and East China can be generalized to parts of other regions of the country as well.

14. Phillip C. C. Huang, *The Peasant Economy and Social Change in North China* (Stanford, 1985).

15. The Treaty of Nanking (1842), which concluded the Opium War, opened up Canton, Amoy, Foochow, Ningpo, and Shanghai to British trade, and further gave the British the right to live in these locations and carry on business. Fourteen more ports were opened under the Treaty of Tientsin (1858) and the Treaty of Peking (1860). By 1900, there were thirty-seven treaty ports; by 1913, fifty. The Treaty of Shiminoseki (1895) substantially expanded the rights of foreigners in the treaty ports and allowed them to invest in China and establish manufacturing enterprises. Official permission was also no longer required to import capital machinery.

16. The rise in Chinese cotton prices during the Civil War and the decline in silk prices in the 1930s are frequently cited examples. The analysis has not gone much further than this.

17. In both 1926 and 1927, for example, Shanghai was blockaded from Upper Yangtse ports. In general, however, the Yangtse region experienced fewer and less severe military and political disruptions than those in North China, though, as Thomas Rawski has pointed out, even the impact of such events in North China has been slightly exaggerated. Rawski, "China's Republican Economy: An Introduction" (University of Toronto-York University, Joint Centre on Modern East Asia, Discussion Paper # 1, 1978).

18. Although it was not necessarily true on a commodity-by-commodity basis, this continued growth of the domestic nonagricultural sector helped to offset the impact of declining international demand for Chinese agricultural goods during the early 1930s.

19. Thomas Rawski, "Economic Growth in Prewar China" (in press).

20. Friedrich Otto, "Sketch of Chinese Agricultural Policy," *Chinese Economic Journal* 2, 5 (May 1928), p. 369.

21. Other factors possibly contributing to growth in agricultural output in the pre–1949 era would be increases in cultivated area, more labor input, or even commercial fertilizers. In a 1935 survey carried out by the National Agricultural Resource Bureau, 36 percent of all households in the region

reported buying commercial fertilizers in the form of oil-cakes. No estimate was provided of the quantity.

22. Albert Feuerwerker, "Economic Trends," in *Cambridge History of China, Republican China, 1912–1949*, Part I (Cambridge, 1983).

23. The remarkably high degree of specialization and exchange that the Chinese economy had achieved explains why in the 1960s and 1970s the costs to the nation's rural sector of highly restrictive commercial policies, including local grain self-sufficiency, were so high. See Nicholas Lardy, *Agricultural Development in China* (Cambridge, 1983).

## Chapter 2. Chinese Agriculture and the International Economy

1. Imperial Maritime Customs, *Decennial Reports, 1882–1891* (Shanghai, 1924), p. 323.

2. Ibid.

3. S. Wells Williams, *The Chinese Commercial Guide*, 5th edition, 1863, cited in Lillian Li, *China's Silk Trade: Traditional Industry in the Modern World, 1842–1937* (Cambridge, 1981).

4. D. K. Liu, *The Silk Industry of China* (Shanghai, 1941), cited in Li, *China's Silk Trade*, p. 88.

5. T. R. Banister, "A History of the External Trade of China, 1834–1881," in Imperial Maritime Customs, *Decennial Reports, 1922–1931*, 2 vols. (Shanghai, 1933), vol. 1, pp. 77–8.

6. Between 1920 and 1928, these exports averaged slightly less than 500 million *yuan*. Over the same period, gross value of agricultural output (GVAO) averaged approximately 14.5 billion *yuan*. See Dwight Perkins, *Agricultural Development in China, 1368–1968* (Chicago, 1969), pp. 130 and 289. On the other hand, failure to recognize this fact has led some scholars to exaggerate the influence of foreign demand on the rural sector. Phillip Huang's *The Peasant Economy and Social Change in North China* (Stanford, 1985) is a case in point.

7. Thomas Rawski, "China's Republican Economy: An Introduction" (Joint Centre on Modern East Asia, University of Toronto-York University, Discussion Paper #1, 1978).

8. The timing differed slightly depending on the commodity.

9. According to one Chinese scholar, by the middle of the Ch'ing Dynasty (1644–1911), there were already more than 50,000 km. of commercial water routes in the interior and approximately 10,000 km. coastally. By comparison, total railroad mileage in all of China was only 16,287 km. in 1935, slightly less than half of which was in Manchuria. The two estimates come from Cheng-ming Wu, "Lun Ch'ing-tai chien-chi wo-kuo kuo-nei shih-chang," *Li-shih yen-chiu* 1 (1983), pp. 96–106, and Ch'in-yu Wang, *Chin-tai Chung-kuo ti tao-lu chien-she* (Hong Kong, 1969), pp. 73–138, and 84–93.

10. A. J. H. Latham and Larry Neal, "The International Market in Rice and Wheat, 1868–1914," *Economic History Review* 36 (May 1983), pp. 260–80.

11. Ibid., p. 272. Latham and Neal argue that rice and wheat were consumed together in India and other parts of Asia, but typically not elsewhere. Reflecting this, internal rice and wheat prices in India were highly correlated. As an exporter of both grains (rice to Monsoon Asia and wheat to Great Britain), India became the key link between the two international markets and was critical to the formation of the basic international market for food grains.

12. Estimates cannot be made prior to 1900 because data are not available on Indo-China's exports. In addition, Chinese Maritime Customs data do not include until 1889 rice imports into Kowloon, a major port of entry for rice from Hong Kong. Even after 1900, the data have their shortcomings because junks carried rice in and out of South China unrecorded by Maritime Customs. More will be said of this in Chapter 4.

13. Perkins, *Agricultural Development in China*, has estimated Kwangtung average rice production at 186.5 million *picul* for the period between 1914 and 1918 and 1931 and 1937. Imports into Kwangtung, on the other hand, averaged slightly less than 6 million *picul* between 1900 and 1910, or approximately 3 percent.

14. Between 1890 and 1899, some 53 million out of total rice imports of 66 million entered through Kowloon. Rice import figures were taken from Liang-lin Hsiao, *China's Foreign Trade Statistics, 1864–1949* (Cambridge, 1974), pp. 32–3. Data on imports into Kowloon were obtained from Imperial Maritime Customs, *Returns of Trade and Trade Reports*, for Kowloon for those years.

15. Kowloon handled only sailing vessels and declined in importance as the steamer became the preferred means of shipping rice from Hong Kong to Canton.

16. In this regard, Latham and Neal follow the suggestion of Donald McCloskey and Richard Zecher, "How the Gold Standard Worked, 1880–1913," in *The Monetary Approach to the Balance of Payments*, ed. Jacob Frankel and Harry Johnson (Toronto, 1976). The average correlation coefficient between prices in the United States, the United Kingdom, France, and Germany, the four major participants in the North Atlantic wheat market, was 0.83.

17. Some uncertainty exists because most imported rice first passed through Hong Kong, an entrepôt for the trade with South China, but no trade statistics exist for Hong Kong, so the country of origin of this rice is unknown. Maritime Customs reports for these years, however, typically list rice imported into South China as Siamese or French-Indochinese in origin.

18. Annual rice prices for the years 1896–1927, based on these reports, were published in *She-hui yueh-kan*, (February 1929). Annual prices for the years between 1870–95 were later computed by Ta-fan Tsou. In both cases, the authors converted the original prices (given in *taels*) into Chinese

silver dollars per *shih*. I have subsequently converted the prices into Hai-kwan *Tael* (HKT) per cwt. The Chinese silver dollar, or *yuan*, was equal to 0.6218 HKT. Data on the exchange rate between the HKT and the British pound were obtained from Hsiao, *China's Foreign Trade Statistics*, pp. 190–2.

19. Several reasons are cited for this change: first, a shift in the Yellow River rendered the upper portion of the Grand Canal useless; second, the occupation of Soochow by the Taiping rebels between 1860 and 1863 and its ultimate devastation by the imperial army; and third, the introduction of steamships, which made the port of Soochow all but obsolete because it could not accommodate them. On the decline of Soochow, see Linda Cooke Johnson, "The Decline of Soochow and Rise of Shanghai: A Study in the Economic Morphology of Urban Change, 1756–1894," (Ph.D. Dissertation, University of California, Santa Cruz, 1986).

20. Hsi-an K'ung, "Chung-kuo liu-ta-shi ti jen-k'ou chi ch'i tseng chien," in *Chung-kuo li-tai jen-k'ou wen-t'i lun-chi* (Hong Kong, 1965), pp. 209–17.

21. This estimate is based on an examination of the trade reports for these treaty ports. See Imperial Maritime Customs, *Returns of Trade and Trade Reports*, for these years.

22. Latham and Neal, "The International Market in Rice and Wheat," p. 287.

23. Charles Robequain, *The Economic Development of French-Indochina* (London, 1944), p. 220.

24. James Ingram, *Economic Change in Thailand Since 1850* (Stanford, 1955), and "Thailand's Rice Trade and the Allocation of Resources," in *The Economic Development of Southeast Asia*, ed., C. D. Cowan (London, 1970), p. 109.

25. I have not been able to find annual data on the costs of shipping rice from Monsoon Asia to China, but a time series for the costs of shipping rice from Burma to continental Europe between 1869 and 1914 reflect a decline of about two-thirds, from approximately £3.00 per metric ton to slightly below £1.00. These data appeared in E. A. V. Angier, *Fifty Years Freight, 1869–1914* (London, 1920). A second index that appeared in John S. McGee, "Ocean Freight Rate Conferences," in *The Economic Value of the U.S. Merchant Marine* (Evanston, 1961), and which drew on later work by Angier, implies that in the 1920s and 1930s freight rates may have fallen to between one-half and one-third of their level immediately preceding the war.

26. Imperial Maritime Customs, *Returns of Trade and Trade Reports: Wuhu Trade Report for 1893*, p. 169.

27. Imperial Maritime Customs, *Returns of Trade and Trade Reports: Wuhu Trade Report for 1897*, pp. 184–5.

28. The relative efficiency of water transport is made obvious in a comparison of alternative transportation costs undertaken in the mid–1930s by the Ministry of Industry:

| Form of Transport | Cost (Yuan/ton-km.) |
|---|---|
| Pack animal | 0.20–0.35 |
| Human porter | 0.20–0.35 |
| Cart | 0.05–0.17 |
| Junk | 0.02–0.13 |
| Steamship | 0.02–0.16 |
| Railroad | 0.02 |

Source: Bureau of Roads, Ministry of Communications, *Chung-kuo ti kung-lu* (Nanking, 1936), Table 15.

29. Imperial Maritime Customs, *Report of Trade*, 1931, p. 51.

30. Rice shipments out of Changsha's Maritime Customs, for example, were prohibited for major parts of every year between 1928 and 1932. The fact that the correlation coefficient between Changsha and Shanghai is still relatively high may, on the other hand, just signify how easily official restrictions could be circumvented.

31. Although I am primarily interested in establishing the fact that there was a highly integrated regional market, numerous other factors indicate there was also a national grain market. First, the correlation coefficient between monthly prices in Shanghai and an index of monthly wholesale prices for Canton during the period between 1927 and 1937 is 0.87. The correlation between annual rice prices for the same period is 0.83. Second, a high degree of correlation exists between prices in Shanghai and Tientsin. For the years between 1913 and 1933, the correlation coefficient between the retail price of rice in Shanghai and the wholesale price in Tientsin is 0.90. For monthly price data between 1928 and 1932, the correlation coefficient is between 0.81 and 0.96, depending on the variety of rice. Finally, annual rice and wheat prices in Shanghai and Tientsin are correlated (0.72), as are rice and wheat prices in each market (0.75 in Shanghai and 0.86 in Tientsin). The price data for Canton come from Shou-ch'u Ching, *Kuang-chou chih mi-yeh* (Canton, 1938), p. 69; and for Tientsin, from Nankai Institute of Economics, *Nankai Index Numbers, 1935*, pp. 9–11.

32. Here I differ with Chuan and Kraus, who have suggested that the Yangtse rice market was no more integrated in the early twentieth century than it was two hundred years earlier. They have based this claim on a comparison of the coefficient of variation of monthly rice prices for the two periods 1713–19 and 1913–19. The better integrated the market, the smaller the price fluctuations and, therefore, the smaller the coefficient of variation would be. Aside from certain methodological problems that arise because they are missing twenty-seven out of eighty-four observations for the earlier period, it is unlikely that external factors played the same role in price formation in the early eighteenth century as they did in the early twentieth. In the latter period, rice prices were affected by developments in the international rice market as well as by changes in the gold price of silver. Moreover, during World War I, the month-to-month variability in silver prices was three times as great as it was in either the immediate pre- or

post-war period. More will be said of this in Chapter 3, which takes up the question of price formation.

33. In the *Decennial Reports, 1902–1911*, p. 308, the commissioner of the Wuhu treaty port remarked: "Conditions of trade seem to have altered, and for this improved telegraphic facilities are no doubt partly responsible. Instead of sending off promiscuous shipments, which often entailed losses, merchants now keep in touch with the markets and arrange their shipments accordingly." The parallels with the quotes at the beginning of this chapter are obvious. Between 1912 and 1935, the number of telegraph offices in China increased from 565 to 1,346. Data on the development of China's telegraph system are taken from Yu-ching Wen, "Electrical Communications," in *The Chinese Yearbook, 1936–1937* (Shanghai, 1936), p. 1086.

34. The expansion in warehousing and the rapid growth of the modern banking sector were not unrelated. Like their predecessors, the *ch'ien-chuang*, the modern banks discounted bills of exchange and extended short-term credits to commercial and industrial enterprises on the security of physical commodities that were actually deposited in warehouses owned by the banks.

35. This description is a "stylized" view of long-run price formation in China. In the shorter run, there were obviously feedbacks from the interior to the treaty ports and lags with which changes in the treaty ports would be reflected in interior markets. The data at our disposal are not rich enough to sort these out.

36. A study done under the Ministry of Finance in 1932 estimates these costs and shows that they were generally consistent with the differentials that appear between the price series graphed in Figure 2.1. The costs from Changsha were 4.07 *yuan*, from Kiukiang (just north of Nanchang on the Yangtse) 2.95 *yuan*, and from Wuhu 2.66 *yuan*. Presumably these are costs per *shih*. The table below breaks down these costs. Taxes constituted approximately 40 percent of these costs and provided suppliers with good reason to look for outlets other than through Maritime Customs.

| Cost | Changsha | | Kiukiang | | Wuhu | |
|---|---|---|---|---|---|---|
| Transport | 0.970 | *yuan* | 0.691 | *yuan* | 0.450 | *yuan* |
| Middlemen fees | 0.380 | | 0.390 | | 0.260 | |
| Packing | 0.480 | | 0.430 | | 0.480 | |
| Taxes | 1.803 | | 1.100 | | 1.053 | |
| | 0.300 | | 0.200 | | 0.200 | |
| Warehouse costs | 0.037 | | 0.037 | | 0.035 | |
| Miscellaneous | 0.100 | | 0.100 | | 0.180 | |
| Total costs | 4.070 | *yuan* | 2.948 | *yuan* | 2.658 | *yuan* |

*Source:* "Chung-kuo chin-tai mi-yu mao-yi chia-ke tzu-liao," *Chia-ke li-lun yu shih-chien* (February 1982), p. 48. I would like to thank Barbara Sands for calling my attention to these data.

37. This relationship between prices would have also been upset after 1936 with the completion of the Changsha-Canton Railroad, which allowed rice to be shipped directly to Kwangtung from Hunan rather than down

the Yangtse and then coastally. According to one source, Ching, *Kuang-chou mi-yeh*, p. 8, these shipments totaled 2.5 million *picul* in 1937.

38. These data appeared in Lu-luan Chang, "Chiang-su Wu-chin wu-chia chih yen-chiu," *Chin-lu hsueh-pao* 3 (May 1933), pp. 153–216, and were obtained from six market towns in southeastern Wuchin *hsien*. Like the Shanghai series, they appear to be of exceptional quality, a feature that may help explain why they are so supportive of my results. Although it is always easy to point to the quality of data when undesirable results obtain, there may some validity to the argument in this study because I do not always know how the data were gathered.

39. For the logic and assumptions behind this test, see Vernon Ruttan, "Agricultural Product and Factor Markets in Southeast Asia," *Economic Development and Cultural Change* (July 1969), pp. 501–20.

40. When regressions were run for the entire period, 95-percent confidence intervals just failed to include the critical value of 1, implying that the slope coefficients were statistically different from 1. In 1926–7, however, for reasons to be detailed later, markets in the Lower Yangtse were seriously disrupted. When the model is reestimated with dummies for these two years, we accept the hypothesis that the slope coefficient is equal to 1.

41. There actually appears to have been a slight rise in the margin, but, given the secular rise in prices over this period, a slight rise in marketing margins to reflect an increase in costs would not be unexpected.

42. Cheng Wu, *Wan-chung tao-mi ch'an-hsiao tiao-ch'a* (Shanghai, 1936). Other studies that complement this one include: *Shang-hai mi-shih tiao-ch'a*, *Nan-ching liang-shih tiao-ch'a*, and *Tsung-chiang mi-shih tiao-ch'a*, all three of which were carried out by the Institute of Social and Economic Research in Shanghai and published in either 1935 or 1936.

43. Unlike the price data for Wuchin, no explicit mention is made of the source of these data.

44. R. H. Tawney, *Land and Labor in China* (London, 1932), p. 56.

45. Albert Feuerwerker, *The Chinese Economy, 1912–1949* (Ann Arbor, 1968). p. 39.

46. The core areas were usually river valley lowlands or fertile plains with well-developed networks of traditional transport, communication, and marketing. They could also usually be identified by their higher population density, greater urbanization, and higher levels of commercialization. By comparison, the peripheral areas were isolated, with higher transport costs. This made the level of commercialization lower, economic opportunities fewer, and incomes probably lower than in core areas.

47. Albert Feuerwerker, "Economic Trends, 1912–1949," in *Cambridge History of China, Republican China, 1912–1949*, Part I (Cambridge, 1983), p. 89.

48. Rowe's discussion of the structure of the tea trade in Hankow and Hupei appears in *Hankow: Commerce and Society in a Chinese City, 1796–1889* (Stanford, 1984), especially pp. 180–95.

49. This would include having the rice milled by one of the local mills or milling it themselves using the old-style mills.

50. Ramon Myers, *The Chinese Economy: Past and Present* (Belmont, 1980), p. 94.

51. Correlation coefficients again offer empirical support for this hypothesis. In the case of cotton, for example, for the period between 1900 and 1936 the price of China's cotton exports (expressed in dollars) is highly correlated with that for the United States (0.941), as is the price of raw cotton in Tientsin (0.952) for the shorter period between 1913 and 1936. The price in Tientsin and the price of China's cotton exports are also highly correlated (0.959). Over this period, the United States was a leading world exporter of cotton, sending out an average one-and three-quarter million metric tons a year.

52. On the marketing structure for cotton, see H. D. Fong, *Terminal Marketing of Tientsin Cotton* (Tientsin, 1935), and *Yu-O-Wan-Kan ssu-sheng chih mian-chan yun-hsiao* (Nanking, 1937). Both studies suggest a competitive market structure.

53. See, for example, Po-chuang Ch'en, *Hsiao-mai chi mien-fen* (Shanghai, 1936).

## Chapter 3. Price Formation, Marketing, and Output in Agriculture

1. The estimates that follow are based on data in China's Maritime Customs *Returns of Trade and Trade Reports*.

2. See, for example, Friedrich Otto, "Correlation of Harvests with Importations of Cereals in China," *Chinese Economic Journal* 15, 4 (1934), pp. 388–414. Dwight Perkins suggests something very similar when he argues that imports rather than domestic resources fed almost all of the increase in China's urban population in the early twentieth century, a point that I will take issue with later on. See Perkins, *Agricultural Development in China, 1368–1968* (Chicago, 1969), especially pp. 154–5.

3. Perkins, *Agricultural Development in China*, p. 212.

4. The role of import and export points is analogous to that of gold points under the gold standard. Under this system, gold points reflect the allowable differences that can exist in gold prices between countries before it becomes profitable to ship gold between the two. These differences are themselves just a reflection of transportation and other costs of transferring gold, including its opportunity costs.

5. Some scholars might argue that the mere possibility of such flows suffices to return prices back to unprofitable levels of divergence.

6. Actually, even if the system were to work perfectly, one price would not prevail simultaneously in every market. Rather, differences less than the import and export point would be allowed. It is only when the import and export points are too wide that prices can move within wide limits quite independently of each other. With their narrowing, the mutual independence associated with market integration quickly asserts itself.

7. Most of the following paragraph is based on M. K. Bennett and V. K. Wickizer, *The Rice Economy of Monsoon Asia* (Stanford, 1941).

8. According to Wilfred Malenbaum, *The World Wheat Economy* (Cambridge, 1953), in the 1930s world wheat exports averaged 550 to 600 million bushel, of which China absorbed approximately 3 percent.

9. These policies are discussed in James Ingram, *Economic Change in Thailand Since 1850* (Stanford, 1955), and Charles Robequain, *The Economic Development of French-Indochina* (London, 1944).

10. This point is developed more fully below.

11. Until now, I have implicitly assumed that all prices were expressed in a common currency.

12. The equivalency of the HKT in terms of the other local *taels* in wide use are reported below. In general, arbitrage ensured that the actual rates of exchange between these various *taels* never deviated far from the rate given by their silver content.

> 1 HKT = 1.1140 Shanghai *Tael*
> = 1.1900 Canton *Tael*
> = 1.0875 Hankow *Tael*
> = 1.0555 Tientsin *Tael*
> = 1.0436 Kiukiang *Tael*
>
> Source: Hsiao, *China's Foreign Trade Statistics, 1864–1949* (Cambridge, 1974), p. 16.

13. For the best discussion on China's banking and financial system, see Frank Tamagna, *Banking and Finance in China* (New York, 1942).

14. Through April 1933, exchange rates on London, New York, Paris, Hamburg, Java, and Bombay were quoted in their respective currencies per *tael* or 100 *taels*; and those on Hong Kong, Singapore, and Yokohama were in *taels* per 100 units of foreign currency. Thereafter, they were all quoted per 100 Chinese *yuan*.

15. Late 1934 and early 1935 is an exception. The reasons are explained in Loren Brandt and Thomas J. Sargent, "Interpreting New Evidence about China and U.S. Silver Purchases," *Journal of Monetary Economics* (in press).

16. For a discussion of this, see A. J. H. Latham, *The International Economy and the Underdeveloped World, 1865–1914* (London, 1978).

17. Yu-kwei Cheng, *Foreign Trade and Industrial Development in China* (Washington, D.C., 1956).

18. Estimates of China's demand for silver coinage and of world silver production and sales by governments were compiled by Wei-ying Lin, *China under Depreciated Silver, 1926–1931* (Shanghai, 1935).

19. Institute of Social and Economic Research, *Shang-hai mi-shih tiao-ch'a* (Shanghai, 1935).

20. To make a point worth repeating, in more isolated areas not served by water or rail transport, price formation tended to remain as before: a function of local demand and supply.

21. See P'ei-kang Chang, *Kuang-si liang-shih wen-ti* (Changsha, 1938).

22. Perkins, *Agricultural Development in China*, pp. 292–5.

23. Household survey data for Shanghai for the 1930s show that all but 7 percent of grain consumption was rice. The same was probably true for

other cities in the Yangtse. See *Shang-hai shih kung-ren cheng-huo cheng-t'u* (Shanghai, 1934), pp. 26–29.

24. The estimated surplus of these three provinces was between 24 and 30 million *picul*. These estimates are contained in Appendix A of Loren Brandt, "Population Growth, Agricultural Change, and Economic Integration in Central and Eastern China, 1890s–1930s" (Ph.D. Dissertation, University of Illinois, 1983).

25. This view is expressed by Perkins, *Agricultural Development in China*, pp. 98–101. Moreover, in a sampling of farm households carried out in 1912 by the National Agricultural Research Bureau (NARB), 23 percent of farm families were found to be part-owners and 28 percent tenants. By comparison, the average in NARB surveys carried out between 1931–7 was 24 percent and 31 percent, respectively, or too small of an increase to argue with any confidence that tenancy was rising. These data are discussed in more detail in Chapter 6.

26. Ching-chih Sun, *Hua-tung ti-ch'u ching-chi ti-li* (Peking, 1959), pp. 405–6.

27. John L. Buck, *Land Utilization in China: Statistical Volume* (Chicago, 1937), Table 8, p. 296.

28. Tao-fu Hsu, *Chung-kuo chin-tai nung-yeh sheng-ch'an chi mao-yi t'ung-chi tzu-liao* (Shanghai, 1983).

29. Buck, *Land Utilization in China* (Chicago, 1937), p. 217.

30. Naosuke Takamura, *Kindai Nihon mengyō to Chūgoku* (Tokyo, 1982), p. 98.

31. Between 1927 and 1936, net yarn exports averaged a quarter of a million *picul*. See Liang-lin Hsiao, *China's Foreign Trade Statistics, 1864–1949* (Cambridge, 1974), pp. 38–9 and 86.

32. Richard Kraus, "Cotton and Cotton Goods in China, 1918–1936" (Ph.D. Dissertation, Harvard University, 1968).

33. Cheng-ming Wu, *Chung-kuo tzu-pen chu-yi yu kuo-nei shih-chang* (Peking, 1985), p. 110.

34. Albert Feuerwerker, "Handicraft and Manufactured Cotton Textiles in China, 1871–1910," *Journal of Economic History* 30, 2 (1970), pp. 338–78. Feuerwerker discounted the possibility that output may have been as high as 8 million because it would imply too high a level of output for the late 1920s given Buck's data on the growth of cotton acreage and the Cotton Manufacturers' Association's estimates on cotton output for the 1930s. Whereas the association's estimates now appear too low, 8 million may not be out of line after all.

35. These would include estimates by Perkins, *Agricultural Development in China*, p. 283; T. C. Liu and K. C. Yeh, *The Economy of the Chinese Mainland: National Income and Economic Development, 1933–1959* (Princeton, 1965), p. 135; and Kang Chao, *The Development of Cotton Textile Production in China* (Cambridge, 1977), p. 224.

36. Data compiled by Richard Kraus show no decline in yields between 1918 and 1936. See "Cotton and Cotton Goods in China, 1918–1936."

37. This is more than twice the level suggested by Buck's data on

marketing. His underestimation of the percentage of cotton marketed arises from the fact that he simply took an arithmetical average of the marketing rates in the localities surveyed to calculate national (regional) rates. The data reveal, however, a positive correlation between the percentage of cotton output marketed in each *hsien* and the percentage of cultivated acreage that was planted. He should have taken a weighted average of the form:

$$\Sigma \%_i * Q_i / \Sigma Q_i$$

where $\%_i$ is the percentage of the crop output marketed in *hsien* i and $Q_i$ is the output of that crop in the same *hsien*. Some appreciation of the bias can be obtained by examining Buck's data on cotton marketed in the Yangtse. Several *hsien* that devoted less than 1 percent of acreage to the crop were included in the average. If we recompute the average, omitting these observations, the percentage of cotton marketed would increase from 45 percent to 60 percent, an increase of approximately a third.

38. This would have consisted of overseas cotton imports of approximately 1 million *picul* and an additional 3 million *picul* to accommodate the demand for alternative uses, including handicraft spinning.

39. Shang-hai shih mien-fang chih-kung-yeh tung-yeh kung-hui ch'ou-pei-hui, *Chung-kuo mien-fang t'ung-chi shih-liao* (Shanghai, 1950), pp. 1–3. It should be pointed out that a slightly higher percentage earlier in the period would bias the estimated increase in the industry's demand for cotton by several hundred thousand *picul* at most.

40. This is discussed in David Faure, "Export and the Chinese Farmer: The Rural Economy of Kiangsu and Kwangtung, 1870–1937" (unpublished, 1987). Information on the landholdings of land reclamation companies in the early thirties in Kiangsu can be found in Ministry of Industry, *Chung-kuo shih-yeh chih: Chiang-su sheng* (Shanghai, 1933), pp. 231–2.

41. The growth between 1914–16 and 1931–3 was 43.1 percent, the same percentage growth implied by Buck's data for the years 1914–19 and 1930–33.

42. These data are contained in Chiao-t'ung pu yu-cheng tsung-chu, *Chung-kuo t'ung-yu ti-fang wu-chan-chi* (Shanghai, 1937), in the sections on marketing for the three provinces.

43. I have used the term minimum because I have excluded various alternative demands for cotton from my calculations.

44. *The China Weekly Review*, February 16, 1935, pp. 404–5. I would like to thank Tim Wright for this citation.

45. Imperial Maritime Customs, *Report of Trade, 1929*, p. 33.

46. Imperial Maritime Customs, *Report of Trade, 1932*, p. 44.

47. Nan-kai ta-hsueh ching-chi yen-chiu suo pien, *Nan-kai chih-shu tzu-liao hui-pien* (Peking, 1958), pp. 97–8.

48. U.S. Bureau of the Census, *The Statistical History of the United States from Colonial Times to the Present* (New York, 1965), p. 546.

49. Indian data are for fiscal years beginning on July 1 of the correspond-

ing calendar year; fiscal year 1927, for example, begins on July 1, 1927, and runs through June 30, 1928.

50. Po-chuang Ch'en's *Hsiao-mai chi mien-fen* (Shanghai, 1936) provides a description of price formation in the wheat market almost identical to the one provided for the rice and cotton markets.

## Chapter 4. The Accelerated Commercialization of Agriculture

1. The commercialization of Chinese agriculture is documented in Wen-chih Li and You-yi Chang, eds., *Chung-kuo chin-tai nung-yeh-shih tzu-liao*, 3 vols. (Peking, 1957). The volumes compile original source materials on agriculture between 1840 and 1949. Their outlook and tone, however, is pessimistic. They view the era's rapid commercialization of agriculture as one source of the increasing impoverization that supposedly marked the period. Ramon Myers's "The Commercialization of Agriculture in Modern China," in *Economic Organization in Chinese Society*, ed. W. E. Willmott (Stanford, 1972), provides an excellent, slightly more optimistic description of the commercialization process.

2. See, for example, Phillip C. C. Huang, *The Peasant Economy and Social Change in North China* (Stanford, 1985); Ramon Myers, *The Chinese Peasant Economy: Agricultural Development in Hopei and Shantung, 1890–1949* (Cambridge, 1970); and Ernest P. Liang, *China: Railways and Agricultural Development, 1875–1935* (Chicago: University of Chicago, Department of Geography, Research Paper No. 203, 1982).

3. Liang, *Railways and Agricultural Development*, p. 11.

4. In addition, the introduction in the 1880s and 1890s of the steam launch, which took junks in its tow, made traditional transport more cost-effective. See, for example, the discussion in the *Decennial Report* for 1892–1901 in the section on Nanking. Yet, as Note 28 of Chapter 2 suggests, the steamship may not have reduced shipping costs (*yuan*/per ton) directly so much as it reduced the time it took to ship goods. In reducing the time, of course, the steamship may very well have reduced transactions costs.

5. Between 1920 and 1928, exports of agicultural and processed agricultural products from all of China averaged less than 500 million *yuan* in 1933 prices. The total value of agricultural output also in 1933 prices was in the vicinity of 15 billion *yuan*. See Dwight Perkins, *Agricultural Development in China, 1368–1968* (Chicago, 1969), pp. 130 and 289.

6. This assessment is based on a detailed examination of Maritime Customs grain trade data. Although overseas rice and wheat imports into Shanghai and the Lower Yangtse increased in the 1920s and 1930s, they were more than offset by rice and flour exports to other parts of China.

7. G. William Skinner, "Regional Urbanization in Nineteenth Century China," in *The City in Late Imperial China*, ed. G. William Skinner (Stanford, 1977).

8. Alternative definitions of urban central places yield very similar estimates.

9. The population of the Middle Yangtse as a whole was 75 million in the early 1890s and that for just Hupei, Hunan, and Kiangsi was 65 million. Almost 70 percent of the population of Kiangsu, Chekiang, and Anhwei lived within the Lower Yangtse. The urbanization rate in those parts of Kiangsu, Chekiang, and Anhwei falling outside the Lower Yangtse probably did not exceed 6 percent.

10. *Chung-kuo t'ung-chi nien-chien, 1984* (Peking, 1985), p. 81.

11. Kam Wing Chan and Xueqiang Xu, "Urban Population Growth and Urbanization in China since 1949: Reconstructing a Baseline," *China Quarterly* 104 (December 1985), p. 592.

12. Provincial estimates for 1953 are taken from R. J. R. Kirkby, *Urbanisation in China: Town and Country in a Developing Economy, 1949–2000* (London, 1985), pp. 262–3.

13. Annual estimates appear in *Chung-kuo t'ung-chi nien-chien, 1984*, p. 81.

14. One set of estimates shows that, between 1936 and 1949, total output expressed in 1936 prices declined by 39 percent, and in industry alone by almost a half. These estimates are in Yu-ruo Wang, "Lun liang-tz'u shih-chieh ta-chan chih-chien Chung-kuo ching-chi te fa-chan," *Chung-kuo ching-chi yen-chiu*, February 1987, pp. 97–110.

15. Perkins, *Agricultural Development in China*, pp. 290–296. Additional urbanization data for several provinces in the region are included in Kuo-ch'i Li, "Yu Su Che liang-Hu Ssu-ch'uan chi Min Yueh chi-sheng tou-shih ren-kou chuang-t'ai lun Ch'ing-wei min-ch'u wo-kuo nan-fang ch'e sheng te tou-shih-hua hsian-hsiang," in Kuo-chi han-hsueh hui-yi lun-wen chi, *Li-shih k'ao-ku tsu*, pp. 1505–40.

16. Kirkby, *Urbanisation in China*, p. 150.

17. The basic data are those of Hsin-yi Chang, *Chung-kuo nung-yeh k'ai-kuang chan-chi*, cited in Pao-san Wu, *Chung-kuo kuo-min so-te, 1933-nien* (Shanghai, 1947), vol. 1, p. 151, with additional data for Kwangsi, Chinghai, and Sikang provided by Wu.

18. T. C. Liu and K. C. Yeh, *The Economy of the Chinese Mainland* (Princeton, 1965), pp. 102–3.

19. For fifteen localities that Buck surveyed in the region, the average farm size (measured in cropping area) declined by only 8 percent between 1890 and 1930, from 0.88 hectares to 0.81. For these fifteen localities plus six more, average farm size declined by less than 5 percent between 1910 and 1930. By comparison, population increased by 26.3 percent between 1893 and 1933. Buck's data appear in *Land Utilization in China: Statistical Volume* (Chicago, 1937), p. 288. The population estimates are by Perkins, *Agricultural Development in China*, p. 212.

20. For example, if grain consumption by the nonagricultural population were 20 percent lower, the percentage increase would have been 7.5 percent rather than 8.4 percent. Data on per capita grain consumption

by the nonagricultural population are very limited, but one cannot rule out the possibility that they consumed less grain per capita. In a 1929–30 survey of 305 working-class households living in Shanghai, for example, annual grain consumption per adult male equivalent was 4.15 *picul*, or slightly more than a *catty* a day, all but 7 percent of which was rice. By comparison, Buck's nutritional survey data for the farming population imply an average consumption per adult male equivalent of 5.5 *picul*. The Shanghai data can be found in Shang-hai shih cheng-fu she-hui chu, *Shang-hai shih kung-ren sheng-huo cheng-t'u* (Shanghai, 1934), pp. 26–29. Additional information on urban consumption can be found in Bureau of Statistics, Ministry of Industry, *Wu-hsi kung-ren sheng-huo-fei chi ch'i chih-shu* (Nanking, 1935), and C. C. Chang, *China's Food Problem* (Shanghai, 1931), vol. 8.

21. This estimate is based on provincial data for the years 1914–16 and 1918 and 1931–7 relating to acreage in major grains and six cash crops: soybeans, peanuts, sesame, rapeseed, tobacco, and cotton. The data for Hupei and Hunan have not been used because of problems with the grain figures for the earlier years. For the other four provinces, acreage in cash crops more than doubled. Measured as a percentage of the combined acreage in grains and cash crops, cash-crop acreage increased roughly 7 percent. At yield and price levels for the 1930s, output per *mou* of cash-crop production was typically higher than that for grains, which suggests that the share of cash crops in the total value of agricultural output increased by slightly more than the acreage figures suggest. By comparison, Perkins's aggregate data show an increase of 4.4 percent between 1914–18 and 1931–6.

22. The lower marketing ratio for the 1890s was suggested by the experience of cotton and my view that self-processing declined. This point is elaborated below.

23. Calculations in Chapter 5 suggest that agricultural output may have increased by as much as 50 to 60 percent over this period. Under these circumstances, an increase in marketed surplus from 23.5 percent to 39.8 percent of total agricultural output would imply almost a tripling of market surplus measured in absolute terms, or annual increases of 2.5 percent.

24. There were other reasons for grain sales. Some farm households engaged in grain arbitrage to increase caloric intake. This might entail selling wheat to buy sorghum or potatoes, which offered more calories per *yuan*. Some farm households may have had to sell grain immediately after the harvest to repay debts, only to have to buy grain to eat later in the year. Despite much discussion of the second situation, I have not found much evidence of it in farm survey data.

25. Buck's data are for the percentage of calories from grain purchased on the market. Because calories per kilogram of the various types of grain were very similar, a similar percentage would apply to consumption in physical terms.

26. Applying this same method of estimation to the whole of China and

including in the calculations the contribution of grain imports gives estimates of market surplus and marketed output of roughly 33 percent and
43 percent, respectively.

27. Calculated on the basis of data in Tables 5, 9, 10, and 16 in Po-chuang
Ch'en, *Ping-han yan-hsien nung-tsun ching-chi tiao-ch'a* (Shanghai, 1937).

28. John L. Buck, *Chinese Farm Economy: A Study of 2,866 Farms* (Chicago, 1930), p. 199.

29. Hui-sun T'ang et al., *Chung-kuo nung-chia ching-chi chih chi-chang
te yen-chiu* (Nanking, 1936), p. 436.

30. Calculated from figures in Thomas Rawski, "Economic Growth in
Prewar China" (in press).

31. John Chang, *Industrial Development in Pre-Communist China* (Chicago, 1969), p. 71.

32. Ibid., p. 76.

33. The concept of core areas was briefly discussed in Note 46 of Chapter 2.

34. Thomas Rawski, "The Economy of the Yangtse Region, 1850–1980"
(paper presented at the conference on Spatial and Temporal Trends and
Cycles in Chinese Economic History, Bellagio, Italy; Toronto, 1984), p. 32.

35. Between 1891 and 1895, the output of agriculture, forestry, and fish-
ing constituted approximately 40 percent of Japanese GDP; that of manufacturing, mining, and construction plus facilitating industry 13 percent;
and the remainder was commerce and services. In the early 1890s, Japan
had a population of 40 million, roughly the same as that of the Lower
Yangtse core in the 1930s. Data on the composition of output and population
in Japan were taken from Kazushi Ohkawa and Miyohe Shinohawa, eds.,
*Patterns of Japanese Economic Development: A Quantitative Appraisal* (New
Haven, 1979), Table A12, pp. 278–9 and 392–3.

36. Stephen Hymer and Stephen Resnick, "A Model of an Agrarian Economy with Nonagricultural Activities," *American Economic Review* 59
(March 1969), pp. 493–506.

37. On this point, see Donald McCloskey and Richard Zecher, "How the
Gold Standard Worked, 1880–1913," in *The Monetary Approach to the Balance of Payments*, ed. Jacob Frenkel and H. G. Johnson (Toronto, 1976).
Arbitrage in related markets, for example, would have tied prices for some
of the coarser grains like sorghum or millet to the price for wheat.

38. U.S. Bureau of the Census, *The Statistical History of the United States
from Colonial Times to the Present* (New York, 1965), Series E 15, pp.
116–17.

39. These data have been compiled in *Nan-kai chi-shu tzu-liao hui-pien,
1913–1952* (Peking, 1958).

40. A brief discussion in the appendix at the end of this chapter outlines
the construction and shortcomings of the index in more detail.

41. Agricultural price indices for Wuchin, Kiangsu province, for the years
between 1910 and 1932, and an index for Szechwan for 1910–34 suggest as
much. These can be found in Lu-luan Chang, "Chiang-su Wu-chin wu-chia
chih yen-chiu," *Chin-lu hsueh-pao* 3 (May 1933), and Lien Wang, "Farm

Prices in Szechwan, 1910–1934," *Economic Facts* 9 (October 1938), pp. 416–17.

42. Between 1931 and 1935, the price of silver doubled, from £0.0609 per troy ounce to £0.1208 in England and from $0.2954 to $0.5923 in the United States.

43. The Nankai index shows wholesale agricultural prices falling from 106.82 in 1930 (1926 = 100) to 64.26 in 1934, while the Shanghai index fell from 113.2 to 77.4 over the same period. The latter index can be found in *Shang-hai chieh-fang ch'ien-hou wu-chia tzu-liao hui-pien* (Shanghai, 1958), p. 135.

44. The latter can also include the price of processed agricultural goods.

45. See, for example, Tse-yi P'eng, "Ch'ing-tai ch'ien-chi shou-kung-yeh te fa-chan," *Chung-kuo shih yen-chiu* 1 (January 1981), pp. 43–60, and Cheng-ming Wu, "Lun Ch'ing-tai chien-chi wo-kuo kuo-nei shih-chang," *Li-shih yen-chiu* (January 1983), pp. 96–106. Both authors have based their interpretations on estimates of the volume of interregional commodity circulation. After declining in the pre-Taiping years, this trade took off again and soon surpassed earlier levels. William Rowe in his book on Hankow offers additional support for this view of a nationally integrated commercial economy.

46. According to one estimate, approximately 2.5 million *picul* of cotton, or a quarter of total output, entered into interregional trade in China prior to the Opium War. See Cheng-ming Wu, "Wo-kuo pan chih min-ti pan feng-chien kuo-nei shih-chang," *Li-shih yen-chiu* (February 1984), pp. 110–21.

47. These percentages are based on estimates provided in Table 5.11.

48. Wu, "Wo-kuo pan chih min-ti pan feng-chien kuo-nei shih-chang."

49. Its construction is also discussed in the appendix to this chapter.

50. Although for the years that my indices overlap with the Nankai series the behavior of the two series is very similar, my series actually imply a more serious deterioration in the terms of trade during World War I. With the exception of 1919, the Nankai series suggests only a modest decline in agriculture's terms of trade over this period.

51. Price indices for agricultural and manufactured goods between 1867 and 1922 included in *Ti-yi-t'zu Chung-kuo lao-tung nien-chien* (Peking, 1928) suggest an increase in the terms of trade of 60 percent. Unfortunately, no information is provided on the original source or construction of these indices.

52. McAlpin's data show agriculture's terms of trade rising by almost 50 percent between 1861–5 and 1911–15, with much of that rise occurring after 1885. The terms of trade decline during World War I, but then recover through the 1920s, only to fall again sharply in the early 1930s. See McAlpin, "Price Movements and Fluctuations in Economic Activity," in *Cambridge Economic History of India* (Cambridge, 1983), pp. 878–904.

53. If labor was originally underutilized and the farm household was operating within its production possibility curve, the amount of labor allocated to agriculture could actually increase without any reduction in time allocated to Z goods. The extent to which labor was actually underutilized

is difficult to say, however, because we do not have estimates of the amount of time that was allocated to "non-market" Z-type activities. Japan's agriculture was even more commercialized than China's. But a 1929 survey of 219 Japanese farm households shows that they still devoted approximately 30 percent of their labor time to "domestic work," or what we might call household production. In some cases, the percentage was much higher, but in others it was as low as 5 to 10 percent. How much these differences reflect differences in the relative opportunity cost of labor in agriculture remains to be seen. See Norinsho Nomukyoku, *Noka keizai chōsa* (Tokyo, 1930).

54. No differentiation is made between increases in overseas and domestic demand or in the source of the nonagricultural goods supplied to the rural sector. Unquestionably, however, the long-run transformation of a predominantly rural economy like China's was at the turn of the century would depend heavily on its ability to develop an indigenous sector capable of meeting some of this demand.

55. Technological change in the production of a Z-type good or the goods superiority to its manufactured counterpart may guarantee continued production.

56. Ester Boserup, *The Economics of Agrarian Change under Population Pressure* (Chicago, 1965). Dwight Perkins also emphasizes the role of changes in population density and labor supply in explaining changes in cropping intensity.

57. Li and Chang, *Chung-kuo chin-tai nung-yeh-shih tzu-liao*, vol. 2, pp. 229–40.

58. Data in *Chung-kuo shih-yeh chih: Che-kiang sheng*, sec. IV, pp. 184–5, put acreage in mulberry in Chekiang at over 2.5 million *mou* in the late 1920s. This is roughly 8 percent of cultivated area. Even allowing for some contraction in mulberry acreage in the 1930s because of declining world demand, over 40 percent of the land cultivated in Chekiang was in cash crops in the 1930s. Acreage data for Kiangsu are lacking, but cocoon production estimates for the province imply that 1 to 1.5 million *mou* were in mulberry. Data on cocoon production can be found in *Shina sanshigyo taikan*, pp. 10–12 and are cited by Lillian Li, *China's Silk Trade* (Cambridge, 1981), p. 107. In Wuhsi *hsien* alone, acreage in mulberry was reportedly 20 to 30 percent of total cultivated area, or 300,000–400,000 *mou*. Total cultivated acreage in Kiangsu was 92 million *mou*, so less than 2 percent of the cultivated area was in mulberry. Given the possibility that silk output figures are too low (Li, p. 102), these acreage estimates for mulberry may be low as well.

59. Exports of raw silk are measured here in physical terms. Data on silk exports are contained in Liang-lin Hsiao, *China's Foreign Trade Statistics, 1864–1949*, pp. 109–10.

60. Mei-yu Chu, *Chung-kuo ch'a-yeh* (Shanghai, 1937), pp. 49–50.

61. Table 4.3 shows that 367 million *mou* out of the total cultivated area of 1,471 million *mou* were in these cash crops. With the multiple-cropping index in the 1930s at 140, approximately 18 percent of sown area would have been devoted to these cash crops. Data on acreage in cash crops in the

People's Republic of China can be found in *Ch'uan-kuo t'ung-chi nien-chien*, p. 137.

62. Nicholas Lardy, *Agriculture in China's Modern Economic Development* (Cambridge, 1983).

63. Kang Chao, *Man and Land in Chinese History* (Stanford, 1986), p. 199.

64. Applying Buck's regional estimates of multiple-cropping to provincial acreage data, for example, yields an estimate of 150 for the 1930s.

65. Information on cotton and soybeans is based on data collected by the Nationalist Government's newly formed Statistical Bureau under the direction of Hsin-yi Chang, which were later compiled in the Japanese source: Toa kenkyujō, *Shina nōgyō kiso tōkei shiryō* (Tokyo, 1940), pp. 47–48.

66. Additional information on cotton production in Hupei is provided in *Hu-pei sheng nien-chien, 1937*.

67. Imperial Maritime Customs, *Wuhu Trade Report*, for these years.

68. Imperial Maritime Customs, *Hankow Trade Report*, for these years and output data in Perkins, *Agricultural Development in China*.

69. The data may underestimate the degree of specialization. In some of the larger counties, soil types and growing conditions differed substantially. If production of a particular cash crop was confined to one portion of a county, specialization at the farm level may have proceeded further than more aggregate data would suggest.

70. Buck, *Land Utilization in China: Statistical Volume*, p. 69. The fact that these localities were more commercialized on average may have imparted a positive bias to this estimate, but such a bias may have been either partially or totally offset by the larger-than-average size of those farms surveyed.

71. Po-chuang Ch'en, *Ping-han yan-hsien nung-tsun ching-chi tiao-ch'a*, Tables 9 and 10.

72. Lardy, *Agriculture in China's Modern Economic Development*, p. 34. Aside from possibly reflecting lower levels of specialization, this may also reflect a higher degree of income equality following land reform. Households that may have owned or rented small amounts of land, earned supplementary income hiring out, and obtained grain from the market may have become less dependent on the market when their farm holdings increased.

73. Lardy suggests, on the other hand, that in the 1950s part of provincial grain "exports" were used to meet the grain deficits of specialized producers. Between 1938 and 1958, however, the population living in urban centers larger than 100,000 increased by 40 million. Over roughly the same period, overseas grain imports declined by 1.5 million metric tons, while soybean exports rose. Under these circumstances a doubling of total provincial grain exports from 3.5 million to 7 million metric tons between the 1930s and 1950s would seem to have left little for specialized producers.

74. Buck, *Land Utilization in China: Statistical Volume*, p. 349.

75. Buck, *Land Utilization in China*, p. 357.

76. Ministry of Industry, National Agricultural Research Bureau, *Crop Reports* 4, 7 (July 15, 1936), p. 201.

77. Perkins, *Agricultural Development in China*, p. 361. Aside from grains, the two largest items in 1908 were silk and opium. Perkins's data for 1928 are very similar to those for 1936, with some minor differences arising from the exclusion of Manchuria from trade statistics after 1931.

78. The question naturally arises that, because Maritime Customs did not record junk trade, does this growth represent no more than a diversion of trade from traditional to modern carriers? Thomas Rawski has recently examined this question in some detail and concluded that the newer modes supplemented rather than displaced traditional forms and that the growth in Maritime Customs figures represents a genuine expansion in trade. My analysis of agricultural marketing provides additional support for this view. The growth in the cotton trade, for example, was tied to the growth and concentration of the industry in Shanghai that occurred in the early twentieth century; it could not possibly represent a diversion. Moreover, much of the increased marketing of grain to feed the expanding urban and non-agricultural population occurred totally outside Maritime Customs. In Anhwei, for example, only about a quarter of estimated rice exports of 12 to 15 million *picul* were shipped through Wuhu Maritime Customs. A similarly low percentage of Hunan's rice exports went through Changsha. Finally, hardly any of the almost 20 million *picul* of domestic wheat used by the modern milling industry in Kiangsu were transported through Maritime Customs. Rawski estimates that between 1895 and 1936 the volume of freight transport by all modes (rail, steamship, junk, and land) increased around 3 percent a year, or slightly higher than my estimate of the rate of growth of agriculture's market surplus in the region. Rawski's estimates are taken from "Economic Growth in Prewar China" (in press), Chapter 4, Table 4.10.

79. This is based on the assumption that per capita GNP was roughly 60 *yuan*. This figure is suggested by Liu and Yeh's national income estimates and those of Dwight Perkins. See Liu and Yeh, *The Economy of the Chinese Mainland*, p. 99, and Perkins, "Growth and Changing Structure of China's Twentieth-Century Economy," in *China's Modern Economy in Historical Perspective*, ed. Dwight Perkins (Stanford, 1975).

80. By comparison, data for four North China treaty ports (Newchang, Tientsin, Chefoo, and Kiachow) imply just the opposite, with overseas exports expanding at a real rate of 7.5 percent, but inter-treaty-port shipments at 3.00 percent.

81. A post office survey carried out in the early 1930s is an excellent source of information about specialization at the county level. For each county, the survey provides information on major items of exports (agricultural, manufactured, handicraft, forestry and mineral products, and so forth), their volume and destination. These data are provided in *Chung-k'uo t'ung-yu ti-fang wu-chan-chih* (Shanghai, 1937).

82. Liu and Yeh estimate that in the 1930s there were 87.54 million male "man-labor units" solely in agriculture and an additional 42.95 million jointly in agriculture and subsidiary occupations. Of this latter group, 2.80 million "man-labor units" were in trade and transportation. This represents

the labor of roughly 8.5 million males who devoted a third of their time to this sideline. See Liu and Yeh, *The Economy of the Chinese Mainland*, pp. 184–5.

83. These same kind of differences are found in North China villages, where it was not uncommon for 20 percent or more of all households to be classified as nonagricultural. Data on occupational distribution at the village level compiled by the South Manchurian Railroad can be found in Minami Manshū Tetsudō Kabushiki Kaisha, Kito chiku noson jittai chosahan, *Kitō chiku nai nijugo ka son nōson jittai chōsa hōkokusho*, 2 vols. (Tientsin, 1936), and *Kitō chiku nai sentaku nōnson jittai chōsa gaiyō hōkokusho* (Tientsin, 1936).

84. See Buck, *Land Utilization in China*, p. 311. Fairly consistent information on the role of by-employment is provided by the survey of households living along the Peking-Hankow Railroad. For the 1,231 owner-operated farms surveyed, net subsidiary income averaged 64.32 *yuan*, or 34.30 percent of total net income; and, for 225 tenants, it was 41.1 percent. Excluding animal husbandry from sidelines, about one-quarter of a household's income came from other than farm sources. In some cases, net subsidiary income (including that from animal husbandry) amounted to almost 50 percent, but in others it was as low as 15 percent. The major subsidiary activities were handicraft textiles, 111 households; semi-skilled labor, 115 households; transportation, 96 households; and marketing and distribution, 96 households.

85. In a survey of four villages in East China, approximately two-thirds was in cash. Hui-sun T'ang et al., *Chung-kuo nung-chia ching-chi chih chi-chang te yen-chiu* (Nanking, 1936).

## Chapter 5. Productivity Change and Incomes in the Rural Sector

1. On Tokugawa Japan, see Susan B. Hanley and Kozo Yamamura, *Economic and Demographic Change in Preindustrial Japan, 1600–1868* (Princeton, 1977).

2. The marginal product of labor can be falling and average productivity rising. As long as the marginal product of labor is above the average product, the later will be rising with additions to labor. It is only when the marginal product of labor falls below the average product that the average product itself begins to fall.

3. See Dwight Perkins, *Agricultural Development in China* (Chicago, 1969); Phillip Huang, *The Peasant Economy and Social Change in North China* (Stanford, 1985); and Kang Chao, *Man and Land in Chinese History: An Economic Analysis* (Stanford, 1986). Perkins actually argues that per capita agricultural output remained roughly constant over this period. Much of this increase in output, however, occurred in Manchuria, implying that in China proper output failed to grow commensurately with the population. If one assumes that the composition of the population (agricultural versus

nonagricultural) did not change—Perkins does not appear to entertain that it might have—this suggests that, in China proper, average and probably marginal productivity were falling. Myers's work on the influence of the commercialization process on North China modifies this slightly, but he says no more than that average productivity probably remained constant over this period. See Ramon Myers, *The Chinese Peasant Economy* (Cambridge, 1970).

4. Empirical support for the proposition that factors of production were remunerated at levels equal to or near their marginal products has been provided by Ramon Myers and Scott Dietrich, "Resource Allocation in Traditional Agriculture: Republican China, 1937–1940," *Journal of Political Economy* 79 (July-August 1971), 887–96; and Thomas Wiens, "The Microeconomics of Peasant Economy: China, 1920–1940" (Ph.D. Dissertation, Harvard University, 1973). Further support will be offered in the next chapter.

5. John L. Buck, *Land Utilization in China: Statistical Volume* (Chicago, 1937), p. 305. A slightly higher percentage is suggested by his *Chinese Farm Economy: A Study of 2,866 Farms* (Chicago, 1930), p. 234.

6. In a survey of 1.75 million households in sixteen provinces carried out in the early 1930s by the National Land Commission, only 1.57 percent of these households were classified as landless laboring households. The average for Kiangsu, Chekiang, Anhwei, Kiangsi, Hupei, and Hunan was less than 1 percent. See Tu-ti wei-yuan hui, *Chuan-kuo t'u-ti tiao-ch'a pao-kao kang-yao* (Nanking, 1937), p. 34.

7. In village-level surveys carried out in five diverse counties in Kiangsu, the following percentages of farming households hired out in agriculture at some point during the year: Nantong, 36.2 percent (34 out of 94 households); Changshu, 75.0 percent (30 out of 40); Sungkiang, 60.3 percent (38 out of 63); Taitsang, 48.1 percent (25 out of 52); and Wuhsi, 46.3 percent (37 out of 80). See Minami Manshū Tetsudō Kabushiki Kaisha, Shanhai Jimusho, Chōsashitsu, *Kōso-shō Jōjuku-ken nōson jittai chōsa hōkokusho* (Dairen, 1939); *Kōso-shō Mushaku-ken nōson jittai chōsa hōkokusho* (Dairen, 1941); *Kōso-shō Nantsū-ken nōson jittai chōsa hōkokusho* (Dairen, 1941); *Kōso-shō Shōkō-ken nōson jittai chōsa hōkokusho* (Dairen, 1940); and *Kōso-shō Taisō-ken nōson jittai chōsa hōkokusho* (Dairen, 1940);

8. "Tenure of Land in China and the Condition of the Rural Population," *Journal of the China Branch of the Royal Asiatic Society* 23 (1889), pp. 58–143.

9. These include Cheng-mo Ch'en, *Ko-sheng nung-kung ku-yung hsi-kuan chi hsu-kung chuang-kuang* (Nanking, 1935), and "Ko-sheng nung-kung kung-tzu t'ung-chi," *T'ung-chi yue-pao* 13 (Sept.-Oct. 1933), pp. 99–106.

10. Buck, *Land Utilization in China: Statistical Volume*, pp. 151–2.

11. The reports offer no indication, however, that 1888 was unrepresentative.

12. Kang Chao, *Man and Land in Chinese History: An Economic Analysis*,

pp. 218–19. Presumably these were wages paid during the farming season. A *sheng* equals 0.01 *shih*. A Ch'ing *shih* of grain weighed approximately 130 *catty*. An equally low level of real wages for roughly the same period is implied by wage data in Wen-chih Li's *Chung-kuo tzu-pen-chu-yi meng-ya wen-t'i t'ao-lun chi* (Peking, 1957), pp. 652–3, and grain price data that have been collected recently in the Chinese archives by Lillian Li, Yeh-chien Wang, and Peter Perdue, just to name a few.

13. Thomas Wiens, "The Microeconomics of Peasant Economy: China, 1920–1940," (Ph.D. Dissertation, Harvard University, 1973), p. 471.

14. On this point, see the Note to Table 5.2. In the case of Szechwan, Wiens's estimate is 100 percent higher than Buck's. For other parts of China, the two estimates are roughly consistent. This may explain the exceptionally low level of wage grain equivalencies I report for Szechwan.

15. Buck, *Land Utilization in China: Statistical Volume*, pp. 317–20. The total wage was 82.50 *yuan*, of which 45.50 *yuan* was the value of income paid in kind.

16. Data for the early Meiji on the full wage paid annual contract laborers in agriculture along with rice price data can be found in Mataji Umemura et al, *Estimates of Long-term Economic Statistics of Japan Since 1868*, vol. 9, (Tokyo, 1966). For Tokugawa Japan, see Hanley and Yamamura, *Economic and Demographic Change in Preindustrial Japan*.

17. Grain supplied approximately 80 percent of all calories. Vegetables and small amounts of meat and fish supplemented the diet.

18. This finding can be easily reconciled, especially if increases in labor productivity (measured here by output per worker) are resulting as much from increases in labor input per individual gainfully engaged in agriculture as they are from increases in output per days each individual worked. Given the increasing cropping intensity of the period, I believe this was probably the case in Chinese agriculture. This also points out a pitfall in using monthly or daily wage data by themselves to measure productivity change during such a period.

19. George Jamieson, "Tenure of Land in China and the Condition of the Rural Population," *Journal of the China Branch of the Royal Asiatic Society* 23 (1889), pp. 58–143.

20. Because roughly two-thirds of all households in Central and East China lived in core areas, the bias in Buck's data may not be all that great. For a definition of core areas, see Note 46, Chapter 2.

21. Thomas Rawski has performed a similar exercise using the data for all 100 counties. He elected to deflate each series by an index of prices paid for agricultural and nonagricultural prices rather than by index for agricultural prices alone because he was primarily concerned with income changes. For inferences regarding productivity change, agricultural prices should be used by themselves as the numeraire.

22. The estimates are contained in Buck's *Land Utilization in China: Statistical Volume*, p. 305. It is generally acknowledged, however, that Buck's survey was biased in favor of larger farms. Given that the percentage

of income earned from nonagricultural sources declined with increasing farm size, Buck's data probably underestimates the time allocated to non-agricultural activities.

23. Of the fifty-three localities in the Yangtse Rice-Wheat Region and Rice-Tea Region that Buck provides data for, eleven devoted 30 percent or more of their labor-time to sidelines and earned roughly a quarter of their incomes from these sources. Similarly high percentages are found in a detailed survey of localities along the Peking-Hankow Railroad and in many other surveys carried out for individual counties such as those for Kiangsu cited in Note 7 above. Regarding the former, see Po-chuang Ch'en, *Ping-han yan-hsien nung-tsun ching-chi tiao-ch'a* (Shanghai, 1937).

24. I am ignoring here questions of risk, capital immobility, and so forth.

25. All this discussion is in terms of homogeneous labor. Obviously, wages differed depending on the workers skill, education, and sex. Wages for female farmhands, for example, averaged two-thirds that for males. In Ting *hsien*, Hopei, wages were quoted for three classes of agricultural workers.

26. A survey carried out in 952 *hsien* in 22 provinces in 1935 found that approximately 20 percent of all rural households were engaged in handicraft textiles on a part-time basis, though for many this was probably purely for their own consumption only. See National Agricultural Research Bureau, *Crop Reports* 4, 11 (November 15, 1936), p. 292. In a Lower Yangtse village surveyed by Hsiao-tung Fei, *Peasant Life in China* (London, 1939), p. 124, nearly every household had a wooden loom, but only two were still actually using it. Handcraft cloth production as either a sideline or for own use had long ago been given up because all but a few households were consuming manufactured cloth.

27. Kang Chao, *The Development of Cotton Textile Production in China* (Cambridge, 1977).

28. Minami Manshū Tetsudō Kabushiki Kaisha, Shanhai Jimusho, Chō-sashitsu, *Kōso-shō Nantsū-ken nōson jittai chōsa hōkokusho* (Dairen, 1941), Appendix, Table 11.

29. There is no monthly production data, but some impression of labor allocation to handicraft textiles in Nantong over the course of the year may be obtained from the percentage of output marketed each month: January, 6.0 percent; February, 5.4 percent; March, 10.3 percent; April, 11.3 percent; May, 7.4 percent; June, 5.2 percent; July, 6.9 percent; August, 10.0 percent; September, 9.6 percent; October, 11.0 percent; November, 8.6 percent; and December, 8.4 percent. May, June, and July were the busiest agricultural months. These percentages, based on data for 1932, 1933, and 1936, were reported by Chung-p'ing Yen, *Chung-kuo mien-fang-chih shih-kao* (Peking, 1955), p. 278.

30. Because the Sino-Japanese War had partially disrupted the rural economy at the time of the survey, these data may actually *underestimate* off-farm activity in this village.

31. The survey indicated that in most of these households both males and females were engaged in handicraft textiles, but it does not state how the labor was divided between the sexes.

32. The total value of output was 7,500 *yuan*, so value-added per labor day is equal to (0.20 * 7,500)/4,000 or 0.40 *yuan*.

33. In 1931 value-added in weaving was thirty cents (or 0.30 *yuan*) per piece for big cloth (which sold for 1.80 *yuan*) and twenty cents per piece for export cloth (which sold for 1.20 *yuan*). On the "improved" wooden looms that were most widely in use, two pieces of cloth could be produced per ten-hour working day. See Sidney Gamble, *Ting Hsien: A North China Rural Community* (Stanford, 1954), pp. 302–3. I have excluded spinning from the calculations because much of it was done by teenage girls and elderly adults. Spinning reportedly earned five to six *cents* per day.

34. See, for example, Yen, *Chung-kuo mien-fang-chih shih-kao* (Peking, 1955). For a similar interpretation about handicrafts more generally, see Tse-yi P'eng, ed., *Chung-kuo chin-tai shou-kung-yeh shih tzu-liao* (Peking, 1957), especially vols. 2 and 3.

35. Ramon Myers, "Cotton Textile Handicraft and the Development of the Cotton Textile Industry in Modern China," *Economic History Review* 18 (September 1965), pp. 614–32; Albert Feuerwerker, "Handicraft and Manufactured Cotton Textiles in China, 1871–1910," *Journal of Economic History* 30 (June 1971), pp. 338–78; Bruce Reynolds, "The Impact of Foreign Trade and Industrialization: Chinese Textiles, 1875–1931," (Ph.D. Dissertation, University of Michigan, 1975); Chao, *The Development of Cotton Textile Production in China*; and Richard Kraus, "Cotton and Cotton Goods in China, 1918–1936" (Ph.D. Dissertation, Harvard University, 1968).

36. If I erred, it has probably been to overestimate handicraft yarn production and underestimate handicraft cloth production. The reasons for this will become obvious.

37. A careful examination of yarn import data and estimates of factory output suggest that much of the handicraft yarn decline occurred within a period of fifteen years between the late 1880s and early 1900s.

38. On this matter, I have roughly followed Feuerwerker, "Handicraft and Manufactured Cotton Textiles in China, 1871–1910."

39. Yen, *Chung-kuo mien-fang-chih shih-kao* p. 24.

40. Cheng-ming Wu, *Chung-kuo tzu-pen chu-yi yu kuo-nei shih-chang* (Peking, 1985), pp. 188–92.

41. Between 1871–80 and 1901–10, the price of raw cotton imports and exports increased by slightly more than 50 percent, while the price of manufactured yarn imports and the price of handicraft cloth exports remained roughly constant. The data on cotton imports and exports and manufactured yarn imports are contained in Liang-lin Hsiao, *China's Foreign Trade Statistics 1864–1949* (Cambridge, 1974), pp. 38–9 and 85–6. The data on handicraft cloth exports can be found in Hsien-ting Fong, *Chung-kuo chih mien-fang chih-yeh* (Shanghai, 1934), p. 327.

42. T. C. Liu and K. C. Yeh, *The Economy of the Chinese Mainland: National Income and Economic Development, 1933–1959* (Princeton, 1965), pp. 521–2.

43. The 50-percent revision is suggested by information drawn from local gazetteers by Wu, *Chung-kuo tzu-pen chu-yi yu kuo-nei shih-chang*, pp. 188–92, on value-added in spinning during the Ch'ing. For the 1700s, the value of the yarn that could be spun from 100 copper cash of cotton was 130 to 140 cash, implying value-added (measured as a percentage of the price of yarn) of 23.1 percent (30/130) or 28.6 percent (40/140). If one assumes that value-added in the 1870s was 50 percent higher than it was in the 1930s, when measured as a percentage of the price of yarn, value-added would be 27.6 percent.

44. The new wooden looms were originally imported "in the thousands" from Japan, but later were also made in China. See Ralph Odell, *Cotton Goods in China* (Washington, 1916), p. 186.

45. Shih-wen Chang, *Ting-hsien nung-tsun kung-yeh tiao-ch'a* (Peking, 1935), p. 97. For a brief summary of the technical innovations of these new looms, see Kraus, "Cotton and Cotton Goods in China," pp. 132–3, and Chao, *The Development of Cotton Textile Production in China*, pp. 185–6.

46. This is the view of both Chao and Kraus, who have done detailed studies of the handicraft textile sector. Odell, *Cotton Goods in China*, notes how the low cost of these looms allowed many Chinese households to buy them.

47. The number of improved wooden looms increased from 20 to 122 between 1912 and 1932, and the number of iron looms increased from zero to 69. See Gamble, *Ting Hsien: A North China Rural Community*, pp. 302–3 and Table 96.

48. Minami Manshū Tetsudō Kabushiki Kaisha, Hokushi Keizai Chō-sajo, *I-ken dofugyō chōsa hōkokusho* (Minami Manshu Tetsudo Kabushiki Kaisha Chosabu, 1942), p. 34.

49. Tzu-chien Wang, *Chung-kuo t'u-pu-yeh tzu ch'ien-t'u* (Shanghai, 1936), p. 131, and Tse-yi P'eng, *Chung-kuo chin-tai shou-kung-yeh shih tzu-liao* (Peking, 1957), vol. 3, pp. 21, 107, 690, cited in Chao, *The Development of Cotton Textile Production in China*.

50. Chung-p'ing Yen, *Chung-kuo mien-fang-chih shih-kao*, p. 24.

51. Gamble, *Ting Hsien: A North China Rural Community*, p. 300.

52. Wu, *Chung-kuo tzu-pen chu-yi yu kuo-nei shih-chang*, p. 190.

53. Feuerwerker, "Handicraft and Manufactured Cotton Textiles in China, 1871–1910."

54. The latter estimate is based on the dimensions of the three kinds of cloth most frequently woven in Ting *hsien* during the early twentieth century.

55. Given that much of the substitution of manufactured for handicraft yarn did not really begin until the late 1880s, the timing of this increase can be reasonably reduced to a forty-five to fifty-year period rather than a sixty-year one.

56. Including the value of income-in-kind, Buck estimated the average daily wage paid in agriculture over the entire year at 0.45 *yuan*.

57. Gamble, *Ting Hsien: A Rural North China Community*, p. 301.

58. The estimated level of handicraft cloth production is suggested by fragmentary data compiled by Yen, *Chung-kuo mien-fang-chih shih-kao*, pp. 257–64. Production was very specialized and much of the output was concentrated in a few key counties in each province. For example, in Kiangsu: Nantong, Kiangnin, Wuchin, Changshu, and Kunming; in Chekiang: Pinghu, Haining, and Shaohsing; and in Hupei: Kuangkang and Laokan.

59. Perkins, *Agricultural Development in China*, p. 212.

60. Sectoral changes are discussed more fully in Chapter 4.

61. As noted at the outset, in light of the substantial reduction in rice output in Central and East China in Perkins's estimates, it would appear that this assumption holds only in the aggregate and not for individual regions.

62. A priori, there is no reason for the increases implied by these calculations to be the same as those for the wage data. Although the wage data are measures of marginal productivity, in equation 3 we are estimating the average product of labor. Only in the case of a Cobb-Douglas production function are the rates of growth of marginal and average productivity the same. Although in Chapter 6 we estimate a profit function that assumes production technology to be Cobb-Douglas, work that I have done on prewar Japanese agriculture reveals that all elasticities of substitution were significantly less than one. Assuming a Constant Elasticity Substitution (CES) production function with two inputs, labor and land, the ratio of the rate of growth in average to marginal product of labor declines with a decline in $\sigma$, the elasticity of substitution. Assuming, for example, that $\sigma$ equals 0.67, $\delta$, the distribution parameter, equals 0.33, and A, the efficiency parameter, equals 1, a 100-percent increase in the marginal product of labor implies an increase in average productivity of 60 percent. The differences in the rate of growth of real wages in the rural sector and average productivity as implied by Table 5.10 are too great to believe that they can be attributed solely to a non-Cobb-Douglas production technology.

63. This range of estimates is suggested by the wage data and productivity estimates for the handicraft textiles.

64. See Miyohei Shinohara, *Structural Changes in Japan's Economic Development* (Tokyo, 1970), p. 245, Table 7.

65. Calculated on the basis of the following relationship:

$$\%\triangle(Q_A/\text{Pop}) = \%\triangle(Y/\text{Pop})e_Y + \%\triangle P * e_P$$

where $\%\triangle(Q_A/\text{Pop})$ is the percentage change in per capita agricultural consumption, $\%\triangle(Y/\text{Pop})$ and $\%\triangle P$ are the percentage changes in income per capita and the relative price of agricultural goods, and $e_Y$ and $e_P$ are the income and price elasticity of demand.

66. Thomas Rawski, "Economic Growth in Prewar China" (in press), Chapter 6.

67. John Buck, *Land Utilization in China* (Chicago, 1937), pp. 458–9.

## Chapter 6. The Distributive Consequences of Commercialization

1. Carl Riskin's *China's Political Economy* (New York, 1987), Chapter 2, typifies much of the thinking on this issue.

2. This, of course, is not to say that other kinds of inequality, such as that between regions, may not have increased because of the commercialization process. Commercialization tends to favor areas with access to inexpensive transport; however, these are not the kinds of differentials that have concerned the literature linking commercialization with income inequality.

3. See Phillip Huang's *The Peasant Economy and Social Change in North China* (Stanford, 1985) for a recent expression of this viewpoint.

4. T'u-ti wei-yuan hui, *Ch'uan-kuo t'u-ti tiao-ch'a pao-kao kang-yao* (Nanking, 1937). The summary reports the distribution of own landholdings for the entire sample only. For both the distribution of cultivated holdings and incomes, it provides information at the provincial level as well.

5. The Gini coefficient can assume a value between zero and one; the higher the value, the higher the degree of inequality of distribution implied.

6. The households surveyed cultivated a total of 24,188,622 *mou*, 19,650,458 of which they owned. Although some of the remaining 4.5 million *mou* may have been rented in from other rural households (rather than absentee landlords living in cities and towns) living in non-surveyed areas, in a random sample such as this such acreage would have been offset by holdings of surveyed households outside their own villages that they rented out.

7. The latter is the weighted average of the Land Survey's provincial estimates and Dwight Perkins's figures for cultivated area.

8. For discussions of permanent tenancy, see Evelyn Rawski, *Agricultural Change and the Peasant Economy of South China* (Cambridge, 1972), pp. 19–24; John Shepard, "Rethinking Tenancy: Spatial and Temporal Variation in Land Ownership and Concentration in Late Imperial China" (unpublished, 1986), pp. 34–8; and Yung-tian Liu, "Ch'ing-tai ch'ien-ch'i te nung-yeh tsu-tien kuan-hsi," *Ch'ing-shih lun-tsung* 2, 1980, pp. 69–70.

9. In Chinese, this system was referred to as *yi t'ien liang chu*, which translates as "one field, two owners," or more eloquently "two lords to a field."

10. T'u-ti wei-yuan hui, *Ch'uan-kuo t'u-ti tiao-ch'a pao-kao kang-yao*, p. 45. Some of the differences in estimates of permanent tenancy may be attributed to differences in definition. Shepard, for example, identifies strong and weak forms of permanent tenancy; weak tenancy could be acquired when the tenant paid the equivalent of three years of rent as a

deposit. Rental deposits were paid on approximately 30 percent of the land in all China and nearly 50 percent in Central and East China. It is difficult to say on how much of this land the tenant actually benefited from the weaker form of permanent tenancy. Data on rental deposits are taken from Cheng-mo Ch'en, *Chung-kuo k'o-sheng te ti-tsu* (Shanghai, 1936), p. 61.

11. Dwight Perkins, *Agricultural Development in China, 1368–1968* (Chicago, 1969), p. 101, presents some fragmentary data showing roughly similar percentages for the 1880s and 1890s.

12. T'u-ti wei-yuan hui, *Ch'uan-kuo t'u-ti tiao-ch'a pao-kao kang-yao*, p. 34. Other data compiled by Kang Chao and Chung-yi Chen, *Chung-kuo t'u-ti chih-tu shih* (Taipei, 1982), pp. 309–10, for four counties in Kiangsu also reveal a very low percentage of households earning a living as long-term agricultural workers.

13. The increase in the demand for labor that accompanied commercialization provided more opportunities for household members to hire out. Because of this, an increase in the number of annual laborers is very misleading.

14. To provide an example from North China, in Michang village, Fengrun county, Hopei, 17 out of 120 households had a member hiring out as an annual laborer. Eleven of these households, however, owned or rented land, the average of which was over twelve *mou*. For one other household, nonagricultural activity were reported to be the primary source of income. Only five households, or 4.2 percent of the village total, could strictly be classified as landless laboring households. Moreover, for only 9 of the 17 would the income earned as an annual laborer probably have exceeded that earned from farming. So, using a more liberal definition of a landless laboring household, the percentage of households so classified is less than commonly believed. These data are taken from Minami Manshū Tetsudō Kabushiki Kaisha, Kito Noson Jittai Chosahan, *Dainiji kitō nōson jittai chōsa hōkokusho: tōkeihen, Dai sanban: Hōjun ken* (Dairen, 1936).

15. Kang Chao, *Man and Land in Chinese History* (Stanford, 1986), pp. 25–7.

16. Ibid., pp. 121–3. *Fen-chia* literally means splitting up of the family. When this occurred, land (and other wealth) were divided equally among the male heirs.

17. In his *The Income of the Chinese Gentry* (Seattle, 1962), p. 145, Chung-li Chang suggests that about a third of all land was rented in the 1880s.

18. See, for example, Ramon Myers, *The Chinese Peasant Economy* (Cambridge, 1970), pp. 220–22; Chao and Chen, *Chung-kuo t'u-ti chih-tu shih*, p. 202; and Loren Brandt, "Review of Phillip Huang's 'The Peasant Economy and Social Change in North China,' " *Economic Development and Cultural Change* 35, 3 (April 1987), p. 676.

19. In this regard, see John Shepard, "Rethinking Tenancy" (unpublished, 1986).

20. The data compiled by the National Land Commission can be compared

with that gathered in a 1934 survey undertaken by the NARB covering over 600 localities. This survey divided farm households into five rather than thirteen size categories. The NARB survey shows a smaller percentage of farms in the category "less than 10 *mou*," slightly higher percentages in the next three size categories, but roughly the same percentage in the largest size category. The degree of inequality in cultivated holdings suggested by the two surveys is very similar.

*Size distribution of farms (in* mou*)*

|            | Less than 10 | 10–20 | 20–30 | 30–50 | More than 50 |
|------------|-------------|-------|-------|-------|--------------|
| Kiangsu    | 40.5%       | 31.2% | 11.9% | 11.3% | 5.1%         |
| Chekiang   | 53.5        | 31.4  | 8.4   | 4.7   | 2.0          |
| Anhwei     | 35.3        | 27.6  | 14.2  | 14.4  | 8.5          |
| Kiangsi    | 47.2        | 33.5  | 10.7  | 5.2   | 3.4          |
| Hupei      | 49.9        | 33.9  | 8.9   | 5.1   | 2.2          |
| Hunan      | 48.4        | 33.7  | 10.2  | 5.2   | 2.5          |
| Average    | 45.8        | 31.9  | 10.7  | 7.7   | 3.9          |

*Source:* NARB, *Crop Reports* 3, 4 (April 15, 1935), pp. 85–87.

21. The table below shows the distribution of farms by size of cultivated area for Japan. By all indications, the increasing concentration of farms in the 0.5–2.0 hectare category actually began much earlier, though no estimates can be provided. If farms in Central and East China are divided into similar categories, 43.26 percent would be less than 0.5 hectare, 48.49 percent would be between 0.5 and 2.0 hectare, and only 8.25 percent would be larger than 2.0 hectare.

*Size distribution of farms, 1908–1937*
*(excluding Hokkaido)*

|      | Below 0.5 Hectares | 0.5–1.0 Hectares | 1.0–2.0 Hectares | 2.0–3.0 Hectares | Above 3.0 Hectares |
|------|--------------------|------------------|------------------|------------------|--------------------|
| 1908 | 38.1%              | 33.3%            | 19.6%            | 5.8%             | 3.2%               |
| 1917 | 37.0               | 34.2             | 20.6             | 5.8              | 2.5                |
| 1927 | 35.3               | 35.1             | 22.0             | 5.6              | 2.0                |
| 1939 | 34.0               | 33.8             | 24.9             | 5.6              | 1.7                |

*Source:* Ouchi Tsutoma, *Nihon ni okeru nominso no bunkai* (Tokyo, 1969), cited (with corrections) in Richard Smethurst, *Agricultural Development and Tenancy Disputes in Japan, 1870–1940* (Princeton, 1986), p. 77.

22. Buck, *Land Utilization in China: Statistical Volume*, p. 55, found that the various size categories of farms rented roughly the same percentage of land (measured as a percentage of their cultivated acreage). If smaller farms rented a higher percentage, the percentage of land cultivated by farms smaller than 30 *mou* would have been even higher.

23. Huang, *The Peasant Economy and Social Change in North China.*

24. Albert Berry and William Cline, *Agrarian Structure and Productivity in Developing Countries* (Baltimore, 1979).

25. See, for example, Thomas Rawski, "China's Republican Economy: An Introduction," 1978; Ramon Myers, *The Chinese Economy: Past and Present* (Belmont, 1980); and Albert Feuerwerker, "Economic Trends, 1912–1949," in *Cambridge History of China, Republican China, 1912–1949*, Part I (Cambridge, 1983). My analysis of product markets in Chapter 2 supports this view.

26. In models of farm household behavior such as A. K. Chayonov's, *The Theory of the Peasant Economy* (Homewood, 1966) and A. K. Sen's, "Peasants and Dualism with or without Surplus Labor," *Journal of Political Economy* 74 (1966), pp. 425–50, in which there is no labor market, the amount of labor that an individual household supplies to farm production depends directly on its subjective evaluation of work. With an active labor market, this subjective evaluation determines the total supply of labor by the household, but not its total demand for labor in farm production. The latter is determined by conditions of profit maximization.

27. The attention that I am giving to North China data can easily be justified given the impact of Huang's work and the similarity in agriculture between these villages and some in Central and East China. Although there were regional differences in China, I still believe that markets in commercialized areas worked well and were competitive. If my analysis is to be taken seriously, it is necessary to show that the data from North China are consistent with the interpretation now being put forward.

28. More formally, I tested the relationship between farm size and land productivity by regressing gross farm output per unit of cultivated area (GFOCA) on the log of cultivated area (lnCA) using the pooled data. Lacking local price indices, the data for Wukuan have been deflated by the Nankai wholesale price index for agricultural goods for Tientsin, a major outlet for the market surplus of the region. This index appears in Nan-k'ai ta-hsueh ching-chi yen-chiu-so, eds., *Nan-k'ai chih-shu tzu-liao hui-pien, 1913–1952* (Peking, 1958), p. 12. The *t*-statistics are in parenthesis.

$$\text{GFOCA} = 33.11 + 1.31(\text{lnCA})$$
$$(5.05) \quad (.63)$$

$$R^2 = 0.007 \quad n = 57$$

The small *t*-value for the coefficient on lnCA and the low explanatory power of the model (as measured by $R^2$) do not support a systematic relationship between farm size and land productivity in these localities.

29. By comparison, Huang found in his sample of fourteen that net profits (and, therefore, net profits per unit of cultivated area) were negative for four of the five small (less than thirty *mou*) farms, but positive for the remaining nine farms. He attributes this to the greater use of labor on small farms, of which more is said below, and uses this finding to support the view that smaller farms were less efficient.

30. On the basis of oral testimony he obtained, Huang noted that a wage laborer worked a longer day at greater intensity than family members did on their own farms. According to Buck, on the other hand, women and children performed between 20 and 30 percent of the work on farms in North China. On some of these smaller farms, the adult male hired out as a monthly or annual laborer, so remaining household members performed most of the work on the family farm.

31. John L. Buck, *Chinese Farm Economy* (Chicago, 1930).

32. Buck used relative prices to convert non-grain crops into their grain equivalency.

33. Buck's data do not provide information on crop selection by farm size category. Data compiled by Ramon Myers for various villages in East-Central China in the 1930s, however, show the same degree of similarity as seen in Table 6.5. See his "The Commercialization of Agriculture in Modern China," in *Economic Organization in Chinese Society*, ed. W. E. Willmott (Stanford, 1972). In a survey of 3,412 farms carried out in Chia-hsing, Chekiang province, the percentage of acreage devoted to rice and mulberry was very similar among three sizes of farms. Farms larger than fifty *mou* devoted 46.36 and 8.35 percent of their land to rice and mulberry; farms between twenty and fifty *mou*, 41.95 and 11.01 percent; and farms smaller than twenty *mou*, 41.74 and 11.05 percent. Institute of Pacific Affairs, *Agrarian China* (Chicago, 1938), p. 74. This is a compilation of Chinese articles on rural China introduced by R. H. Tawney. Like much of the literature of the period, its outlook is pessimistic.

34. Even if there is not a well-developed rural labor market that offers off-farm wage opportunities, we would still expect land to be leased until differences in the marginal product of labor across farm sizes disappeared. Only in the case where neither set of markets is working well would we find small farms using land more intensively. More formally, if imperfections are present in at least two of the factor markets (that is, markets for land, labor, capital, and draft animals), the factor price ratios that peasant households implicitly face will differ. Assuming profit maximization, this implies that optimal factor combinations will differ among farm households, as will output/input ratios.

35. Berry and Cline have attributed the tendency for land productivity to decline with increasing farm size to these imperfections and the differences in decision making they give rise to. For an alternative explanation which assumes that farmers face identical factor prices, see Gershon Feder, "The Relation between Farm Size and Farm Productivity: The Role of Family Labor, Supervision, and Credit Constraints," *Journal of Development Economics* 18 (1985), pp. 297–313.

36. Farm households in North China were not only aware of local opportunity costs, but were equally informed of and profoundly influenced by interregional wage differences. According to Thomas Gottschang, these same households "year in and year out weighed the information they received about job possibilities and wage levels in Manchuria against local conditions, with an eye to sending off a son or a brother when the difference

promised a positive return to their investment." See Gottschang, "Economic Change, Disasters, and Migration: The Historical Case of Manchuria," *Economic Development and Cultural Change* 35 (April 1987), pp. 461–90.

37. Huang, *The Peasant Economy and Social Change in North China*, arrived at the same conclusion, but did not try to relate this finding to the fact that a market for draft-animal services existed.

38. See Pan Yotopoulus and Lawrence Lau, "A Test for Relative Economic Efficiency: Some Further Results," *American Economic Review* 63 (March 1973), pp. 214–23, and a number of earlier papers cited therein.

39. Thirty *mou* can be used to set off smaller farms that relied primarily on family members for labor from those that depended more heavily on hired farmhands. In North China at that time, an adult male could farm approximately fifteen *mou* by himself. Assuming that the average household had two male equivalents, it would take thirty *mou* to absorb the supply of family labor. Any "average-sized" household with landholdings exceeding thirty *mou* would presumably have to hire in some labor, but any smaller would probably try to hire out. My experimentation with cutoff points on both sides of thirty *mou* yielded qualitatively and quantitatively similar results.

40. In the estimation results reported, capital services are defined as the sum of expenditure on fertilizer, seed, and feed, plus depreciation and maintenance on fixtures and implements. The results are very robust to the use of alternative measures of either capital services or the capital stock.

41. Once family labor has been valued, the daily wage rate, W, can be found by dividing the sum of wages paid in cash and kind to hired labor and the imputed value of family labor by the total number of hired and family member workdays.

42. On the first of these points, see Note 30.

43. The rationale for using 85 percent is as follows. In the cotton-growing areas of North China, women and children provided slightly less than 30 percent of self-supplied labor. Imputing each day of this labor at the commonly used rate of 70 percent of the value of its adult male counterpart, and assuming an additional 10 percent difference in the value of a labor day supplied by the family and one supplied by hired labor, I arrived at a weight in the vicinity of .85.

44. It is of interest to note that weighting family labor on smaller farms at 70 percent would eliminate most of the differences in reported labor use with larger farms. Because I have no independent basis for identifying those households on which the contribution of women and children exceeded the average, I have decided to use only one weight for all farms.

45. See Arnold Zellner, "An Efficient Method for Estimating Seemingly Unrelated Regressions and Tests for Aggregation Bias," *Journal of the American Statistical Association* 57 (June 1962), pp. 348–68.

46. This increases my confidence in the tests for absolute price efficiency that are discussed below. In other similar studies, the large standard errors of the coefficients on the price variables in the profit equation make it very unlikely that a null hypothesis of absolute price efficiency could ever be

rejected. See, for example, Mahmoud Kahn and Dennis Maki, "The Effects of Farm Size on Economic Efficiency," *American Journal of Agricultural Economics* 61 (February 1979), pp. 64–9, and Ronald Trosper, "American Indian Relative Economic Efficiency," *American Economic Review* 68 (September 1978), pp. 503–16.

47. Once I failed to reject a particular hypothesis, I reestimated Model I with that restriction imposed in order to increase the efficiency of estimation. These estimates are provided in columns $I_B$ and $I_C$ of Table 6.14. Their use is explained below.

48. A type-II error is the acceptance of the null hypothesis when the alternative is true.

49. The results of these tests are in general agreement with earlier work by Ramon Myers and Scott Dietrich, "Resource Allocation in Traditional Agriculture: Republican China, 1937–1940," *Journal of Political Economy* 79 (July-August 1971), pp. 887–96; and Thomas Wiens, "The Microeconomics of Peasant Economy: China, 1920–1940," (Ph.D. Dissertation, Harvard University, 1973). Myers and Dietrich found on the basis of the same data that the allocation of factors of production among crops was reasonably efficient; and Wiens, using only the data for Michang village, arrived at a similar conclusion.

50. See Yotopoulus and Lau, "A Test for Relative Economic Efficiency," especially pp. 217–18.

51. Estimates of the same elasticities can be obtained directly from the production function by ordinary least squares, but are generally statistically inconsistent because of the existence of simultaneous equation bias.

52. By comparison, Myers and Dietrich, "Resource Allocation in Traditional Agriculture," found in the estimation of production functions for each crop with two inputs (land and labor) that in Michang and Matsun, cotton, corn, kaoliang (sorghum), wheat, and millet generally experienced increasing returns to scale, but that, in Wukuan, cotton, wheat, and millet all reflect decreasing returns. Their estimation, however, made no adjustment to labor.

53. Some support for this view appears in Dennis Chinn's work. Utilizing Buck's aggregate cross-sectional data, Chinn found in the estimation of a Cobb-Douglas production function that included both conventional inputs as well as indices for land fragmentation and tenancy that fragmentation was negatively related to output in four of Buck's eight regions, including the two regions that contain the villages I examined. See Chinn, "Land Utilization and Productivity in Prewar Chinese Agriculture: Preconditions for Collectivisation," *American Journal of Agricultural Economics* 59 (August 1977), pp. 559–64.

54. Berry and Cline, *Agrarian Structure*, address some of the key issues.

55. Ronald Trosper, "American Indian Relative Ranching Efficiency," *American Economic Review* 68 (September 1978), pp. 503–16.

56. Unlike the earlier tests for the influence of farm size on relative economic efficiency, the present ones cannot test separately for the effects of tenancy on price and technical efficiency, but only on overall economic

efficiency. With more observations on pure tenants, the sample could be divided and tests for relative economic efficiency between tenants and owners carried out along the same lines as before.

57. These test results can be interpreted as tests for differences in efficiency with any influence of tenancy now controlled for.

58. To make perhaps an obvious point, if real wages paid farm laborers were rising, the returns to tenantry had to be rising as well. After all, a tenant household could decide to hire out the labor of one of its members rather than rent in additional land. From the perspective of the landlord, he had to offer the tenant at least as good as (if not better) terms as the tenant could earn as a wage laborer for him to agree to farm.

59. I am assuming that the percentage going to other inputs, most notably intermediate inputs such as fertilizer, seed, and so forth, remained the same.

60. Perkins, *Agricultural Development in China*, p. 312.

61. Noboru Niida, *Chūgoku hōseishi kenkyū*, vol. 3, p. 768, cited in Chao, *Man and Land in Chinese History*, p. 170.

62. The difference between the stipulated and actual rents represents the concessions that landlords ceded tenants.

63. Liang-lin Hsiao, *China's Foreign Trade Statistics, 1864–1949* (Cambridge, 1974), pp. 74–5, and "Chinese Egg and Egg Products," *Chinese Economic Journal and Bulletin* 14, 2 (1935).

64. Because an even higher percentage of land was rented out in Central and East China, it can be inferred that the degree of inequality of own landholdings was probably slightly higher than 0.72.

65. This has been the case in three North China (Hopei) villages that Barbara Sands and I are presently analyzing. In Michang, Fengrun county, the Ginis for household income and household income per capita were 0.488 and 0.391; in Chienlianggezhuang, Changli county, 0.409 and 0.346; and in Dabeiguan, Pinggu county, 0.43 and 0.349. The difference between the two measures leads me to believe that the Gini for rural household incomes on a per capita basis in Central and East China was in the vicinity of 0.35, and possibly lower.

66. Michael Todoro, *Economic Development in the Third World*, 2d ed. (New York, 1981), pp. 128–9. Because these estimates are for the entire economy and not just the rural sector, they are not exactly comparable. But, with 88 percent of the region's population rural, only a substantially higher degree of income inequality in the urban sector would lead to a degree of inequality significantly higher than that found for the rural sector alone.

67. Although a number of other estimates suggest even lower degrees of inequality in rural Taiwan, the estimates for 1972 and 1975 are preferred because they are based on more representative samples. See Terry Y. H. Yu, "Farm Family Income Distribution by Region in Taiwan," in *Income Distribution by Sectors and Overtime in East and Southeast Asian Countries*, ed. Harry T. Oshima and Toshiyuki Mizoguchi (Quezon City, Philippines and Tokyo, Japan, 1979), p. 177.

68. These included Michang village of Fengjun *hsien* in Hopei province for the three years, 1937, 1938, and 1939; Matsun village of Huolu *hsien*,

also in Hopei, for 1939; and Wukuan village of Changte *hsien* in Honan province for 1940. See Minami Manshū Tetsudō Kabushiki Kaisha, *Nōka keizai chōsa hōkoku, Hokushi keizai shiryō no. 5* (Fengjun hsien, Michang village, 1937); *Hokushi keizai shiryō no. 12* (Fengjun hsien, Michang village, 1938); *Hokushi keizai shiryō no. 36* (Fengjun hsien, Michang village, 1939); *Hokushi kezai shiryō no. 25* (Changte hsien, Wukuan village, 1940); and *Hokushi keizai shiryō no. 32* (Huolu hsien, Matsun village, 1939).

69. Full citations are in Notes 3 and 49.

70. On the basis of a sample of over 500,000 households taken by the National Land Commission, the average amount of land cultivated per farm household in North China was 21.5 *mou*. See T'u-ti wei-yuan hui, *Ch'uan-kuo t'u-ti tiao-ch'a pao-kao kang-yao* (Nanking, 1937), p. 24.

## Chapter 7. Conclusion

1. Based on estimates of gross value of agricultural output contained in Mataji Umemura et al., *Estimates of Long-Term Economic Statistics of Japan Since 1868: Agriculture and Forestry*, Vol. 9 (Tokyo, 1966), pp. 152–3.

2. See Thomas Wiens, "The Microeconomics of Peasant Economy: China, 1920–1940" (Ph.D. Dissertation, Harvard University, 1973), and Ying Ting, *Chung-kuo shui-tao tsai-p'ei hsueh* (Peking, 1961), cited therein.

# References

Angier, E. A. V., *Fifty Years Freight, 1869–1914*. London: Fairplay, 1920.

Archibald, Sandra O., and Loren Brandt, "A Flexible Model of Factor Biased Technological Change: An Application to Japanese Agriculture." Unpublished, 1987.

Banister, T. R. "A History of the External Trade of China, 1834–1881." In *Decennial Reports, 1922–1931*. Compiled by Chinese Imperial Maritime Customs. 2 vols. Shanghai, 1933. I, 1–193.

Bennett, M. K., and V. K. Wickizer. *The Rice Economy of Monsoon Asia*. Stanford: Stanford University Press, 1941.

Berry, Albert, and William Cline. *Agrarian Structure and Productivity in Developing Countries*. Baltimore: Johns Hopkins University Press, 1979.

Bhatty, I. K. "Inequality and Poverty in Rural India." In *Poverty and Income Distribution in India*, edited by P. K. Bardhan and T. N. Srinivisan. Calcutta: Statistical Publishing Society, 1974.

Boserup, Ester. *The Economics of Agrarian Change under Population Pressure*. Chicago: University of Chicago Press, 1965.

Brandt, Loren. "Population Growth, Agricultural Change, and Economic Integration in Central and Eastern China, 1890s–1930s." Ph.D. Dissertation, University of Illinois, 1983.

———. "Chinese Agriculture and the International Economy, 1870s–1930s: A Reassessment." *Explorations in Economic History* 22 (1985), pp. 168–93.

———. "Review of Phillip Huang's 'The Peasant Economy and Social Change in North China.' " *Economic Development and Cultural Change* 35, 3 (1987), pp. 670–82.

———. "Farm Household Behavior, Factor Markets, and the Distributive Consequences of Commercialization." *Journal of Economic History* 47, 3 (1987), pp. 711–37.

Brandt, Loren, and Thomas J. Sargent. "Interpreting New Evidence about China and U.S. Silver Purchases." *Journal of Monetary Economics* (in press).

Buck, John L. *Chinese Farm Economy: A Study of 2,866 Farms*. Chicago: University of Chicago Press, 1930.

———. *Land Utilization in China*. Chicago: University of Chicago, 1937.

———. *Land Utilization in China: Statistical Volume*. Chicago: University of Chicago, 1937.

Bureau of Social Affairs. City Government of Greater Shanghai. *Shang-hai shih kung-ren cheng-huo cheng-t'u.* Shanghai: Chung-hua shu-chu, 1934.

Chan, Kam Wing, and Xueqiang Xu. "Urban Population Growth and Urbanization in China Since 1949: Reconstructing a Baseline." *China Quarterly* 104 (1985), pp. 583–613.

Chandra, Bipan. "Reinterpretation of 19th Century Indian Economic History." *Indian Economic and Social History Review* 5, 1 (1968), pp. 35–76.

Chang, C. C. *China's Food Problem.* Shanghai: China Institute of Pacific Relations, 1931.

Chang, Chung-li. *The Income of the Chinese Gentry.* Seattle: University of Washington Press, 1962.

Chang, Jen-chia. *Konan no kokumai.* Translation of 1936 Report by the Hunan Provincial Economic Research Institute. Tokyo: Seikatsusha, 1940.

Chang, John. *Industrial Development in Pre-Communist China.* Chicago: Aldine, 1969.

Chang, Lu-luan. "Chiang-su Wu-chin wu-chia chih yen-chiu." *Chin-lu hsueh-pao* 3 (1933), pp. 153–216.

Chang, Pei-kang. *Kuang-si liang-shih wen-ti.* Changsha: Commercial Press, 1938.

Chang, Shih-wen. *Ting-hsien nung-tsun kung-yeh tiao-ch'a.* Peking, Chieh-hua yin-shu chu, 1936.

Chao, Kang. *The Development of Cotton Textile Production in China.* Cambridge: Harvard University Press, 1977.

———. *Man and Land in Chinese History: An Economic Analysis.* Stanford: Stanford University Press, 1986.

Chao, Kang, and Chung-yi Chen. *Chung-kuo t'u-ti chih-tu shih.* Taipei: Lian-ching ch'u-pan shih-yeh kung-szu, 1982.

Chayonov, A. K. *The Theory of the Peasant Economy.* Homewood, Ill.: Irwin, 1966.

Chen, Han-seng. *The Present Agrarian Problem in China.* Shanghai: China Institute of Pacific Relations, 1933.

———. *Industrial Capital and Chinese Peasants: A Study of Chinese Tobacco Cultivation.* Shanghai: Kelly and Walsh, 1939.

Ch'en, Cheng-mo. *Ko-sheng nung-kung ku-yung hsi-kuan chi hsu-kung chuang-kuang.* Nanking: Chung-shan wen-hua chiao-yu-kuan, 1935.

———. *Chung-kuo k'o-sheng te ti-tsu.* Shanghai: Commercial Press, 1936.

Ch'en, Po-chuang. *Ping-han yan-hsien nung-tsun ching-chi tiao-ch'a.* Shanghai: Chiao-t'ung ta-hsueh yen-chiu so, 1937.

Cheng, Yu-kwei. *Foreign Trade and Industrial Development in China.* Washington, D.C.: University Press of Washington D.C., 1956.

China. Bureau of Roads. Ministry of Communications. *Chung-kuo ti kung-lu.* Nanking: National Economic Council, 1936.

China. Bureau of Statistics. Ministry of Industry. *Wu-hsi kung-ren sheng-huo-fei chi ch'i chih-shu.* Nanking: National Government of China, 1935.

China. Chiao-t'ung pu yu-cheng tsung-chu, ed. *Chung-kuo t'ung-yu ti-fang wu-chan-chih.* Shanghai: Commercial Press, 1937.

China. Imperial Maritime Customs. *Decennial Reports.* 1882–1891, 1892–1901, 1902–1911, 1912–1921, and 1922–1931.

China. Imperial Maritime Customs. *Returns of Trade and Trade Reports* (annual). 1870–1936.

China. National Agricultural Research Bureau. *Crop Reports* (monthly). 1931–1937.

China. Shih-yeh pu. Guo-chi mao-yi chu. *Chung-kuo shih-yeh chih: Chekiang sheng.* Shanghai: Shih-yeh pu, 1933.

China. Shih-yeh pu. Guo-chi mao-yi chu. *Chung-kuo shih-yeh chih: Chiang-su sheng.* Shanghai: Shih-yeh pu, 1933.

China. Shih-yeh pu. Guo-chi mao-yi chu. *Chung-kuo shih-yeh chih: Hu-nan sheng.* Shanghai: Shih-yeh pu, 1935.

*China Weekly Review.*

"Chinese Egg and Egg Products." *Chinese Economic Journal and Bulletin* 14, 2 (1935).

Ching, Shou-ch'u. *Kuang-chou chih mi-yeh.* Canton: Bank of Kwangtung, 1938.

Chinn, Dennis. "Land Utilization and Productivity in Prewar Chinese Agriculture: Preconditions for Collectivisation." *American Journal of Agricultural Economics* 59 (1977), pp. 559–64.

Chu, Hsi-chou, ed. *Mi.* Nanking: Bank of China, Economic Research Unit, 1937.

Chu, Mei-yu. *Chung-kuo ch'a-yeh.* Shanghai: Chung-hua shu-chu, 1937.

Chuan, Han-sheng, and Richard Kraus, *Mid-Ch'ing Rice Markets: An Essay in Price History.* Cambridge: Harvard University Press, 1975.

*Ch'uan-kuo t'u-ti tiao-ch'a pao-kao kang-yao.* Nanking: T'u-ti wei-yuan-hui, 1937.

*Chung-kuo mien-fang t'ung-chi shih-liao.* Shanghai: Shang-hai shih mien-fang-chih kung-yeh tung-yeh kung-hwei chou-pei-hui, 1950.

*Chung-kuo t'ung-chi nien-chien.* Peking: Chung-kuo t'ung-chi ch'u-pan she, annual.

Cressey, G. B. *China's Geographical Foundation.* New York: McGraw-Hill, 1934.

Faure, David. "The Rural Economy of Kiangsu Province, 1870–1911." *Journal of the Institute of Chinese Studies of the Chinese University of Hong Kong* 9, 2 (1978), pp. 365–469.

———. "Export and the Chinese Farmer: The Rural Economy of Kiangsu and Kwangtung, 1870–1937." Unpublished, 1987.

Feder, Gershon. "The Relation between Farm Size and Farm Productivity: The Role of Family Labor, Supervision, and Credit Constraints." *Journal of Development Economics* 18 (1985), pp. 297–313.

Fei, Hsiao-tung. *Peasant Life in China.* London: Kegan Paul, Trence, Trubner and Co., 1939.

Feng, Ho-fa, ed. *Chung-kuo nung-tsun ching-chi tzu-liao.* 2 vols. Shanghai: Li-ming shu-tien, 1935.

Feuerwerker, Albert. *The Chinese Economy, 1912–1949*. Ann Arbor: Center for Chinese Studies, 1968.

———. "Handicraft and Manufactured Cotton Textiles in China, 1871–1910." *Journal of Economic History* 30 (1970), pp. 338–78.

———. "Economic Trends, 1912–1949." In *Cambridge History of China, Republican China, 1912–1949*, Part I. Cambridge: Cambridge University Press, 1983.

Fong, Hsien-ting. *Chung-kuo chih mien-fang chih-yeh*. Shanghai: Commercial Press, 1934.

———. *Terminal Marketing of Tientsin Cotton*. Tientsin: Chihli Press, 1935.

French Indochina. Government general de L'Indochine. Direction des affaires economiques. Service de la statistique generale. *Annuaire Statistique de L'Indochine*. Hanoi, 1927–.

Gamble, Sidney. *Ting Hsien: A North China Rural Community*. Stanford: Stanford University Press, 1954.

Gottschang, Thomas. "Economic Change, Disasters, and Migration: The Historical Case of Manchuria." *Economic Development and Cultural Change* 35 (1987), pp. 461–90.

Great Britain. *Statistical Abstract for British India*. Issues for years 1911–12 through 1936–37. Calcutta: Superintendent Government Printing.

Han, Ch'i-tung. *Chung-kuo pu-chi mao-yi t'ung-chi, 1936–40*. Peking: Scientific Press, 1951.

Hanley, Susan B., and Kozo Yamamura. *Economic and Demographic Change in Preindustrial Japan, 1600–1868*. Princeton: Princeton University Press, 1977.

Hsiao, Liang-lin. *China's Foreign Trade Statistics, 1864–1949*. Cambridge: Harvard University Press, 1974.

Huang, Phillip C. C. *The Peasant Economy and Social Change in North China*. Stanford: Stanford University Press, 1985.

Hymer, Stephen, and Stephen Resnick. "A Model of an Agrarian Economy with Nonagricultural Productivities." *American Economic Review* 59 (1969), pp. 493–506.

Ingram, James. *Economic Change in Thailand Since 1850*. Stanford: Stanford University Press, 1955.

———. "Thailand's Rice Trade and the Allocation of Resources." In *The Economic Development of Southeast Asia*, edited by C. D. Cowan. London: Allen & Unwin, 1964.

Institute of Social and Economic Research. *Nan-ching liang-shih tiao-ch'a*. Shanghai, 1935.

———. *Shang-hai mi-shih tiao-ch'a*. Shanghai, 1935.

———. *Tsung-chiang mi-shih tiao-ch'a*. Shanghai, 1936.

Jamieson, George. "Tenure of Land in China and the Condition of the Rural Population." *Journal of the China Branch of the Royal Asiatic Society* 23 (1889), pp. 58–143.

Johnson, Linda Cooke. "The Decline of Soochow and Rise of Shanghai: A Study in the Economic Morphology of Urban Change, 1756–1894." Ph.D. Dissertation, University of California-Santa Cruz, 1986.

Kahn, Mahmoud, and Dennis Maki. "The Effects of Farm Size on Economic Efficiency." *American Journal of Agricultural Economics* 61 (1979), pp. 64–9.

Kaneda, Hiromitsu. "Long-term Changes in Food Consumption Patterns in Japanese Agriculture." In *Agriculture in Economic Growth: Japan's Experience*, edited by Kazushi Ohkawa et al. Tokyo: University of Tokyo Press, 1969.

Kirkby, R. J. R. *Urbanisation in China: Town and Country in a Developing Country, 1949–2000*. London: Croom Helm, 1985.

"Ko-sheng nung-kung kung-tzu t'ung-chi." *T'ung-chi yueh-pao* 13 (1933), pp. 99–106.

Kraus, Richard. "Cotton and Cotton Goods in China, 1918–1936." Ph.D. Dissertation, Harvard University, 1968.

K'ung, Hsi-an. "Chung-kuo liu-ta-shih ti jen-k'ou chi ch'i tseng chien." In *Chung-kuo li-tai jen-k'ou wen-t'i lun-chi*, pp. 209–17. Hong Kong: Lung-men shu-tien, 1965.

Lardy, Nicholas. "Consumption and Living Standards in China, 1978–1983." *China Quarterly* 100 (1984), pp. 849–65.

———. *Agriculture in China's Modern Economic Development*. New York: Cambridge University Press, 1983.

Latham, A. J. H. *The International Economy and the Underdeveloped World, 1865–1914*. London: Croom Helm, 1978.

Latham, A. J. H., and Larry Neal. "The International Market in Rice and Wheat, 1868–1914." *Economic History Review* 36 (1983), pp. 260–80.

Li, Lillian. *China's Silk Trade: Traditional Industry in the Modern World, 1842–1937*. Cambridge: Harvard University Press, 1981.

Li, Wen-chih. *Chung-kuo tzu-pen-chu-yi meng-ya wen-t'i t'ao-lun chi*. Peking: San-lien shu-tien, 1957.

Li, Wen-chih, and Chang You-yi, eds. *Chung-kuo chin-tai nung-yeh-shih tzu-liao*. 3 vols. Peking San-lien shu-tien, 1957.

Liang, Ernest P. *China: Railways and Agricultural Development, 1875–1935*. Chicago: University of Chicago, Department of Geography, 1982. Research Paper No. 203.

Lieu, D. K. *The Silk Industry of China*. Shanghai: Kelly and Walsh, 1941.

Lin, Wei-ying. *China under Depreciated Silver, 1926–1931*. Shanghai: Commercial Press, 1935.

Liu, T. C., and K. C. Yeh. *The Economy of the Chinese Mainland: National Income and Economic Development, 1933–1959*. Princeton: Princeton University. 1965.

McAlpin, Michelle. "The Effects of Expansion of Markets on Rural Income Distribution in Nineteenth Century India." *Explorations in Economic History* 12 (1975), pp. 289–302.

———. "Price Movements and Fluctuations in Economic Activity." In *Cambridge Economic History of India*. Cambridge: Cambridge University Press, 1983.

McCloskey, Donald, and Richard Zecher. "How the Gold Standard Worked, 1880–1913." In *The Monetary Approach to the Balance of Payments*, edited by Jacob Frenkel and Harry Johnson. Toronto: University of Toronto Press, 1976.

McGee, John S. "Ocean Freight Rate Conferences." In *The Economic Value of the U.S. Merchant Marine*, edited by Edward Johnson. Evanston, Ill.: Transportation Center, Northwestern University, 1961.

Malenbaum, Wilfred. *The World Wheat Economy.* Cambridge: Harvard University Press, 1953.

Minami Manshū Tetsudō Kabushiki Kaisha. Hokushi Keizai Chōsajo. *I-ken dofugyō chōsa hōkokusho.* Dairen: Minami Manshu Tetsudo Kabushiki Kaisha Chosabu, 1942.

——. Kito Noson Jittai Chosahan, *Dainiji kitō nōson jittai chōsa hōkokusho: tōkeihon, Dai ichiban: Heikoku ken.* Dairen, 1937.

——. ——. *Dainiji kitō nōson jittai chōusa hōkokusho: tōkeihon. Dai sanban: Hōjun ken.* Dairen, 1937.

——. ——. *Dainiji kitō nōson jittai chōsa hōkokusho: tōkeihon. Dai yonban: Shōrei ken.* Dairen, 1937.

——. Shanhai Jimusho. Chōsashitsu. *Kōso-shō Jōjuku-ken nōson jittai chōsa hōkukusho.* Dairen: Minami Manshu Tetsudo Kabushiki Kaisha Shanhai Jimusho Chōsashitsu, 1939.

——. ——. ——. *Kōso-shō Mushaku-ken nōson jittai chōsa hōkokusho.* Dairen: Minami Manshu Tetsudo Kabushiki Kaisha Shanhai Jimusho Chōsashitsu, 1941.

——. ——. ——. *Kōso-shō Nantsū-ken nōson jittai chōsa hōkokusho.* Dairen: Minami Manshu Tetsudo Kabushiki Kaisha Shanhai Jimusho Chōsashitsu, 1941.

——. ——. ——. *Kōso-shō Shōkō-ken nōson jittai chōsa hōkokusho.* Dairen: Minami Manshu Tetsudo Kabushiki Kaisha Shanhai Jimusho Chosashitsu, 1940.

——. ——. ——. *Kōso-shō Taisō-ken nōson jittai chōsa hōkokusho.* Dairen: Minami Manshu Tetsudo Kabushiki Kaisha Shanhai Jimusho Chosashitsu, 1940.

Mizoguchi, Toshiyuki. "Income Distribution by Sectors and Overtime in East and Southeast Asian Countries." In *Income Distribution by Sectors and Overtime: Selected Papers Presented for the CAMS-Hitotsubashi Seminar Held at Norita on September 5 to 7, 1977,* edited by Harry T. Oshima and Toshiyuki Mizoguchi. Quezon City, Philippines: Council for Asian Manpower Studies, 1978.

Myers, Ramon. "Cotton Textile Handicraft and the Development of the Cotton Textile Industry in Modern China." *Economic History Review* 18 (1965), pp. 614–32.

——. *The Chinese Peasant Economy: Agricultural Development in Hopei and Shantung, 1890–1949.* Cambridge: Harvard University Press, 1970.

——. "The Commercialization of Agriculture in Modern China." In *Economic Organization in Chinese Society,* edited by W. E. Willmott. Stanford: Stanford University Press, 1972.

——. *The Chinese Economy: Past and Present.* Belmont: Wadsworth, Inc., 1980.

Myers, Ramon, and Scott Dietrich. "Resource Allocation in Traditional Ag-
    riculture: Republican China, 1937–1940." *Journal of Political Economy*
    79 (1971), pp. 887–96.
Nan-kai ta-hsueh ching-chi yan-chiu-so, ed. *Nan-kai chih-shu tzu-liao hui-
    pien.* Peking: T'ung-chi chu-pan she. 1958.
Nanking University, Department of Economics. *Yu-O-Wan-Kan ssu-sheng
    chih mian-chan yun-hsiao.* Nanking: Nanking University Press, 1936.
Odell, Ralph. *Cotton Goods in China.* Washington: Government Printing
    Office, 1916.
Ohkawa, Kazushi, and Miyohe Shinohawa, eds. *Patterns of Japanese Eco-
    nomic Development: A Quantitative Assessment.* New Haven: Yale Uni-
    versity Press, 1979.
Otto, Friedrich. "Sketch of Chinese Agricultural Policy." *Chinese Economic
    Journal* 2, 5 (1928).
———. "Correlation of Harvests with Importations of Cereals in China."
    *Chinese Economic Journal* 15, 4 (October 1934), pp. 388–414.
P'eng, Tse-yi, ed. *Chung-kuo chin-tai shou-kung-yeh shih tzu-liao.* 3 vols.
    Peking: Scientific Press, 1957.
———. "Ch'ing-tai ch'ien-chi shou-kung-yeh te fa-chan." *Chung-kuo shih
    yen-chiu* 1 (1981), pp. 43–60.
Perkins, Dwight. *Agricultural Development in China, 1368–1968.* Chicago:
    Aldine, 1969.
———. "Growth and Changing Structure of China's Twentieth-Century
    Economy." In *China's Modern Economy in Historical Perspective,* edited
    by Dwight Perkins. Stanford: Stanford University Press, 1975.
Rawski, Evelyn. *Agricultural Change and the Peasant Economy of South
    China.* Cambridge: Harvard University Press, 1972.
Rawski, Thomas. "China's Republican Economy: An Introduction." Toronto:
    University of Toronto-York University, Joint Centre on Modern East
    Asia, Discussion Paper #1, 1978.
———. "The Economy of the Yangtse Region, 1850–1980." Paper presented
    at the conference on Spatial and Temporal Trends and Cycles in Chinese
    Economic History, Bellagio, Italy. Toronto, 1984.
———. "Economic Growth in Prewar China." In press.
Reynolds, Bruce. "The Impact of Foreign Trade and Industrialization:
    Chinese Textiles, 1875–1931." Ph.D. Dissertation, University of Mich-
    igan, 1975.
Reynolds, Lloyd. *Economic Growth in the Third World, 1850–1980.* New
    Haven: Yale University Press, 1985.
Riskin, Carl. *China's Political Economy.* New York: Oxford University
    Press, 1987.
Robequain, Charles. *The Economic Development of French-Indochina.* Lon-
    don: Oxford University Press, 1944.
Rowe, William. *Hankow: Commerce and Society in a Chinese City, 1796–
    1889.* Stanford: Stanford University Press, 1984.
Ruttan, Vernon. "Agricultural Product and Factor Markets in Southeast
    Asia." *Economic Development and Cultural Change* 17, 4 (1969),
    pp. 501–20.

Sen, A. K. "Peasants and Dualism with or without Surplus Labour." *Journal of Political Economy* 74 (1966), pp. 424–50.

*Shang-hai chieh-fang ch'ien-hou wu-chia tzu-liao hui-pien.* Shanghai: Shang-hai ren-min ch'u-pan she, 1958.

Shepard, John. "Rethinking Tenancy: Spatial and Temporal Variation in Land Ownership and Concentration in Late Imperial China." Unpublished, 1986.

Skinner, G. William. "Regional Urbanization in Nineteenth Century China." In *The City in Late Imperial China*, edited by G. William Skinner. Stanford: Stanford University Press, 1977.

Smethurst, Richard. *Agricultural Development and Tenancy Disputes in Japan, 1870–1940.* Princeton: Princeton University Press, 1986.

Sun, Ching-chi. *Hua-tung ti-ch'u ching-chi ti-li.* Peking: Scientific Press, 1959.

Takamura, Naosuke. *Kindai Nihon mengyō to Chūgoku.* Tokyo: Tokyo Daigaku Shuppankai, 1982.

Tamagna, Frank. *Banking and Finance in China.* New York: Institute of Pacific Relations, 1942.

T'ang, Hui-sun et al. *Chung-kuo nung-chia ching-chi chih chi-chang te yen-chiu.* Nanking: Shi-yeh pu chung-yang nung-yeh-shih yen so, 1936.

Tawney, R. H. *Land and Labor in China.* London: Allen & Unwin, 1932.

*Ti-yi-t'zu Chung-kuo lao-tung nien-ch'ien.* Peking: Pei-p'ing she-hui tiao-ch'a pu, 1928.

Ting, Ying. *Chung-kuo shui-tao tsai-p'ei hsueh.* Peking: 1961.

Toa kenkyujō. *Shina nōgyo kiso tōkei shiryō.* Vols. 1 and 2. Tokyo: Tanaka Seizo, 1940.

Trosper, Ronald. "American Indian Relative Economic Efficiency." *American Economic Review* 68 (1978), pp. 503–16.

Umemura, Mataji et al. *Estimates of Long-Term Economic Statistics of Japan Since 1868: Agriculture and Forestry.* Vol. 9. Tokyo: Toyo Keizai Shinposha, 1966.

United States Bureau of the Census. *The Statistical History of the United States from Colonial Times to the Present.* New York: Horizon Press, 1965.

Wang, Ch'in-yu. *Chin-tai Chung-kuo ti tao-lu chien-she.* Hong Kong: Lungmen shu-tien, 1969.

Wang, Lien. "Farm Prices in Szechwan, 1910–1934." *Economic Facts* 9, (1938), pp. 416–17.

Wang, Yu-ruo. "Lun liang-ts'z shih-chieh ta-chan chih-chien Chung-kuo ching-chi te fa-chan." *Chung-kuo ching-chi shih yen-chiu* 2 (1987), pp. 97–110.

Wen, Yu-ching. "Electrical Communications." In *The Chinese Yearbook, 1936–1937.* Shanghai: Commercial Press, 1936.

Wiens, Thomas. "The Microeconomics of Peasant Economy: China, 1920–1940." Ph.D. Dissertation, Harvard University, 1973.

Williams, S. Wells. *The Chinese Commercial Guide.* 5th ed. Hong Kong: A. Shortrede, 1863.

Wu, Cheng. *Wan-chung tao-mi ch'an-hsiao chih tiao-ch'a.* Shanghai: Chiao-t'ung ta-hsueh yen-chiu so, 1936.

Wu, Cheng-ming. "Lun Ch'ing-tai chien-chi wo-kuo kuo-nei shih-chang." *Li-shih yen-chiu* 1 (1983): 96–106.

———. "Wo-kuo pan chih min-ti pan feng-chien kuo-nei shih-chang." *Li-shih yen-chiu* (February 1984), pp. 110–21.

———. *Chung-kuo tzu-pen chu-yi yu kuo-nei shih-chang.* Peking: Chung-kuo she-hui k'o-hsueh ch'u-pan she, 1985.

Wu Chih, *Hsiang-tsun chih-pu-yeh ti-yi-ke yen-chiu.* Shanghai: Commercial Press, 1941.

Wu, Pao-san. *Chung-kuo kuo-min so-te, 1933 nien.* 2 vols. Shanghai: Chung-hua Shu-chu, 1947.

Yen, Chung-p'ing. *Chung-kuo mien-fang-chih shih-kao.* Peking: Scientific Press, 1955.

Yotopolous, Pan, and Lawrence Lau. "A Test for Relative Economic Efficiency: Some Further Results." *American Economic Review* 63 (1973), pp. 214–23.

Yueh, Ssu-ping. *Chung-kuo ts'an-ssu.* Shanghai: Shih-chih shu-chu, 1935.

Zellner, Arnold. "An Efficient Method for Estimating Seemingly Unrelated Regressions and Tests for Aggregation Bias." *Journal of the American Statistical Association* 57 (1962), pp. 348–68.

# Index